Not a Normal Country

Not a Normal Country

Italy After Berlusconi

Geoff Andrews

Pluto  Press

LONDON • ANN ARBOR, MI

First published 2005 by Pluto Press
345 Archway Road, London N6 5AA
and 839 Greene Street, Ann Arbor, MI 48106

www.plutobooks.com

British Library Cataloguing in Publication Data
A catalogue record for this book is available from the British Library

ISBN   0 7453 2368 5 hardback
ISBN   0 7453 2367 7 paperback

Library of Congress Cataloging-in-Publication Data

Andrews, Geoff, 1961–
    Not a normal country : Italy after Berlusconi / Geoff Andrews.
        p. cm.
    Includes bibliographical references and index.
    ISBN 0–7453–2368–5 (hardback) — ISBN 0–7453–2367–7 (pbk.)
    1. Politics and culture—Italy—History—20th century. 2. Politics and
culture—Italy—History—21st century. 3. Berlusconi, Silvio, 1936– 4.
National characteristics, Italian. 5. Political
parties—Italy—History—20th century. 6. Political
parties—Italy—History—21st century. I. Title.
    DG583.5.A53 2005
    306.2'0945'090511—dc22

                                                            2005006760

10   9   8   7   6   5   4   3   2   1

Designed and produced for Pluto Press by
Chase Publishing Services Ltd, Fortescue, Sidmouth, EX10 9QG, England
Typeset from disk by Stanford DTP Services, Northampton, England
Printed and bound in the European Union by
Antony Rowe Ltd, Chippenham and Eastbourne, England

For Italian friends

Contents

List of Photographs

Preface and Acknowledgements

In May 2001, Silvio Berlusconi became Italy's Prime Minister when his House of Liberties coalition was elected with 45.4 percent of the vote in the Chamber of Deputies and 42.5 percent in the Senate, compared to 43.8 and 39.2 percent respectively for the centre-left Olive Tree coalition. Berlusconi's Forza Italia became the largest party in Italy with 29.5 percent of the vote. Divisions between the centre-left parties and Rifondazione comunista, the refounded Communists, who stood on separate election tickets, contributed to Berlusconi's victory. The minutiae of this election have already been described in the journals of conventional political science. Future analysis will discuss Berlusconi in light of the ruptures of the Italian party system, electoral swings and shifts in voting behaviour; some, no doubt, will predict another 'period of transition' in Italian politics.

These bare facts, however, only tell us part of the story of Silvio Berlusconi's rise to power. His political ascendancy is deeply connected to particular moments in recent Italian history, the paradoxes of Italian culture and the long-term crisis of the state. Moreover, it is a story that remains incomplete, his own future in 2005 being as precarious as that of his country, now deep in economic crisis and political paralysis. Despite Berlusconi's declining popularity from 2002 onwards, the centre-left has a propensity to clutch defeat from the jaws of victory. Electoral scenarios notwithstanding, Berlusconi's legacy is likely to be significant for some years to come.

In writing a book of this kind I wanted to avoid some of the limitations of conventional academic analysis. Indeed, the fast-moving events which unfolded in Italy since 2001 warranted a different approach. When I started my research six months before Berlusconi came to power in May 2001, I was not sure where it would take me; I had only a feeling that something profound was happening. I wanted to follow and capture what seemed to be ground-breaking and significant developments. Initially, this was Berlusconi's world; his populism, together with the historical revisionism and xenophobia of his allies, was pushing Italy into some of its darkest hours.

Subsequently, I found another Italy in the making; one of resistance, idealism and association, but whose short-term future was uncertain. A new postmodern paradigm seemed to be opening up in the Berlusconi era, bringing two distinct and conflicting responses, described in this book as populism and associationism. This new paradigm meant that while political parties remained powerful, they faced new challenges to their legitimacy, while other conventions of 'normal' politics were left behind. To do justice to the immediacy of these developments, my methods of inquiry drew on interviews, diaries of events and investigative journalism in very different regions of Italy. I was fortunate in this respect to be working in the age of the Internet, low-cost airlines and mobile phones, which variously enabled me to make contacts, find new leads and organise my time. As I started writing it also became apparent that on many occasions I was simply lucky to be in the right place at the right time.

While the book is essentially about politics, it is also a reminder that much of politics in Italy takes place beyond parties and involves movements, loosely organised networks and other forms of association. Italian politics also remains profoundly informed by cultural and regional variation, while political actors include film directors and other intellectuals, priests and magistrates. It confirms the view that Italy is not a normal country, and that the boundaries between orthodoxies and heresies are constantly shifting.

Writing the book has also been a personally liberating experience. The opportunity to travel and write outside the narrow constraints of contemporary academic life was a rare privilege, while respite from the tedium of British politics was also welcome. The book was only made possible by the extraordinary generosity of Italians, most of whom I did not know until I arrived in their city, town or village. Intrigued, if not bemused, by what I was doing, they provided me with every kind of help and hospitality imaginable; interviews were arranged, often at very short notice; accommodation was provided if I needed it; discussions with people who wanted to tell me about their country carried on long into the night. I was driven around beautiful cities, narrow (and sometimes mean) streets, coastal villages and remote hilltops.

Only in Genoa in July 2001, a city militarised for the duration of the G8 summit, were my movements restricted.

In particular I would like to thank the following for their help. In Bologna, my base for much of the time and where I did most of the writing, I owe a lot to Simona Lembi, now an *assessore* for culture in the *Provincia*, who arranged interviews and kept me up to date on political developments in her city; Ruben Bombardi, for welcoming me to Bologna, acting as my lawyer and helping me decipher Umberto Bossi's political dialect; Roberto Grandi, for his insight into the postmodern condition in Italy; Andrea Chiarini of *La Repubblica*; and Antonio and Davide at the Osteria Tempo Perso, for showing a British person how to pour beer properly. At nearby Marzabotto, I am grateful to Bruno Sidoli of the Fondazione scuola di pace di Monte Sole for organising my visit and to Francesco Pirini and Franco Lanzarini for telling me the story of their families, describing, with dignity, the massacre that took place in the autumn of 1944 and of their hopes and optimism for the future.

I'm grateful to Matteo Patrono and Ida Dominjianni of *Il Manifesto* in Rome for offering their reflections on the state of the Italian left on the very gloomy election evening of 13 May 2001. Matteo, along with Marco Capecelatro, Luigi Coldagelli and Lele Capurso, also organised great lunches in Rome. Rory Carroll, *The Guardian*'s former Italy correspondent, was good company in Rome and Genoa in the early stages of my work.

In Bari, Livia Cantore and Alessandro Cobianchi of ARCI arranged a series of interviews, including one with the mayor at very short notice, and took me to their favourite pizzeria. They also introduced me to Sajjad Sardar, who told me the story of his courageous journey to Italy.

I am grateful to Chiara Samanta Farella in Matera for showing me her city, including its vibrant nightlife, help with translations and more; Antonio Foschino, for his knowledge of the history of Matera and for providing photos; Serafino Paternoster, for arranging an interview with the mayor at short notice. In Scanzano Jonico, Pino Mele drove me around, took me to the *campobase* for an organising meeting and introduced me to Don Filippo Lombardo. Giorgio Braschi generously provided his photos of the Scanzano demonstrations.

In Bra, I was introduced to the wonderful Slow Food movement, shown the world's first 'slow' university, the University of Gastronomic Sciences, and met Carlo Petrini with the help of Anna Eastman and Sandra Abbona of the Slow Food press office, who also provided photos.

In Pordenone, Mick and Carolyn Walton provided great hospitality, and looked on with mild disapproval as I tackled the *senatur*.

In Florence, Paul Ginsborg kindly gave me the benefit of his expertise on contemporary Italian history and told me about the Laboratorio per la democrazia. Maud Bracke and Luca Stellati discussed the Italian left with me.

I am grateful to Donatella Gariffo of the Sicilian Renaissance Institute for organising my interview with Leoluca Orlando in Palermo. On Sicily's east coast, Natalie Guziuk, Ezio Mongiovi, Luca Lo Presti and Laura Nicolosi drove me around and, along with Ignazio Barbagallo, Gianni and Fabrizio Samperi and (on one occasion) Philosophy Football FC, shared fabulous Sicilian hospitality.

Some of my writing on Italy has appeared elsewhere and I am grateful to Anthony Barnett and Paul Hilder at *Open Democracy*, my fellow editors at *Soundings* and Mandy Garner at the *Times Higher Education Supplement* for their encouragement. James Newell of the Italian Politics Group of the Political Studies Association and Ivor Gaber of Goldsmiths College, University of London, both organised conferences at which I was able to try out some of my ideas. The Politics and International Studies department at the Open University generously provided a sabbatical and funding for the early part of my research. I am grateful to colleagues for their interest in my work.

I was fortunate to talk again to former tutors Gino Bedani and David Selbourne, who first introduced me to Italian politics many years ago.

Ethlyn Boothe, Sarah Grindrod and Richard Wachala provided invaluable technical help in the latter stages of the book. I am grateful to David Castle and the staff at Pluto for their encouragement and help at all stages.

Finally, Italian friends in London: Alessandra Buonfino, Ilaria Favretto (who also showed me Milan), Benedetta Mascalchi and Filippo Ricci listened with curiosity and offered gentle encouragement as I recounted tales of my travels in their country. Numerous discussions of food, football and politics with Filippo over the last five years have vastly expanded my knowledge of Italy.

All translations are my own, unless otherwise indicated.

Geoff Andrews
London, 2005

Italy, with political hotspots.

Introduction:
Not a Normal Country

In December 2000, I read a newsflash on the Internet that there had been a bomb explosion at the Rome offices of *Il Manifesto*, Italy's left-wing daily newspaper. The previous week I had been in Rome with the paper's sports editor, Matteo Patrono. I made urgent inquiries about Matteo's well-being and received an evocative email two hours later, telling me he was OK (he was out of the office at the time of the bomb) and that nobody apart from the bomber had been seriously injured. However, the intention had been to kill and he described to me the anxiety and fear about the wider implications of the incident.

Over the next few days I followed the story in the Italian newspapers. It appeared that the perpetrator of the bomb was a neo-Fascist, with links to right-wing extremist groups. There seemed to be bigger questions in the minds of commentators, however. Some warned of a return to the *'anni di piombo'* ('years of lead') in the 1970s, when terrorist groups of the left and right combined to bring instability to Italy's creaking political system. In particular, the latest bomb attack provided further confirmation, if any were needed, that the crisis of the state in those years had never been resolved. This was despite the *'mani pulite'* ('Clean Hands') investigations of the early 1990s led by the magistrates into political corruption which brought about the downfall of Italy's ruling Christian Democrats after the *Tangentopoli* ('Bribesville') scandal and the anti-Mafia reforms which followed the murders of the magistrates Giovanni Falcone and Paolo Borsellino in the same period.

Another name was being mentioned in the inquisitions and discussions at this time. Silvio Berlusconi, Italy's richest man, who had large media business interests, had spent a short time as Prime Minister in 1994, in a rapid rise to power that seemed to confirm the 'abnormality' of Italian politics in a period when its political system had virtually collapsed overnight. Now, less than six months before the next general election, opinion polls inexplicably put his party, Forza Italia, and prospective allies,

1

Alleanza Nazionale (National Alliance) and the Lega Nord (Northern League), ahead again, with the centre-left government, which had seen three different Prime Ministers in over four years, losing its way. With a long-standing interest in Italian politics, but not finding in conventional academic accounts sufficient explanations for these developments, I wanted to know what was going on. Why, for example, was Berlusconi, a figure who had connections to the previous discredited Prime Minister Bettino Craxi, and an entrepreneur who had started to monopolise the media, able to make such headway in Italy? More precisely, how were we to understand his appeal to ordinary Italians? What were we to make of the new Italian right, composed not only of Berlusconi, but 'post-Fascists' and what seemed to be Padanian nationalists? What was the legacy of the two dominant political cultures in Italy, namely political Catholicism after the demise of the Democrazia cristiana (Christian Democrats, or DC) and the Partito Comunista Italiano (Italian Communist Party, or PCI), following the collapse of Communism in Eastern Europe? Where was political life beyond the parties? And, in particular, what was the viability of Italy becoming a 'normal country' – the frequently declared objective of Italian politicians of left and right?

As I started my journey at the beginning of 2001, one that took me the length and breadth of the country, I began to get answers to some of these questions – inevitably, however, new ones appeared. Berlusconi's subsequent election in May 2001 was made possible by the splits and ineffectiveness of the Italian centre-left, his power as a media entrepreneur and his appeal as a successful businessman. Yet it soon became clear that the Berlusconi phenomenon had deeper origins in the crisis of the Italian state and owed much to the historical revision of Italy's Fascist past and the anti-Fascist postwar consensus that shaped the first Italian Republic. Its novelty, moreover, lay in its response to an impasse that followed the crisis in party politics in which the dominant interests of parties, the DC in particular, had been bound up with the state. This *'partitocrazia'* had allowed little room for other sorts of political forces.

In the age of political disengagement, and the centrality of new technology and marketing, Berlusconi represented a challenge to the essence of modern politics, notably in his preference for bypassing political norms and structures. He was not a typical politician and, moreover, seemed to celebrate this fact with a certain style and panache. The centre-left had appeared best-placed to take advantage of *Tangentopoli*. The revamped DS was the party that most escaped claims of corruption, and articulated a language of modernity and new beginnings. Yet in government it looked tired as well as divided. It had failed to convince the public of its project. Berlusconi, on the other hand, had a lot to say.

His approach to politics contrasted sharply with that of the Christian Democrats, who had ruled Italy uninterrupted for nearly 50 years. After 1992, the party was in ruins; a small remaining rump, cobbled together in the Unione democratici cristiana (UDC), took its place in Berlusconi's Casa delle libertà (House of Liberties) coalition, while the more progressive Catholic centre reorganised under Romano Prodi in the Margherita ('Daisy') party. Such was the disarray among Catholic politicians that for a while they continued to share the same headquarters in Palazzo del Gesù. The Catholic political hegemony was over, while Italy's Catholic *culture* was fragmenting in the face of social change. While the DC had relied on clientelism, the corrupt web of favours which had helped sustain its 'regime', it had also derived loyalty from a sense of social solidarity and cohesion, reproduced in social, familial and cultural rituals, without ever succeeding in imbibing a strong civic consciousness or sense of state.

This culture was now dissolving, providing Italy with greater uncertainty, insecurity and generational conflicts, yet more freedom and individuality in personal lives. Widespread grief at the death of Pope John Paul II in April 2005 cannot disguise the overall decline of the church's authority in modern Italy. Attendances at mass and other church events showed a continual decline, while a gradual liberalisation of attitudes towards homosexuality, cohabitation, divorce and abortion continued throughout the 1990s and into the first part of the millennium. Despite Berlusconi's promise in late 2003 of a 'baby bonus' of 1000 euros for mothers who have a second child, Italy still has one of the lowest birth rates in the world, with women conceiving later in life in order to pursue careers; births outside marriage and divorce rates remain lower than the European average, however. The Italian population is now one of the oldest. Such demographic changes often have direct influence on political change. What is clear is that the Catholic factor in Italian politics was now much more complex. Conservative family structures largely remained with, for example, many young people continuing to live at home until their 30s, particularly in the South. Pictures of the Madonna and busts of Padre Pio, the beatified saint, adorned houses and piazzas throughout Italy, as a reminder that Catholic faith remained important. Yet these factors must be seen alongside greater liberal freedoms, large generational differences and weaker political alignment. The family itself remained for many commentators the focal point of social life and identity.[1]

Italian Communism, the other dimension of Italy's 'mass' political culture, predictably declined after the fall of the Berlin Wall. A name change from the Italian Communist Party to the Party of the Democratic Left (later Left Democrats), however, was not enough to arrest a crisis in identity, as splits, revisions, self-analysis and new challenges all brought into doubt the party's future ideological and strategic role. The PCI, as the party most embedded in the legacy of the Resistance, had been able to cohere solidarity amongst trade unions and social movements, and this allowed it to organise a significant part of Italy's cultural life. In this it was helped by impressive cohorts of intellectuals. It also retained a strong local presence leading to long periods in control of municipal councils, for which it gained a broad respect for good government, notably in the 'Red Belt' of Tuscany, Umbria and Emilia Romagna. The problem it faced was as a party of permanent opposition; apart from a brief period in government in the immediate postwar years and a surge in support in the mid 1970s, it was never able to dismantle the hegemony of the Christian Democrats, who were backed by both the Vatican and the White House. Ironically, for the party least affected by *Tangentopoli*, it was unable to take advantage of the Christian Democrats' collapse because of its own crisis following the fall of the Berlin Wall.

The passing of the PCI meant that the two dominant political traditions of modern Italy were now at an end. In this Catholic–Communist polarity, a conflict had been played out at all levels of Italian society, ranging from festivals and the formation of different trade union federations to sport, where strong rivalry existed between the two main cyclists in the 1950s, the Communist Gino Bardoli and the Christian Democrat Fausto

Coppi (cycling at the time being Italy's leading sport). The composition of the two parties (the PCI, for example, had 2 million members at its peak), together with their roles in Italian society, made them the clearest example of mass parties in Europe. This delineated the political parameters of Italian politics, made more complex by the Cold War, and the domination of the DC, with (as we now know) US support and Mafia cooperation. The end of this uniquely Italian settlement created a vacuum for new political forces. Ironically, in the realignment of Italian politics that took place after *Tangentopoli*, Catholics and Communists often found themselves on the same side, in the Ulivo (Olive Tree) coalition.

Italy is a country where the presence of history is always apparent. Wherever you go, historical monuments adorn piazzas, partisans are remembered in memorials, streets have been named after historical figures, intellectuals and artists, and the regular celebration of festivals – religious, cultural and political –reaffirms the past as a constant source of constraint on the present and future. In the aftermath of the crisis of 1992–94, however, many politicians and commentators were preoccupied with rewriting or trying to forget the past. There was an urgent need to move on from the crisis in the state, a weak civil society, institutional incompetence, the lack of national identity, the legacy of the Mafia and corruption. Many talked about 'years of transition', though towards what was rarely made clear. Even amongst scholars of Italian history, there is little agreement over the precise moment the First Republic ends or, indeed, whether the changes of the early 1990s, such as the collapse of the old parties, the arrival of a new electoral system and the prospect of alternating governments, were sufficient to constitute a new 'Second Republic'. Some have argued that the continuation of multiple parties, institutional inefficiency and parliamentary inertia have reflected the same problems of the pre-1992 period.

Underlying much of this emphasis on transition and the urgent need for new beginnings is the search for normality. Postwar politics in Italy, of course, was rarely 'normal'. Almost uninterrupted rule by one party, in alliance with numerous smaller ones, with Communists supplying the main opposition, was not normal by any definition. Italy has produced more than 50 governments since 1945, though the extent of DC hegemony throughout most of the period makes them more akin to cabinet reshuffles. The *anni di piombo*, which saw violence on a major scale from right and left extremes, as well as conspiracy on behalf of the state, also marked out Italy from its European neighbours. There is no strong social democratic tradition in Italy, nor historically has there been a conventional party of the right, while the numbers of smaller parties has continued to escalate.

The race for normality seemed to characterise the approaches of all the political parties, including many of the new ones. The National Alliance 'came in from the cold', gave up its 'neo-Fascist' heritage, became 'post-Fascist' and, under the leadership of Gianfranco Fini, has even sought the ground of the mainstream European right, though its agenda, as the example of Monte Sole will show later in the book, is derived from a significantly revisionist account of Italy's troubled past. Fini's appointment as Foreign Minister in November 2004 marked a new high in his own personal goal of becoming a statesman as well as a further breakthrough in his party's attempts to claim a new legitimacy.

The need for normality was also prominent on the left. The ex-Communist PDS, under the leadership of Massimo D'Alema, for a short period attempted to mimic a Blairite 'third way', while Walter Veltroni, another of its leaders, became convinced of the example of the American Democrats. Models and examples from other countries, particularly the US and the UK, seemed particularly attractive in this moment of reconstruction. All parties, meanwhile – with the exception of the 'regionalist' Northern League – talked ambitiously of resolving strong regional variations, including those between North and South, which had divided Italy in the past, in the pursuit of new national reconciliation. The very use of the terms 'centre-left' and 'centre-right' to describe the two contending and uniquely Italian coalitions, largely made up of post-Fascists, xenophobic regionalists (or 'Padanian nationalists') and ex-Communists, also seemed an optimistic attempt to normalise Italy's politics.

This need to make Italy normal, as Perry Anderson has put it, 'expresses a longing to resemble others who are superior to it'.[2] It reflects a real, if exaggerated, belief that things are always better elsewhere; a view confirmed, perhaps, by Italy's relatively weak sense of national identity. This has continued to be a feature of the post-1992 governments. The Ulivo government of 1996–2001 was strongly focused on gaining entry into the euro, and close cooperation with European governments and centre-left parties in other countries. However, the Berlusconi government has taken this search for 'international legitimacy' to a new level. Although more 'Eurosceptic' than the previous administration, much energy has been spent exaggerating Italy's prestige in the world order, while no opportunity for photocalls with allies, notably George W Bush and Tony Blair, has been missed. Berlusconi has been explicit about the material benefits for Italy that will come with close alliance with the world's leading statesmen. This extends to stressing strong personal ties, including the 'private' visit of Tony Blair to Villa Certosa, Berlusconi's Sardinian retreat, in August 2004.[3]

PAST IMPERFECT: FUTURE TENSE

Notwithstanding this almost uniform need to break with the past in order to arrive at a normal political system, past events are always round the corner, often reappearing when least expected. Despite the novelty of Berlusconi, whose political origins and development are discussed in the first chapter of this book, many aspects of the crisis of 1992–94 and politics since then have longer origins, which make the transition to a normal country – whatever that means – more problematic.

The 1970s, a period in which the lack of 'sense of state' was graphically demonstrated by fears of a right-wing coup and 'left-' and 'right-'wing terrorism, remains a crucial period for subsequent developments, including those discussed in this book. These include the crisis of identity on the left, the first signs of corruption and Mafia collaboration in the DC, and the challenge to the *partitocrazia* from civil society, notably the autonomous youth and student movements. This period marked the beginning of the end of the Christian Democratic–Communist paradigm. But it was the crisis of the state that was most significant. In a series of articles in *Corriere della Sera* and *Il Mondo* in 1975, Pier Paolo Pasolini, one of Italy's leading intellectuals, accused the ruling Christian Democrats of corruption, collaboration with the CIA and complicity with the Mafia. They were guilty of a further 'moral crime', according to Pasolini, for failing to find and punish the neo-Fascists who carried out bombings in major Italian cities.

Pasolini himself was murdered later that year, allegedly by a male prostitute he had met in Ostia outside Rome; even this was a cause of speculation and numerous conspiracy theories.

The decade of violence reached its climax in March 1978 when Aldo Moro, the former Italian Prime Minister and President of the Christian Democrats, was kidnapped on his way to parliament, where he was about to sign an historic agreement between the DC and the PCI. This agreement was to be the apex of the PCI's influence, making the government of the country impossible without their support. In the following weeks before his eventual murder, Moro was the central figure in an episode that said much about Italy's long-running crisis of the state. Moro had risen through the ranks of the DC and was known to be a shrewd and effective politician. His role had been crucial in maintaining good terms with the Communists who, under their popular and innovative leader, Enrico Berlinguer, had embarked on a strategy defined as the 'historic compromise', in which they would attempt to engage with progressive sections of Catholic opinion as a long-term solution to their political isolation. With their electoral support gradually increasing and reaching its peak in the mid 1970s, the DC became unable to rule effectively without the PCI's support; as a result, concessions and bargaining took on an increasing importance.

As Leonardo Sciascia has argued in his detailed study, the Moro case raised questions at the heart of Italy's crisis, namely the impossibility of reforming the DC leadership, the corruptions of power, secrecy in defence of party interests and, above all, the confusion between a 'sense of state' and the occupation and manipulation of power. In the 54 days of negotiation between Moro, his kidnappers and the political class, Moro himself seemed to become aware of many of these contradictions. As he tried to save himself by requesting that the DC show its humanity and negotiate with the Red Brigades, he became increasingly critical of their intransigence and more aware of the realities of power. As Sciascia writes:

> He had lived for power and by power up to nine o'clock on the morning of 16 March. But now he knows it is the others who possess it. And in the others he perceives its ugly, idiotic, cruel countenance.[4]

In their earlier statements, the DC leadership had praised Moro for his 'great statesmanship'. In fact, as Sciascia reminds us, he was not a great statesman but a great politician: 'neither Moro nor the party he presided over ever had a "sense of the state"'.[5] As the friction increased, Moro's former allies in the DC leadership put out statements of a different kind, in which they distinguished the 'new' from the 'old' Moro: 'He is not the man we knew, whose spiritual, political, juridical vision inspired our participation in the establishment of this Republican constitution.'[6] Moro's response was: 'I do not wish to be surrounded by those in power...Let none of those responsible seek to hide behind the call of an imaginary duty. All things will come to light. Soon they will come to light.'[7]

The Moro case continues to have repercussions for contemporary Italian politics. The absence of a sense of state remains, despite the language of reform and modernisation. This crisis, as we shall see, has intensified in the Berlusconi years. If anybody needs reminding of the crisis of the state, they need look no further than the figure of Giulio Andreotti, the leading Christian Democrat in the postwar years and one of those attacked by Moro from his prison. In the aftermath of *Tangentopoli* and Mafia murders, a new law was passed which made it possible to try politicians, and Andreotti was brought to court in 1993 on charges of 'Mafia association'. A further case of conspiracy to murder was also made and he was initially found guilty of this offence and sentenced to 24 years in prison. The murder for which he was convicted was that of Mino Pecorelli, an investigative journalist who allegedly was about to publish revelations about Andreotti's Mafia links based on diaries kept by Aldo Moro while in captivity. Presumably, these were the things that Moro promised, on the eve of his murder, would 'soon come to light'.

In 2004, following typically long, drawn-out trials, Andreotti was finally released on appeal due to 'insufficient evidence'. The lack of evidence on the question of Mafia links was a result of the difficulty of proving Mafia association *after* 1980 (Mafia association only became a crime in Italy in 1982). There was no difficulty in proving Mafia associations before then. As the appeal court stated: 'The court finds that Andreotti's real, enduring and friendly openness towards *mafiosi* did not last beyond the spring of 1980.'

The response from Italy's political class to Andreotti's release says much about the failure of Italian politicians to take historical and political responsibility for the past. It also confirms the continuing disjuncture between the political class and civil society, a feature of this book. Much of the centre-left as well as the centre-right welcomed the verdict, and Andreotti was variously lauded as 'a great statesman' or 'wise leader'. Now a life senator, he is a regular pundit in the Italian media, frequently asked to comment on historical events or topical issues.

The Moro case also contained significant implications for the future of the Italian left. His murder meant the end of Berlinguer's patient political strategy, the 'historic compromise'. Though he continued to lead the PCI until his death in 1984 under a new strategic idea of the 'democratic alternative', the party never recovered its support and lacked a clear political identity. This problem was not resolved – indeed, it was amplified – by the birth of the party's successor, the PDS. The division it created, with a minority of the party leaving to form Rifondazione comunista, mirrored to some extent the differing reactions to Berlinguer's earlier strategy. The majority two-thirds, loyal to the PCI's leadership, remained together in the new party and sought a new alliance with reformed Christian Democrats, while the remaining third, which reflected many of those critical of Berlinguer, sought a more radical alternative. However, the historic compromise was constructed by a mass party from a long period of opposition under severe Cold War constraints. The new party needed to find an ideology and sense of identity that drew on its existing support. Since its foundation it has never managed to do this, nervously glancing over its shoulder at its past while peering hopefully through rose-tinted spectacles at the prospect of turning itself into the British Labour Party or the American Democrats. Weak leadership and a declining membership have meant that the PDS (DS from 1998) has made little headway in providing a new alternative. Aldo Moro and Enrico Berlinguer were the last two great leaders in Italian politics; the failure to replace them has been a significant factor in Berlusconi's success.

On 9 May 1978, the same day that Moro's body was found in Rome, the death of a young Sicilian, Peppino Impastato, was also reported in the press. He had been found dead near a railway line in Cinisi, a small town in Sicily, not far from Palermo. Impastato had been a member of a left-wing opposition party (Democrazia proletaria, or Dp) and had campaigned throughout his young life against the Mafia. The son of a *mafioso*, he was brought up close to the headquarters of the local Mafia boss, Tano Badalamenti, who was to be imprisoned in the US for Mafia association in the 1980s. At the time, it was claimed that Impastato had died attempting to blow up the railway line, in a death compared to that of the left-wing publisher Giangiacomo Feltrinelli in 1972. It was not until a major film was made of his life, 22 years later, that the case was reopened and the suspicions of his family and friends were confirmed – namely, that he had been murdered on the instructions of Badalamenti.[8]

Impastato's murder and the attempts to cover it up were also indicative of this shady era of Italian politics, in which fear, conspiracy and secrecy did battle with hope, protest and idealism. His short life also says much about the politics of the 1970s and its idealistic and militant youth movements, as significant in their own way as the Paris student revolt of 1968. In Cinisi, Impastato had founded a free radio station, Radio Aut, which he used to undermine the Mafia through satire, music and political polemic. This movement, which included arguments for workers' control, direct action against multinational corporations and student occupations, was formed in opposition not only to the corruptions and repressions of the Italian state, but also as a critique of the PCI, the historic compromise and the limitations of party politics. In many ways, as later chapters will show, its mix of culture and politics, direct action and grassroots mobilisation prefigured the anti-global capitalist movements which grew from the late 1990s and which, in Italy, reached their peak at the time of the G8 summit in Genoa in July 2001. The hopes of Italy's youth continued to drive oppositional politics in the era of Berlusconi as they did in the era of Andreotti in the 1970s.

It is also possible to discern the wider political and historical significance of this event. Impastato's death was overlooked partly because it coincided with the Moro case. It was also overlooked because of the marginalisation of Sicily and the South in general, which contain Italy's most economically underdeveloped regions, and have long suffered most from political corruption and clientelism under the control of the Mafia. This view of the South is partly behind the advance of the Northern League, whose electoral support grew in light of its denunciation of the corruptions in Rome and wider stereotypical assumptions about 'lazy southerners'. Yet, the case of Impastato demands that the South be taken seriously. His campaign for justice has been followed by wider evidence of resistance and the renaissance of a civic spirit in the South. The 'Palermo Spring', led by Leoluca Orlando in the mid 1980s, brought big changes to Sicily's capital and in particular new confidence in the fight against the Mafia, leading to the imprisonment of many *mafiosi*. The type of courage demonstrated by Impastato and other anti-mafia campaigners was no longer an isolated phenomenon but was now part of a mainstream alternative movement.

Meanwhile, the economic development of Puglia and parts of Basilicata, along Italy's heel, offered new opportunities as well as a new confidence. In the Berlusconi years, the South, often the target of the governing coalition's wrath and the recipient of many broken promises of economic and social reform, began to strike back. The new associations and movements, not conditioned by Italy's party system and often stretching beyond the boundaries of left and right, brought new life to Italy's body politic, presenting an alternative to Berlusconi's populism. This civic spirit also challenged long-standing assumptions about apathy, conservatism, and the corrosive aspects of Italian familism.

The Berlusconi years can therefore only be understood within the context of the upheavals of Italian political history. Berlusconi himself is connected to the previous era by his membership from 1978 of Propaganda 2 (P2), the conspiratorial and anti-Communist organisation made up of a cross-section of Italy's power elite, which included three government ministers and 44 MPs, leading army officers, newspaper editors and bankers. Its purpose was to infiltrate and fund key areas of Italy's public institutions in order to halt the rise of the left.[9] Berlusconi's rise to power was cemented in the Milan world of the 1980s, where he made his money and contacts and became close friends with Bettino Craxi, Italy's Prime Minister in the mid 1980s, who was later convicted of corruption.

The Berlusconi years do, however, mark a departure in fundamental ways that suggest new political faultlines and trajectories distinct from the politics of the past. Berlusconi started to impose himself in the vacuum that followed the collapse of the DC and the crisis on the left. He flourished in the aftermath of the decline of the *partitocrazia* and the general contempt held by Italians for their politicians. This era marked the arrival of the businessman as politician. As the first part of this book shows, the Berlusconi phenomenon was one response to the crisis of the state and the erosion of trust in conventional politics. It was a postmodern response in that it altered the traditional relationship between the citizen and politics through the use of new global media, created a different role for the political party (Forza Italia, for example, was a business party founded on a network of football clubs) and prospered in the wake of the two grand narratives in Italian politics, namely political Catholicism and Communism. It was also a *populist* response in that it appealed directly to citizens, often as consumers, while pushing at the boundaries not only of formal democratic politics, but legality and constitutional government. This postmodern populism ultimately presented a challenge to politics itself, with the erosion of dissent and the subordination of public interests to private interests.

As I travelled in Italy these shifts became more visible and tangible in all areas of Italian society. Political corruption has not gone away, but lives on in new forms. The stench of uncleared rubbish in Naples, with more than a whiff of the Camorra lurking in the background, was a sufficient enough reminder. The harrowing sirens of the emergency services seemed to signal the end of innocence of another generation as the Genoa G8 protests were broken up by the violence of the *carabinieri* (paramilitary police), apparently buoyed by the encouraging words of Deputy Prime Minister Gianfranco Fini; detained protesters were forced to sing Fascist songs. The increasingly xenophobic opposition to immigrants, evident in the rhetoric of Umberto Bossi and his depleted band of supporters, alarmingly found its way into the conversations of ordinary Italians. Like Tobias Jones in his fascinating and prescient study of Berlusconi, I also found that breaking the rules was not only accepted but expected, and to be cunning was worthy of particular praise.[10] The duplicity of those in power and indifference from those without it was also disconcerting. It was also clear that power in Italy, as Pasolini had argued 30 years before, remained a complex web of intrigue, bureaucracy, conspiracy and inertia. It was exercised differently, however. To witness the influence of Silvio Berlusconi it was necessary only to switch to one of his many TV channels, in a country saturated by television, usually running uninterrupted in the kitchens of most Italian homes. Tune in, for example, to Rete 4, and hear the news delivered by Emilo Fede, for daily denunciations of the magistrates and regular updates of the achievements of his old friend the Prime Minister.

Yet, as I travelled through what remains a beautiful, complex and fascinating country, I encountered another Italy, one where there was a revival of civil society, the birth of a new associationism and a politics that took place outside political parties. Extraordinary energy, organisational endeavour, idealism and a new civic spirit drove many of the movements and associations, often from sections of Italian society where such activity would be least expected. This was an attempt to rebuild politics, inspired by a return of idealism in the movements of the left, though by no means confined to this, as the renaissance in the South and Sicily, and the breadth of alternative hopes and visions – from pacifism to 'slow food' – show.

Italy's long-term future remains uncertain, with the country divided and evidence of its decline increasing. What became most obvious to me was that Italy had not been a 'normal country' before Berlusconi, and was even less of one under his rule, but would not become one in the years following. Attempts by politicians of left and right had not brought this any closer. Those commentators who saw in Gianfranco Fini's post-Fascist National Alliance a 'mainstream' right-wing party, or in Piero Fassino's (and Massimo D'Alema's) Left Democrats a natural evolution to a Blairite third way – one proposition as equally preposterous as the other – were going to be disappointed. Italy will not become a normal country. The question of what country it could become is the focus of this book.

Part I
Berlusconi and Friends

Please Berlusconi, please do something that, when we go to bed at night, will make us all proud to be Italians.
—Roberto Benigni, San Remo Festival, 2002

1

From Salesman to Statesman: The Postmodern Populism of Silvio Berlusconi

What are we to make of Silvio Berlusconi, Italy's longest-serving postwar Prime Minister, richest man and media entrepreneur? Many see his rise to power as carrying dangerous implications for Western democracy. Some compare his unrivalled personal power to that of a latter-day Peron. It was *The Economist*, not previously noted for radical campaigns, which launched the most in-depth inquiry into his activities, declaring him 'Unfit to Govern' during the 2001 election campaign and later compiling an extensive list of his alleged financial irregularities.[1] Others, like the American journalist Joe Klein, apparently seduced by the 'great seducer', regard him as little more than a lovable rogue who, harangued by the Neanderthal left, was merely trying to follow sensible economic policies.[2] As for Italians themselves, there seems to be an enormous gulf of the kind that has long divided Italy. Some regard him with a mixture of horror and ridicule; others, seemingly indifferent to his activities, shrug their shoulders and talk of their admiration for the way he has 'beaten the system'. Few admit to having voted for him.

Berlusconi has certainly wielded more power than any Italian leader since Mussolini. His second spell in office, which began in May 2001, saw unprecedented conflicts with the judiciary, the President of the Republic and what remains of public broadcasting in Italy, while his 'personal dominion' seems more reminiscent of those found in some Latin American regimes than modern Western democracies. Yet the rise of Berlusconi has a peculiarly Italian context, one which says much about Italy's recent history, political crises, decay of public life, failures of the left and new economic elites. It is partly also a Milanese phenomenon, with its roots in the development of Milanese capitalism in the 1980s and partly framed by the fallout of the *Tangentopoli* crisis, which first broke in that city. The status of Berlusconi as an 'anti-politician', who often projects himself and his party (founded with the help of his business associates and built on a network of football clubs) above the organisational, structural and democratic norms of modern political parties, is crucial to understanding the nature of his power and the image he invokes. As such, while there may well be wider significance to be drawn from Berlusconi's brand of populism for the future of politics more widely, it is conceivable only through an analysis of the particular nature of Italy's crisis.

For this reason we cannot ignore the very unusual and uniquely Italian nature of Berlusconi's allies in the House of Liberties, without which he would never have prospered. The Northern League and National Alliance are no more 'normal' than Berlusconi's Forza Italia. One party, rooted in Italy's prosperous north-eastern region, wants regional autonomy – even, at one point in the 1990s, complete independence – and is habitually hostile to Rome; the other, the heir to Mussolini's Fascists, is profoundly nationalist and centralist, with much of its core support in the South. The personal ambitions of the two leaders, Umberto Bossi and Gianfranco Fini, combined with their evident dislike of each other, was destined to make Berlusconi's reign a troubled and volatile one.

Crucially, however, these new parties of the Italian right represented a major historical break with the past. While a small rump of the old Christian Democrats has remained in the form of the UDC, a usually more circumspect part of the House of Liberties, the vacuum left by the DC, which ruled for almost the entire postwar period until its collapse in the early 1990s, has been filled by three parties that were not born out of the anti-Fascist moment of postwar reconstruction. They played no part in the construction of the 'constitutional arch' that, reflecting the anti-Fascist political consensus, shaped the first Italian Republic after 1945.

As a consequence these parties have a more ambiguous relationship to the past, which was used initially to great advantage. Berlusconi himself orchestrated this shift well, presenting himself as a 'new' type of leader and not a professional politician or someone linked to the failures of the old political class. We will see that this carefully cultivated image of himself as a new political actor is a myth. Yet myths often worked for Silvio Berlusconi. They helped him come to power and more than once have rescued him from tight corners. They are central to his particular approach to politics, defined in these pages as postmodern populism.

POSTMODERN POPULISM

Postmodern populism, Berlusconi's mode of governance, helps explain his capacity to exercise power through the global media, his contempt for the conventional norms of politics and his particular way of communicating with his electorate, which also doubles as his media audience. As a phenomenon it had its roots in the crisis of ideological politics that characterised the late 1980s and early 1990s when firstly the Italian Communist Party, the biggest of its kind in Western Europe, turned itself into the Left Democrats following the end of Communism. Then, more dramatically, following the public revelations of its role in the *Tangentopoli* scandal (namely the systematic corruption in which 'kickbacks' and percentage cuts were taken by politicians in exchange for the distribution of contracts to businesses), the ruling Christian Democrats collapsed. As a result, the Christian Democratic–Communist polarity which shaped the ideological contours of postwar Italian politics came to an end. The old *partitocrazia* was over and an opening beckoned for new political forces.

The collapse of Italy's dominant ideological framework was only part of the story however. The decline of *mass* political parties and Fordist forms of work preceded this crisis and were behind widespread socioeconomic shifts in most European countries. In Italy, the link between left-wing politics and its industrial support in manufacturing, which had been particularly strong, now began to fragment. This was particularly notable in the northern industrial cities, where shifting political allegiances provided the Northern League in particular with important political gains. Several writers have noted the populist turn in Italian politics at this time, as voters looked for new and often immediate solutions to this moment of crisis.[3]

The populist appeal of Forza Italia, however, was as a uniquely postmodern political organisation. Founded on a network of football supporters' clubs, it was unlike traditional political parties by virtue of its membership, recruiting from groups not previously involved in politics, and marked further by the absence of any democratic structure or formal organisational framework. Even more significant was the unique and unrivalled power of its leader, who announced the formation of the new political organisation by sending out a video, made at his Milan villa in 1994, just a couple of months before the election that brought him to power for the first time.

It is his style of leadership and unrivalled power that marked Berlusconi out from other political leaders. Consistently critical of professional politicians, he cultivated the image of himself as an outsider, but someone at ease with the technological shifts of the contemporary world. With his position as a media entrepreneur, owner of a football club and reputation as a 'showman', the 'cavaliere' ('knight') brought his audacious business acumen to politics. His personal leadership style, characterised by presidential ambitions, has been refined with great care and detail, in the presentation of his own image as someone much younger than he actually is, and as a successful businessman who can seamlessly extend his own personal success as a salesman to the role of statesman.

Through his unique access to the media, he addressed an 'audience' as much as an 'electorate'; his appeals to loyalty were made to consumers rather than citizens, in the era of post-Fordist, media-driven information societies. The language he chose to adopt in public combined in a unique, uneven and unprecedented way with the content of his TV programmes, while the success of his team, AC Milan, also enabled him to remain in the limelight of popular appeal. As with all forms of populism, but notably in its postmodern version, truth and myth are often entwined, while history is overlooked or rewritten. Yet as Taggart has argued, populism in reality has an 'empty heart'. While it claims to be revolutionary and 'draws great support at times of crisis…[it] is incapable of offering root and branch reform'. In appealing beyond the conventions of 'normal' politics, Taggart argues that populists 'identify themselves with an idealised heartland'. Despite grandiose language invoking 'the people' against bastions of bureaucracy and officialdom, populism reinforces power elites and above all undermines politics. In fact, as Taggart suggests, populism is only 'reluctantly political', and is 'a reaction against the ideas, institutions and practices of representative politics'.[4]

Indeed, Berlusconi has often shown little patience for the political and legal niceties of representative democracies. He has regularly invoked 'the people' against the judiciary, the left or any other imaginary obstacles that got in his way. In doing so he has sought to bypass the constitutional constraints of liberal democracies. As Ginsborg has argued: 'There is no idea of a level playing field...Scant attention is paid to the benign consequences of a balance of powers within the democratic state. Judicial autonomy is regarded with anathema'.[5]

By bringing entrepreneurial values and practices into public life, Berlusconi has altered the terms of political debate within Italy. As we will see, the parameters of postmodern populism not only defined Berlusconi's entrance onto the political stage, but shaped his political values, his conflicts, the nature of his relationship with the Italian people and ultimately the crisis in his leadership

MILANESE BACKGROUND

As Italy's financial centre, home of the Italian stock exchange, the main hub of Italy's fashion world and historically the fount of Italy's modern economic dynamism, Milan, Berlusconi's home city, remains a crucial part of his story. His rise as an entrepreneur took place against the background of Italy's 'economic miracle' of the 1950s and 1960s. It is important to recognise the massive and rapid expansion of the Italian economy from the 1950s, in which Italy moved from being a country with much dependence on agriculture to being one of the biggest exporters in the West. Its relative wealth reached its peak in the late 1980s when it became the fifth largest economy in the West, overtaking the UK in the process. Much of this wealth was driven by the new industrial districts in the North of the country. Milan symbolised this new wealth, which was evident in the fashion houses but also in the lifestyles of its citizens and the emergence of new economic elites. It was the Milan of the 1980s that provided the major opportunities for Berlusconi to increase his economic power, while the 1990s brought the possibility of combining entrepreneurial endeavour with political commitment.

The major economic transformations that took place in this period resulted in what Ginsborg has called a 'new technological paradigm', in which 'no workplace was left untouched, no entrepreneur unaffected'.[6] In particular, the shift from a Fordist workforce to the dominance of a tertiary and service sector combined with major social and political changes to create new forms of social divisions, increasing individualism and hedonism and above all new power elites. The rise of the 'post-Fordist' industries was particularly strong in the new industrial districts of Lombardy, Veneto, Emilia Romagna and Friuli-Venezia Giulia. Typified by Bennetton, they built on the strong Italian tradition of small artisan firms, while new high-tech retailing and design allowed the industries to flourish. This 'molecular capitalism', as Bonomi has called it, was responsible for a new domination of the service sector, which by 1980 already accounted for 48.3 percent of Italy's employment.[7] It also meant that political allegiances built around the industrial working class were fragmenting; this was reflected in greater electoral volatility, with the Northern League in particular benefiting from a new working-class vote.[8] Shifts in consumption patterns, a rise in social mobility and looser family ties also reflected a greater individualism, with new risks and uncertainties. At the same time, the Catholic and Communist ideologies that had helped shape people's ideas were entering profound and deep crisis. Milan, for example, traditionally had strong left movements in the 1960s and 1970s, whose leading political and cultural figures included the publisher Giangiacomo Feltrinelli, the playwright Dario Fo, and more recently, Vittorio Agnoletto, leader of the 'No Global' movement.

These economic changes were of course taking place in all Western countries at this time and in Britain were symbolised by the Thatcherite generation of slick city dealers and 'yuppies'. In Milan, there was unprecedented mobility in a dynamic service industry and it is possible to discern the development of a new entrepreneurial class of business managers and tycoons, an environment ideal for someone of Berlusconi's profile. In Milan, there was a new economic and political elite which, among other things, facilitated the rise to power of Bettino Craxi, Berlusconi's close friend and Prime Minister of Italy, later found guilty of corruption. As Ginsborg describes it, the late 1980s was symptomatic of an era in which the individual entrepreneur was 'cast loose' in a new climate of hedonism and risk-taking: 'The attitudes of Italian managers were found to be dominated by individualism, autocracy, paternalism, a stress upon masculinity and a strong sense of hierarchy'.[9] As we now know, Milan in this period was also the centre of clientelism and corruption, where the political and economic aspirations of much of the elite crossed the boundaries of legality.

Following a strict schooling and graduation in law, Berlusconi entered the booming construction industry in Milan in the early 1960s. Without his own capital he showed an early sign of entrepreneurialism by getting the owner of the bank where his father worked as a clerk to lend him money for his first ventures. After selling his first apartment blocks, with the help of advertisements in *Corriere della Sera*, he made his main breakthrough with the building of Milano 2 between 1970–79. Milano 2 was an enclosed residential area for 10,000 people, built on the outskirts of the city and further cut off by the tight security of its perimeter gates.[10] Its development reflected the new dominant ethos of Milan at this time. With its artificial lakes, six schools and swimming pool, Milano 2 offered some respite from the 'Milano da bere', the 'city you can drink', one that epitomised the fast life of the new rich.[11]

The significance of Milano 2 for Berlusconi's subsequent career was massive. In building the complex he had to deal with local bureaucracies, trade unions and airport authorities (it was close to Linate Airport and he had to win over the airport authorities to alter flight directions). These were the first of many battles in which he saw himself as the creative entrepreneur pursuing greater prosperity in the face of obstructive and politically motivated officials. As with many of his other business ventures, there was some concern over the exact source of his funds for the complex. It was also at Milano 2 that Berlusconi made his first, decisive intervention in the media, with the arrival of TeleMilano, a TV station for Milano 2's residents set up in 1974. This was the same year that he bought his 147-room villa in Arcore near Milan, at an apparently cut price offer, purchased with the help of his new lawyer, Cesare Previti.

FROM MEDIA ENTREPRENEUR TO POLITICIAN

Berlusconi's rise as a media entrepreneur is central to an understanding of his populist appeal in politics. The setting up of TeleMilano provided the chance for his first break into public life. In 1980 he turned it into the private network Canale 5 (Channel 5). The symbolic launching of Canale 5, from the artificial lake at Milano 2, with one of his now legendary quiz shows, connected with an audience that was subsequently to be served a regular diet of imported American soaps, telefilms, cartoons and variety shows. The centrality of TV in the lives of ordinary Italians owes more to Berlusconi's contribution than it does to anyone else. His skilful positioning of these programmes at peak hours on Canale 5 and his two other networks that he purchased in the early 1980s, Rete 4 and Italia 1, brought him into conflict with the state broadcaster, RAI, which at that time had a monopoly of national broadcasting. His actions changed the rules of public broadcasting in Italy. It was the beginning of an acceleration to power that eventually enabled Berlusconi to own three private networks, as well as to appoint the board of RAI. RAI under his control has subsequently moved rapidly towards privatisation.

By the mid 1980s Berlusconi was effectively the first 'supraregional' broadcaster, in the words of media studies professor Philip Schlesinger.[12] He was able to create the 'illusion of a network' by using private channels from the global media market and applying slick commercial criteria in the production, marketing and targeting of his audience, aided significantly by his advertising company, Publitalia, which he had set up in 1979. In doing so he garnered a committed and long-term loyalty from his audience, drawn from particular social groups (including many housewives), which he later cultivated as part of his core electoral support.

In the short term, Berlusconi had to endure battles with RAI that took him to the courts. The first time this occurred was in 1984, when he was taken off the air after he tried to show consecutive episodes of Dallas and Dynasty on his networks at a time when regulations still restricted the scheduling of commercial TV programmes. Berlusconi attempted to get round this ruling by running his programmes concurrently on different channels.

After he was taken off the air, he persuaded his close friend and political patron, Bettino Craxi, who also happened to be Italy's Prime Minister, of his best intentions, while his case was helped by the popularity of the programmes he was showing, as compared to the 'dryer' RAI options. His victory in getting back on air so quickly was his first over public service broadcasters and his first serious conflict with the state. Berlusconi's friendship with Craxi is important in confirming his place as part of a powerful political and economic elite, consolidated on the back of the power and influence derived from his extensive media ownership through Mediaset. Craxi, like Berlusconi, was at home in the new TV world; his Socialist Party was not encumbered by the Catholic morality of the DC. Craxi issued a special decree, allowing Berlusconi to keep on transmitting (though this was initially rejected by the constitutional court). Changes in media regulations in 1990 effectively allowed Berlusconi to extend his TV empire. Craxi had a significant impact in his role as a bridge between two elites – the old political class around Andreotti and the rising business politicians of whom Berlusconi was the unrivalled leader.

Berlusconi's ownership of TV channels was crucial in his attempts, in a populist way, to bring his style and ethos into the public domain. It allowed him to develop an informal relationship with his audience-voters and build a strategy that saw him hold off numerous attempts – through the courts and in the cut and thrust of political battle – to bring him down. The content of his programmes is also revealing. The programmes Berlusconi imported in the 1980s, often using offshore tax revenues that have subsequently been subject to scrutiny, were precursors to contemporary 'reality TV'. According to Umberto Eco, writing in *L'Espresso* in 1983, these kinds of programmes reflected the new era of 'neo-television'. Neo-TV, in Eco's analysis, is to be understood by the way in which

> it talks about itself and about the contact that it establishes with its own public. It does not matter what it says, nor what it might be about, especially as the public, armed with remote control, decides when to let it speak and when to switch channels. In order to survive...neo-TV tries to hold viewers by saying to them: 'I am here, it's me. I am you'.[13]

In contrast to the diet of mainstream TV, historically divided on political grounds between the main parties, with the Christian Democrats maintaining the bulk share of the spoils, neo-TV assumed a different relationship with its public, addressing them as active consumers. It is a relationship that 20 years on has become widespread and global in its impact, incorporating the culture and ethos of American capitalism, with dubbing as the widespread means of 'Italianising' the programmes for domestic consumption. Globalisation and information technology have provided Berlusconi and other media entrepreneurs like Rupert Murdoch the opportunity for greater monopolisation of the media. The move towards the deregulation of the media and culture industry only increased the power of individual entrepreneurs, and in Italy started to challenge the system of party patronage, the privileges of the state and dominant party interests. This not only benefited Berlusconi the media entrepreneur, who by 1977 had also acquired a leading daily newspaper, *Il Giornale*, by 1983 40 percent of Italy's leading publisher Mondadori, and by 1986 shares in AC Milan, one of Italy's greatest football teams; it also helped Berlusconi's accession to political power.

THE ANTI-POLITICIAN COMES OFF THE BENCH

By the time Berlusconi entered politics in 1994, just months before the general election which brought him to power for the first time, he already understood the predicaments of the Italian political crisis and had experienced power through his conflicts with RAI and the state broadcasting establishment. His new political party, Forza Italia, derived from the well-known football chant urging on the national team to greater endeavours, was built on a network of football supporters that had emerged from AC Milan, the club he bought in 1986 and which at the time was Italy's most successful team. Its name and image owed much to the latest marketing techniques, which have subsequently been employed extensively to research Berlusconi's support. His announcement that he was setting up the new party was dramatic and from the start reflected his populist standpoint. He sent a nine-minute video of his political intent to the major TV channels, including his own, in which he promised to 'create a new Italian miracle' based on his skills as an entrepreneur. As the election campaign got under way, Berlusconi used football metaphors repeatedly – in a country where football is a religion – to explain the predicament in which the nation found itself and the need for a new political force. Not only was he 'taking the field', but he was doing so because: 'I heard that the game was getting dangerous and that it was all being played in the two penalty areas, with the midfield being left desolately empty.'[14]

Berlusconi's election broadcasts, carefully managed and presented down to the smallest details (arrangement of his desk, colour of his tie, etc.), were clearly targeted at what he saw as his key electorate – entrepreneurs, housewives and private sector managers – many of whom, of course, were his TV audience. His intention, according to Pezzini, was to 'seduce' his electorate, a strategy that he has employed many times over through his TV channels and one that crystallised the phenomenon Eco had described as 'neo-TV' 20 years earlier.[15]

Though nominally a party, Forza Italia shares none of the underlying structures of conventional political organisations. It has no mass membership, operates through 'clubs' rather than 'sections' or 'branches' and has only held one national conference in the first ten years of its existence. Most of its national executive committee are appointed businessmen. It therefore has little internal democracy, drawing on business friends and contacts of Berlusconi. John Foot, in his book *Modern Italy*, has described Forza Italia as a 'business party'.[16] Certainly it makes for a strong contrast with the Fordist cultures of modern political organisations – in postwar Italy best illustrated by the Italian Communist Party – not only exemplified by their organisational structures, but also visible in their outward culture of a mass working-class membership and blue-collar workforce. The Forza Italia electorate was not formed through traditional forms of political alignment, namely family background or conventional ideological commitment, but through new networks of power and influence. Many of these were virtual, market-driven and sustained through populist endeavour on the part of Forza Italia's leader, who has unrivalled decision-making powers. As such, the party is one of the earliest examples of a post-Fordist political organisation. Unlike the older political cultures, Christian Democracy and Communism, Forza Italia was not entrenched in any one region, though its strength remained in the northern regions, and in the 2001 election, it achieved a major breakthrough in Sicily.[17]

Forza Italia's biggest innovation was that it seemed to call into question the necessity of politics itself. It repudiated the view that politicians rather than businessmen had the answer to modern problems. Many of its members and activists had never previously been involved in politics. Berlusconi has always defined himself firstly as a businessman who does not think in the ways of a politician; his experience of business has given him the background to succeed where conventional politicians have failed.

In the event, his first taste of political power in 1994 was short-lived, his government lasting only nine months. Indeed, the reasons for its decline – disputes with coalition partners and corruption charges – suggested that there was no way back for Berlusconi. He had not carried out the reforms he promised and became entangled in allegations of corruption. Following the defeat of his government, Oscar Luigi Scalfaro, the President of the Republic, resisting calls for an election which Berlusconi was still likely to have won (his populism surviving the difficulties he faced from the political establishment), appointed a team of technocrats under Lamberto Dini to take over in the short term. The subsequent election of 1996 was won by the Olive Tree coalition made up of the DS and the network of centrists under the leadership of Romano Prodi.

Berlusconi was not finished yet, however. There were several reasons why he was able to fight his way back and win the election of 2001. Firstly, the centre-left government of 1996–2001, despite its reforming agenda, refused to pass legislation to address Berlusconi's growing and unresolved conflicts of interest between his media ownership and political aspirations. As Ginsborg records, Massimo D'Alema spent hours in committee with Berlusconi (the latter as leader of the opposition) in an attempt to thrash out new constitutional proposals in order to forge a new constitutional agreement for institutional reform. This new bicameral commission drew up 38 drafts for its proposals to do with reform of parliament, state and government, hoping a new 'normal' two-party system would be formed based around Forza Italia and the Left Democrats. The key to the passing of the commission's proposals was to be a compromise D'Alema worked out with Berlusconi, whereby the latter would be given a guarantee that the powers of magistrates would be curbed. At the time Berlusconi was facing accusations by magistrates of corruption and the falsification of accounts. D'Alema acquiesced as a way of getting the legislation through. In the event, Berlusconi withdrew his support at a later stage. Together with the inability to pass legislation aimed at curtailing Berlusconi's conflicts of interest, these developments meant that the centre-left missed a historic opportunity, with clear results; 'a damning indictment of the reforming capacity of the centre-left', as Ginsborg put it. This meant that Berlusconi in the immediate term would be given a free run in future elections, his credibility seemingly reinforced by the timidity of centre-left reformers.[18]

Secondly, Berlusconi managed to rebuild his relations with his coalition partners. The Northern League, though showing signs of decline after its peak in the early 1990s, succeeded in opening a 'northern question' in Italian politics and pushing it to the top of the political agenda. Here the Northern League found a natural ally in Berlusconi, whose party was rooted in the culture and methods of Milanese capitalism and shared at least some of Bossi's ideas. Both organisations were populist of a sort; Bossi, the straight-talking rabble-rouser who carefully marketed himself as a 'man of the ordinary people', dressing unfashionably, speaking in the Italian dialects of his supporters; and Berlusconi, the slick 'postmodern' populist whose 'people' had different aspirations but were similarly upwardly mobile. The electorate in the North was regarded by both parties as the bedrock of the Italian economy.

Bossi was also moving towards a tough line on immigration, at times reaching xenophobic levels in his vociferous response to what was becoming one of Europe's biggest social and political crises. This uncompromising stance was shared by the National Alliance under Fini's leadership. Yet Fini had a different project: to cohere and situate his revamped party as the 'normal' voice of right-wing opinion in Italy. In addition the UDC, a rump of centre-right Christian Democrats (the centre-left side was now with Prodi under the umbrella network of the Margherita) was willing to go along with the coalition and expected ministerial prizes for bringing previous government experience. By the time of the 2001 election, this coalition had adopted the anti-Communist positions of the DC, while doing enough to carry the global neo-liberal message; it even had a leader who personally embodied the values of enterprise and success.

FROM SALESMAN TO STATESMAN

The audacity of Berlusconi's election campaign in 2001 was exemplified by his distribution of 10 million copies to the Italian electorate of 'An Italian Story', a glossy pictorial tribute to his career to date, in which he was pictured with family members, world leaders (from his earlier period in office), TV presenters, footballers and adoring crowds. It was accompanied by a letter from Guido Possa, the President of 'Club Forza Italia', urging the electors not to miss their 'appointment with history' and to make the 'decisive choice'. Berlusconi's 'contract with the people', in which he promised lower taxes, more prosperity and greater efficiency, made inevitably on one of his TV programmes during the campaign, was likewise not the stuff of ordinary politics. His election posters meanwhile urged the electorate to vote not for a Prime Minister, but for 'President Berlusconi'; alternatively, they recommended him as 'the working-class candidate'. He was not a normal politician.

The most significant aspect of Berlusconi's arrival on the political scene was his ability to expand his business interests unchallenged. Through Fininvest (his holding company) he had a greater stake in his domestic economy than any of the other major global entrepreneurs, one that supplemented in a unique way his political power. It is unlikely that his accession to power in 2001, with the conflicts of interest between his massive media interests and political office as Prime Minister, could have taken place in any other Western European country.

Berlusconi projected himself as an alternative to the *partitocrazia* and as a response to the *Tangentopoli* scandal and the end of Communism. Yet his connections with the previous regime (notably through his close friendship with Bettino Craxi), his membership of P2 (the secret organisation of powerful military, business and political figures), and his growing list of court battles against corruption, refute his status as a moderniser or outsider. His relationship to *Tangentopoli* has often been shrouded in mystery and remains ambiguous; on the one hand, he has tried to distance himself from the fallout, and on the other, he has mounted continuous attacks on the magistrates who carried out the investigations. His friendship with Craxi, found guilty of corruption and eventually dying in exile from Italian justice in Tunisia, had been crucial in Berlusconi's own path to power, and is a clear link between his own political arrival and the end of the previous era. Without Craxi's patronage, he would never have made it as a major TV entrepreneur. As David Lane has suggested, Berlusconi in many ways is the real 'heir of *Tangentopoli*'.[19]

Moreover, during his period in office, there has been little evidence that Berlusconi has any commitment to reforming the political system. Indeed, his premiership showed greater inclination to turn back the tide of political and constitutional reform, while consolidating and extending his own extraordinary hold on power. During this second period in office, Berlusconi's two closest political friends and allies have faced protracted court trials. Cesare Previti, his long-standing lawyer who completed his first business deals, and a co-founder and Forza Italia MP, was sentenced to eleven years in jail in April 2003 for bribing judges on behalf of Fininvest, while Marcello Dell'Utri, Forza Italia's national coordinator, has appeared on charges of Mafia conspiracy.

Berlusconi himself spent much of his period in power avoiding magistrates and seeking to suspend or prevent the growing list of cases being brought against him, variously on charges of bribing judges, financial corruption and Mafia links. Many cases went back to his earlier business ventures. The financing of Fininvest became an issue of contention when it was revealed that the Rasini bank from which Berlusconi borrowed money was used by the Cosa Nostra, the Sicilian Mafia, which also had links to two Swiss companies that had funded many of Berlusconi's financial dealings, including Milano 2. A leading *pentito* (informer) claimed that 20 billion lire of Mafia money had been put into Fininvest, and many details of Berlusconi's funds were incomplete or shrouded in mystery.

Berlusconi's acquittal on charges of bribing a magistrate in December 2004, on the grounds that the case was 'out of time', was his most serious legal challenge and had caused unprecedented constitutional tension in and outside parliament. Berlusconi was the first Italian Prime Minister to face such charges in office. His manoeuvres to avoid prosecution and to shift his trials from what he perceived to be 'left-wing Jacobin' magistrates in his home city of Milan, together with his general disdain for his own country's legal system, dominated the mid-part of his period in office. That he was able to escape prosecution he owed to his political position, while his populist attacks on the judiciary divided the country, leading either to indifference or big protest movements by an energised civil society, led by the film director

Nanni Moretti and other non-politicians. The unlikely sight of striking magistrates became familiar in Berlusconi's Italy.

Berlusconi's determination to use all means at his disposal to protect his position had been made clear during the summer of 2002. Melchiorre Cirami, a magistrate-turned-politician from Agrigento, a town noted for being one of the Cosa Nostra's strongholds in southern Sicily, put forward a bill to the Italian parliament as it went into recess for its summer break. This bill would allow politicians to challenge court proceedings against them if there was grounds for 'legitimate suspicion' of an unfair hearing. In effect it was a regression from the post-*Tangentopoli* reforms passed in 1993, which effectively removed immunity from politicians. In November 2002, after much heated debate, it became law. Further legislation passed in June 2003, shortly before Italy took up the presidency of the European Union, made it necessary to suspend prosecution until Berlusconi left the office of Prime Minister, a decision subsequently rejected in April 2004 by the constitutional court as 'unconstitutional'.

It was Berlusconi's skills as a salesman that had taken him to political office and which allowed him to maintain support amongst the electorate, even if he was continually threatened with court proceedings, had not resolved his conflicts of interest within the first hundred days of his rule as he had promised, and was frequently ridiculed for his growing list of public gaffes. Following earlier 'tasters', such as his assertion in the aftermath of 9/11 that he was 'confident of the superiority of our civilisation over the Muslim world', these reached a peak during the Italian presidency of the European Union between July and December 2003. The proceedings got off to a bad start on the second day with Berlusconi's now infamous 'Nazi kapo' jibe, in which he suggested to Martin Schulz, a German Social Democrat MP, that he would be well suited to play the role of an SS commandant in a forthcoming film. 'Shall we talk about women and football?', Berlusconi had asked a bemused group of foreign leaders as they waited to begin formal negotiations over the proposed new constitution. His quip about a politician being thrown out of a helicopter was also unfortunate, given that the Polish Prime Minister – a key figure in the negotiations – arrived in a wheelchair, having been injured in a helicopter crash the previous weekend. The negotiations failed to reach an agreement between EU member states on voting powers. The presidency was generally seen as a disaster, except by the British Prime Minister, who, in a House of Commons debate, praised Berlusconi's 'skill and tenacity' in chairing the negotiations.[20] His EU gaffes were followed by his claim in September 2003 that Mussolini had 'never killed anyone', that magistrates are 'mad' and that in order to do the job of a magistrate one had to be 'mentally disturbed' and 'anthropologically different'.[21]

Yet, Berlusconi survived to be Italy's longest-serving postwar Prime Minister in one uninterrupted stretch of power. After the legislation on parliamentary immunity was finally rushed through in 2003, following more than two years of conflict with magistrates and the opposition, he declared his intention to call a snap election if found guilty and take the issue to the people.

Berlusconi's unresolved conflicts of interest severely damaged his relationship with Carlo Azeglio Ciampi, Italy's President. Always problematic, it reached a new low in December 2003 when Ciampi refused to sign into law a bill that would give Berlusconi increased power over Italian TV. Ciampi sent a five-page letter outlining his reasons for not signing and warning of the dangers of ignoring the constitution. Berlusconi's response was emphatic: 'I haven't even read them and nor shall I do so.' Opposition leaders accused Berlusconi of violation of the constitution; one even called for his impeachment.

Berlusconi's longevity therefore depended not on his skilful stewardship of the Italian constitution, nor on his skilful diplomacy (as Blair argued) in Brussels. He lacked the shrewd politicking of a Moro or an Andreotti. His populism gave him a form of legitimacy that usurped the norms of politics. Faced with mounting criticism and corruption charges, his response was either to push through legislation quickly or promise to take the issues back to the people. He did not accept the legitimacy of the magistrates who apprehended him and who he consistently accused of left-wing bias. For a while this created the unusual situation whereby many of his critics around the world, and half the Italian population, looked upon him with disdain for his attempts as a statesman, while the other half, including his committed TV audience and electorate, continued to admire his virtues as a salesman.

To be a successful salesman you need *furbo* (cunning); as Tobias Jones has shown, this was a much admired virtue in Berlusconi's Italy, as was the audacity required to take risks and be a showman.[22] This explains the indifference among many Italians to Berlusconi's list of political misdemeanours. In Italy, postmodern populism has undermined public ethos and trivialised constitutional constraints and the values of democracy. Berlusconi has thrived in a place where politics has lost its way, where traditional ideologies have ceased to organise the beliefs and political behaviour of large numbers of people.

1. Italian Prime Minister Silvio Berlusconi (left) looks at British Prime Minister Tony Blair during a press conference inside No 10 Downing Street in London, 27 April 2004. (Photo: Jim Watson/AFP/Getty Images)

POSTMODERN POPULISM AND THE DECLINE OF THE PUBLIC REALM

Berlusconi's rise to power, as the first postmodern populist leader, carries major implications for the future of politics. In the words of the *Washington Post*, he is 'the quintessential antipolitical politician, yet with more power than anyone in Italy since Mussolini'.[23] This power was increased in dramatic fashion when he added the foreign ministry to his other roles following the resignation in January 2002 of Renato Ruggieri, one of the few ministers to have experience of government, who finally lost patience with the 'Europhobia' of Umberto Bossi. Subsequently, following the much publicised crisis over Tremonti's resignation as economy minister in 2004, Berlusconi also took this mantle for a brief period. For all his claims and plans to make Italy a more prosperous nation, most of Berlusconi's reforms have had a very narrow focus: to preserve his own power and consolidate his extensive private interests, including media ownership. These conflicts of interest have been given a veneer of respectability by being debated in the national media, with the postmodern twist that the public forums of debate are in fact Berlusconi's private centres of power.

This exemplifies the 'problem' of dissent that has characterised the Berlusconi years. Satirists on Italian TV, such as Paolo Rossi and Sabina Guzzanti, have been banned. Even the director of the Italian Cultural Institute in London, Mario Fortunato, found his job on the line because of his politics and the fact that he is gay, according to the many intellectuals in London and Italy who organised a campaign in his defence. For many, a turning point was the Genoa Summit in July 2001, when the *carabinieri*, allegedly encouraged by Gianfranco Fini, Berlusconi's Deputy Prime Minister, took a tough line against the demonstrators, beating and interrogating them with methods compared to that adopted by Chilean police in the 1970s. Subsequent investigations found officers guilty of intimidation and corruption. These restrictions on dissent illustrate in particular ways the logic of populism and how it can be the driving force in the degeneration of the body politic.

For many, Berlusconi's main legacy to the Italian nation is the demeaning of public life and the undermining of democratic politics. According to Leoluca Orlando, former anti-Mafia mayor of Palermo and ex-Christian Democrat, who founded the anti-corruption movement La Rete ('The Network'), Berlusconi succeeded in 'creating a culture of illegality'. 'Berlusconi', Orlando told me, 'has nothing to do with normal politics. He has turned individualism into egoism, and introduced competition without rules.' Under Berlusconi, earlier success in combating the Mafia – in which Orlando played a key role – and strengthening legality had been undermined. 'We have become a model for a culture of illegality', he told me. In an earlier interview with the German magazine *Der Spiegel*, Orlando had said that Berlusconi was the new 'Godfather', a comparison which got on the front page of the popular magazine and brought more attention to the German and international public. He explained, however, that he did not mean that Berlusconi was involved in Mafia links in the way that Andreotti and other Christian Democrats had been compromised in the past. Rather, Berlusconi's approach to government, the undermining of public institutions, his exploitation of deregulation and the passing of laws which tried to 'guarantee impunity for a few', gave legitimacy to the 'new Mafia', as much as the DC had done with the old Sicilian Mafia. 'This new Mafia', an animated Orlando explained to me, 'don't need weapons. The government sends out the message that illegality is an option. Do you like your mineral water with gas or without gas? Do you like your car with a radio or without a radio? Do you like your democracy with legality or without legality?'

For Orlando, the key thing was not whether Berlusconi's P2 links had won him influence or whether he had shady dealings with Mafia bosses behind closed doors. 'He can demonstrate to the prosecutors that he has no criminal responsibilities, but it doesn't change my mind.' He raps his fingers on the desk. 'To promote a culture of illegality, you don't need to meet a Mafia boss. The Mafia bosses want to meet Mr Berlusconi', he carried on. 'But they don't need to.'

THE END OF THE DREAM?

For a considerable time after his election in 2001, Berlusconi was able to convey the impression to the electorate that his own success story could be translated into an Italian one. For a long time, many of those Italians who elected him remained indifferent to his public gaffes and low international esteem. They elected him on the basis of his record as a salesman, not as a statesman, and if he was to make them richer they would tolerate his political shortcomings. This changed, however, following the rapid disintegration of the Italian economy from 2003, when it became more obvious that he was defending his own economic interests and failing to provide general prosperity. Moreover, cases of economic fraud provided further evidence during his reign that the deregulatory environment he had created was being exploited by unscrupulous business leaders. The most grievous example was at the food company Parmalat, where massive fraud was discovered in 2003. Its owner Calisto Tanzi was imprisoned, its remaining assets were seized, and its football club, FC Parma, was put into receivership. Many associated Parmalat's demise with Berlusconi's own strategy of freeing business from all restraints and his belief that rules can be broken in order for this to happen, that regulation holds back prosperity and that the promotion of corporate interests outweighs in importance the interests of the public realm.[24]

In addition to Parmalat, FIAT, for so long Italy's flagship company, was in its deepest crisis, with mounting debts. The long-standing airline Alitalia was in severe difficulty, while the collapse of new companies like Volareweb pointed to further economic instability. The industrial districts, the driving force of Italy's wealth in the 1980s and 1990s, were finding it difficult to cope with the exchange rates of the fixed currency. Indeed, after the euro was introduced in 2002, ordinary Italians noticed a sharp rise in inflation in the restaurants and markets, and economic insecurity increased for a range of social groups. Lower taxes – the key election promise – had not been realised. By 2004, the economy was now seen to be faltering badly and the European Union delivered a warning to the government in April that Italy would be in breach of the European Union stability growth deficit ceiling of 3 percent of GDP. This was a point that Romano Prodi, President of the European Commission and future centre-left electoral opponent of Berlusconi, took up with enthusiasm.

At the local and European elections in June 2004, during which Berlusconi caused further controversy by sending out millions of text messages reminding people to vote, the electorate delivered their own verdict, with significant defeats for Forza Italia, whose vote dropped eight points. These included the province of Milan, one of its strongholds. 'Forza Italia has been beaten at home' was the headline in *La Repubblica*. 'Berlusconi is still in the saddle, but the horse is very unruly' declared *Corriere della Sera*. As soon as the election results were made known, the AN and UDC, whose vote had stabilised, took decisive action to strengthen their position in the coalition. Berlusconi was forced to concede blame for the results and admitted that it was 'a signal of discontent to which one must pay attention'. Paying attention was not enough for the UDC, whose leader Marco Follini demanded action; changes to the personnel of the cabinet and a new political direction were the minimum conditions to ensure his party's support. He welcomed the end of 'monarchical government' and dismissed the view that the allies were the problem. It was his own electorate, Follini declared, that had abandoned Berlusconi. Now there must be a major cabinet reshuffle, for it was 'not enough to replace Totti with Cassano' – like the Italian national football team, following another poor international tournament in the same month, a new squad was needed.

Consequently, Giulio Tremonti, Berlusconi's economy minister and a crucial bridge between the Northern League's narrow authoritarian agenda and Berlusconi's 'culture of illegality', was sacrificed. The National Alliance and the UDC made clear that they had had enough. Yet Berlusconi's appetite for power had not yet diminished, as he briefly added the economy ministry to his own portfolio while promising to the European Union to reduce public finances by 7.5 billion euros.

However, a worse crisis followed a disastrous performance by the House of Liberties coalition in the regional elections in April 2005. From holding 8 out of 14 regions, the centre-right parties were left with only Lombardy and Veneto in their northern heartlands. Lost regions included Piedmont and Lazio together with Puglia and Calabria, in the South, where the UDC and the National Alliance had previously been strong. This time Follini went further and resigned along with three other ministers. Nothing short of a new government with new policies favouring the South would entice him back. This was Berlusconi's biggest political crisis and even his populist threat to call early elections had no impact. He received a further blow when Gianfranco Fini, withdrew the support of his National Alliance. His new government, put together after consultation with President Ciampi (in line with convention and effectively a cabinet reshuffle), was remarkably like the old one however, even including Giulio Tremonti, who had been forced to resign the previous year. His voters, however, were not likely to be satisfied, and the 'economic dream' he had promised had never materialised and was now thought to be a meaningless boast. His failures as a statesman were being followed by the failed promises of a salesman.

2
History Matters: The Battle for the Memory of Monte Sole

At the edge of the Apennines, not far from the beautiful medieval city of Bologna, you will find the remains of the old Etruscan city of Misa. Misa lies near the town of Marzabotto and at the bottom of a mountain called Monte Sole or 'Mountain of the Sun'. Monte Sole was the site of some of the earliest communities who lived and worked off the land and up until the last period of the Second World War its population numbered around 2000, scattered around the different villages and farmhouses on the mountain and its surrounds.

The only people you will come across now on Monte Sole are two religious communities who have set up homes there, and the occasional mountain biker. Despite the beauty of the region there are no holiday homes for the Bolognese or converted farmhouses for the British chattering classes. The last indigenous community on Monte Sole was wiped out in three days of massacre during the worst Nazi atrocity committed in Italy during the Second World War. Monte Sole was unlucky to be on the route chosen by the German armies as they retreated from the advance of the allies in autumn 1944.

As in other mountainous regions in this part of Italy, the partisans had put up strong resistance to the Fascist and Nazi troops. Under the direction of the SS, and with the help of local Italian Fascists who knew the mountain well, Field Marshall Albert Kesselring and Major Walter Reder ordered the massacre of all Italian civilians they found in their way. In *Resto del Carlino*, the local newspaper which supported Mussolini's regime, Kesselring warned that the partisans could not be tolerated any further. 'Localities where we find any verification (of their presence) will be burned and destroyed and the people who help them will be hanged in the public square'. He offered local people 5–10 kilograms of salt for every partisan identified.

During the days of the massacre, at its most intense between 29 September and 1 October 1944, 955 Italians were killed. No concessions were made to women and children, partisan or ordinary civilians, laymen or priests, and the deaths included 316 women, 216 young children and 142 elderly people. Whole families were rounded up and shot and, all the way up the mountain, farmhouses were burned to the ground. In some cases mass graves could be found, including batches of 40–50 next to churches and within the grounds of cemeteries. The brutality was shocking even by SS standards.

In his vivid and detailed account of the massacre, the American writer Jack Olsen described the many heroic acts of resistance. These included Sister Antonietta Benni, a nun and teacher at one of the schools who feigned death in the village chapel of Cerpiano and then escorted two of her pupils to safety, and Don Giovanni Fornasini, one of the local priests, who walked to certain death in an attempt to save others in the church at San Martino.[1]

Following the liberation of Italy, in which the partisans played a major part, the process began of commemorating those who died on Monte Sole as well as accumulating evidence in order to bring the perpetrators to justice. It was a long battle not helped in the early years by the mines that prevented any reconstruction of the area. In fact the body of Don Giovanni Fornasini wasn't found until six months after the massacre, in a mound of bushes at the back of the church. The ground was no longer fit for work and none of the survivors could face returning to their former homes.

Trying to bring German officers to court was an even more arduous task. Many in Germany and Austria claimed that the massacre of Monte Sole was a fiction, stirred up by the strong Communist presence among the partisans. Finally, in 1951, Kesselring was caught and sentenced to death by a British court for war crimes, though this was later changed to life imprisonment and subsequently commuted altogether. In his memoirs he claimed that what took place on Monte Sole was merely an 'act of war'. Walter Reder, the SS major, was caught in Austria and eventually transferred to Italy in 1951 where, in court in Bologna, some of those who survived the massacre at Monte Sole (including Sister Benni) gave evidence against him. It transpired that the Monte Sole massacre had followed earlier atrocities carried out under his orders in Poland and the Ukraine. He was sentenced to life imprisonment.

However, the battle over the meaning of Monte Sole continued, and a campaign was launched by former SS members for Reder's release, helped by some revisionist historians. In 1967 Giovanni Bottonelli, then mayor of Marzabotto, received a letter from Reder written from his prison cell, in which he appealed for 'mercy and forgiveness', in order to see his mother before she died. According to Italian law the only way a pardon could be given for war criminals was for the families of the victims to give their assent. Bottonelli therefore invited the families of the victims to a special meeting of the town council in Marzabotto in order to decide whether a pardon would be granted. The vote was 282 against and four in favour of the motion, with one abstention. The subsequent statement of the Marzabotto town council described a pardon as 'unthinkable':

> For the families of the deceased, for the survivors, for the young who want to and must know, we have the responsibility and duty to give proof of the dignity and moral strength of our people. How could we consider ourselves worthy representatives of these people if we had not respected fully its will? What we want is that it never be forgotten that it was not an act of war that was committed here, as Kesselring has said, but a horrendous massacre, an inhuman reprisal against unarmed peoples, an act of cowardice and of hatred and nothing else. For this reason that pardon is unthinkable.[2]

Following the intervention of Prime Minister Bettino Craxi in 1985, however, Reder was freed and returned to Austria, where he died in May 1991. In freeing Reder, Craxi argued that 'the historical memory of the slaughter does not need an old man to be kept in prison'.

It was not until 2002 that a formal pardon was received from a German President for the crimes carried out on Monte Sole. Johannes Rau took the initiative of visiting Marzabotto in April during the annual occasion for reflection for those who gave their lives. Along with Italy's President, Carlo Azeglio Ciampi, and Francesco Rutelli, leader of the opposition, Rau addressed a gathering in the remains of the church of San Martino. As the first state visit of a German President he made a public vow in front of the survivors and families of the victims. 'In this place of sorrow and memory I ask for a pardon in the name of Germany,' he said, adding that he has carried with him 'the violence and immense pain of Marzabotto'.

'Every generation', he continued, 'has to sharpen its guard without interruption or ideology'.[3] Ciampi complimented Rau on his gesture, which he saw as furthering a spirit of reconciliation between the two countries and cementing hopes for a new generation of Europeans. The families of the victims expressed their satisfaction that after 58 years the gesture from Germany had finally arrived and that Rau fully recognised the suffering and sorrow of those who had survived the massacre. It seemed that, with Rau's visit, the historical responsibility had now been taken for the horrendous crimes carried out under the names of Nazism and Fascism.

This reckoning was to be brought into question, however, by the sweeping shifts taking place in Italian politics that brought to power the Berlusconi government in May 2001. This coalition was composed of a new right which had not been formed by the anti-Fascist consensus and which drew on a quite different historical memory from that of the Christian Democrats and Communists who had dominated Italian politics over the previous 50 years. The attempts of the coalition of Forza Italia, the Northern League and the 'post-Fascist' National Alliance to revise the historical legacy of the resistance have been a crucial and recurrent element of the right's strategy. In the mayoral election of 1999, as a warning of what was to follow at a national level two years later, even 'red Bologna', the stronghold of the postwar Italian left and a city awarded a gold medal of honour for its citizens' opposition to Fascism and Nazism, swung to the right.

Before it was ousted, Bologna's left-wing council made the decision in 1998 to set up a 'Foundation School for Peace', to be built on the site of Monte Sole itself. The purpose of the school was to promote peace and understanding through practical projects and exchanges between different communities, nationalities and cultures in order to understand the causes of conflict, violence and prejudice. The memory of what took place in the autumn of 1944 was to be the defining context for the school's activities, a constant reminder of the need to renew the principles of human dignity and social justice.[4]

According to the President of the school, Vittorio Prodi, a local centre-left politician and brother of Romano Prodi, building the school on Monte Sole was essential to aid the 'process of moral and physical reconstruction of the area'. 'We have a duty to study this specific episode', he told me, 'to extract from the sacrifices made by so many in order to educate future generations. We must keep the memory so that others can see it. There is a saying in Marzabotto that the stones speak up on Monte Sole.'

The composition of the school, which is funded by the European Union, is made up of representatives from Marzabotto and Monzuno and Grizzana Morandi, the neighbouring councils, which also lost people in the atrocity, Bologna University, Resistance organisations, pacifist groups and nominations from the various councils, including the city council in Bologna.

The issue of choosing representatives is where the problem started, and Marzabotto and Bologna proved to be a microcosm of the national political faultlines that divided Italians. History had become a central terrain of Italian politics, where the meaning of Fascism and its legacy became contested and never far away from public debate. It made for a strong contrast with Germany, where great introspection and the rebuilding of a democratic culture have been bulwarks preventing the possibility of this kind of debate.

In these Italian history battles, truth and myth have become entangled and questions previously thought to have been resolved have resurfaced. Here, historical 'revisionism' is not merely a concern of the seminar room or the newspaper column, but has a real purchase on the future of Italian political identity. Therefore, when Berlusconi claimed in September 2003 that 'Mussolini never killed anyone'[5] or, in his previous gaffe, compared a modern German politician to an SS commandant, old historical questions resurfaced in a way that continues to impinge on contemporary politics. It seems that whoever 'wins' the historical battle over Italy's past will hold the key to Italy's future.

Although the peace school on Monte Sole had been initiated in 1998, nominations for its representatives did not take place until the building was complete and other preliminaries were finalised in late 2002. Bologna's city council was allowed one representative, and the nomination of Enzo Raisi by the new right-wing Mayor of Bologna, Giorgio Guazzaloca, was a controversial one.

Enzo Raisi was part of the new right-wing leadership of the city council – or '*giunta*', as the executive of Italian councils are called. More significantly he was a leading member of the National Alliance, the second party to Forza Italia in the Berlusconi coalition government and whose leader, Gianfranco Fini, is the deputy Prime Minister. Indeed, in Bologna, it is the National Alliance rather than Berlusconi's Forza Italia that is the main right-wing party. Guazzaloca himself was elected as one of a group of independents on the 'civic list' and as such had no party base, while the National Alliance has strength in the university and in its local organisations. There are also historical connections: Bologna is Fini's home town, while Mussolini himself originated from the same region.

The National Alliance is the successor party to the Movimento Sociale Italiano (MSI), the direct descendants of Mussolini's Fascists, which was established in 1946 by some of his surviving supporters. In postwar Italy, many former Fascists continued to hold public office in the absence of a major trial such as occurred in Nuremberg in Germany. For almost 50 years the MSI stood in opposition to the main tenets of the Italian constitution and its leaders were often prevented from speaking in public squares. Its support never got beyond 7–8 percent and the party underwent splits, notably over whether to turn itself into a more mainstream party. As recently as 1992, Piazza Venezia in Rome, where Mussolini made many of his speeches, was filled with MSI members singing Fascist songs on the anniversary of the 'March on Rome', which had signalled the onset of Fascism 70 years earlier.

After Italy's political crisis and shake-up of 1992–94, the MSI finally decided to come in from the cold and committed itself to the Italian constitution and consequently changed its name to Alleanza nazionale (National Alliance). Crucially, this made it a potential right-wing partner for Forza Italia, which Berlusconi had founded in the same period. Italy was now in a very different political situation following the disintegration of the Christian Democrats and the transformation of the large Italian Communist Party into the Party of the Democratic Left (PDS). These were not only the two main postwar parties but also ones that had drawn their strength from their participation in the Resistance. For the Communists in particular the memory of the Resistance was crucial to their political identity.

Despite its new image, opponents of the National Alliance say that many of the old ideas are still there. At its Congress of 1995, 69 percent of the delegates saw Mussolini's regime in positive terms, according to a poll, while in the same year Fini himself claimed that Mussolini was 'the greatest statesman of the twentieth century'.[6] Since then he has tried to distance himself from this view, condemning anti-Semitism, visiting Auschwitz in 1999 and more recently in September 2002 telling a Tel Aviv newspaper that: 'Italians must take responsibility for Fascist crimes against Jews. They bear a historic responsibility inscribed in history to issue declarations and ask for forgiveness'. Cynics again claimed this was to enhance his reputation, as an emerging statesman, with the Americans. It was, however, the biggest admission yet from the heirs of Fascism that they needed to take some responsibility for the past.

In Bologna, however, there was little sign of this. Right-wing members of the city council initially opposed the peace school and subsequently sent a letter suggesting that the focus of study should go beyond Monte Sole to include all victims of 'totalitarian ideologies', notably 'the numerous victims of the odious anti-clerical ideology in the years 1945–48'.[7] This reference to crimes committed by Tito's Communists in the Trieste region has become a familiar one in the wider history battle that now dominates much of Italian politics.

The reaction to Raisi's nomination from the survivors and families of victims in Marzabotto was one of horror. They wrote a private letter to Mayor Guazzaloca urging him not to go ahead with it, and when that didn't work a petition against Raisi was circulated. A local partisan veterans' group put out a statement condemning the nomination, which they described as

> offensive to the city of Bologna, the holder of the gold medal of honour, for the memory of those massacred by Nazism and the Fascists of Marzabotto, Monzuno and Grizzana and for all partisans who gave their life fighting for liberty in Italy under German occupation and the Fascist regime. There has been no self-criticism on the part of Raisi in respect of the history of Fascism and its culture, only the wish to diminish the contribution of the Resistance for liberty and democracy.[8]

The incumbent mayor of Marzabotto was still a baby when his predecessor called the public meeting to decide the fate of Walter Reder. In 2003, when I interviewed him, Andrea De Maria was 36 years old and had been Marzabotto's first citizen since he was 28. As he drove me up Monte Sole, past the ruins of farm buildings and cottages destroyed in the massacre – which number over 80 in total – he talked of his concerns for Italian democracy. 'It is very important to recognise that Italian democracy was based on the Resistance and the parties which emerged from it', he said. He saw the nomination of Raisi as an attempt to 'de-legitimise' the role of the partisan movement and therefore undermine the anti-Fascist principles on which the constitution was founded. Raisi, he pointed out, was not just an ordinary councillor. He was also a local MP and President of his party in the region. As such he was a political figure, whose party had embarked on an attempt to rewrite the recent past as a way of enhancing its own credibility.

We walked around the ruins of the church of San Martino, where De Maria had accompanied the two state Presidents Rau and Ciampi the previous year. Nearby, a memorial stone for Don Giovanni Fornasini marks the spot where the priest's body was found. Further down the mountain is the new building which houses the peace school. De Maria felt that the 'imposition' of Raisi does not augur well for the future harmony of the school.

This view was shared by the school's President, Vittorio Prodi. 'I have to accept that one of the members of the Foundation School for Peace is inappropriate', he said. He chose his words carefully, over Mortadella and Sangiovese, as he took time out from a business lunch to discuss the problem that was developing at his peace school.

Inappropriate?

'In institutional terms, his nomination was legitimate. However, we also have to consider the impact for the families. For them, it is like an open wound.'

I first interviewed Enzo Raisi during the Italian election campaign of 2001. Then he was in an ebullient mood, with his party poised to form part of the new government. He was just about to introduce Gianfranco Fini to a packed meeting of supporters in Bologna's main piazza. 'We are like your Conservative Party', was his improbable reply when I asked him what his party stood for. What about these people selling busts of Mussolini? 'They are just old men.' What do you think about a 'post-Fascist' party speaking in a piazza adorned by faces of those who died in the Resistance? 'Our members have uncles who were with the partisans.'

Two years on and he appeared a more beleaguered figure, claiming that the left's opposition to his nomination is a political attempt to attack the *giunta* through him, and that the controversy was whipped up by a sensationalist press. He arrived half an hour late for our interview and was dressed in a brown corduroy jacket and mustard-coloured trousers. On the whiteboard in his office, in the magnificent Palazzo D'Accurso overlooking Bologna's Piazza Maggiore, he had scribbled a few mottos that seemed pertinent to his current predicament.

'Only speak when you have something to say.'

'Don't talk if your audience is not listening as a good word is wasted on bad ears.'

I asked him what the role of the Foundation School for Peace should be. 'It is to broaden the understanding for peace and tolerance in the world.' What about the need to preserve the memory of those who died on Monte Sole? 'Of course that is important.' How did he feel about the view that he had not offered any self-criticism or taken any responsibility for the atrocities committed by the Nazis and Fascists? 'Listen,' he said, 'we can't forget that what happened on Monte Sole was carried out by the German army and in particular the SS.' What about the involvement of Italian Fascists? 'Well, it could be that some Italian Fascists were involved, but the tribunal only found Germans guilty of atrocities. Remember, Italy was an ally of Germany.'

I quoted Fini's statement about the need for Italians to take responsibility for crimes against Jews and asked whether as a member of the same post-Fascist party he had a similar duty to the victims of other atrocities, including those on Monte Sole. 'Listen,' he said again. 'This is only speculation. I don't and didn't belong to a Fascist party. The MSI was not a Fascist party. I was born in 1961. To say Fini is responsible for Fascism, is like saying Fassino (the leader of the Left Democrats) is responsible for Stalinism.'

'Many left people', he carried on, 'have this mentality because anti-Fascism is in the business for votes. I respect the families of the victims. They are very important. But some, only a few, are being pushed by local politicians.' (In other press interviews, he said the families were being used as 'an instrument' of the left.)

He wouldn't be drawn on the earlier attempt by the right to extend the remit of the foundation to include people killed by Communists between 1945 and 1948. However, he pointed out that 'the atrocities of the German army were also carried out in Russia and other places and not only here'. He said that the purpose of the school should be to promote peace today and should not be confined to the old battles of the past. 'That's why I am showing the American and Israeli flags', he said somewhat curiously, pointing to his window. They contrasted sharply with the many multicoloured peace flags flying in opposition to the war in Iraq. 'This is the point. I am with the Americans and Israelis. We need to turn over a page and promote peace and tolerance for the future.' He bore what looked like a series of bruises behind his knuckles on his right hand. A *Ring of Fire* video lay on the sofa behind us.

The battle over the memories of Monte Sole not only reflects the historical revisionism at the heart of contemporary Italian politics, it also became embroiled in the propensity for cover-ups that is now characteristic of Italian public life and which turned the Italian state into the most degenerative body politic in Europe. Indeed, Monte Sole itself became the subject of parliamentary debate during 2003. A documentary programme shown on German TV in 2002 claimed more people than Reder and Kesselring should have been brought to trial for the atrocities on Monte Sole and that many were still alive. Lawyers for the families raised the case and attempts were made to set up a parliamentary commission that would investigate what the press quickly dubbed 'Italy's cupboard of shame'.

In order for a parliamentary commission to be set up, the proposal needed to go through both the Chamber and Senate, the two houses of the Italian parliament. Though it passed the Chamber of Deputies with only one vote against, it was held up in the Senate. A series of referrals and amendments were put forward that critics feared would 'bury' the commission before it has started. The amendments were proposed by Melchiorre Cirami of Forza Italia, who had already come to prominence with his controversial bill making it possible for politicians to oppose magistrates if there was 'legitimate suspicion' of the latter's political motives. The real purpose, many claimed, had been to protect Prime Minister Berlusconi from his current court cases, in which he was accused of bribery and corruption.

This time Cirami's amendments, supported by the majority of the government, were used to block the commission and with it the chance of a full investigation. According to Enrico Cecchetti, the MP who proposed the bill, 'any extension of this terrible chain of referrals, with the power to return to the Chamber with amendments of the law, will provoke further pain and a source of distrust in the institutions'.[9]

But the problem was not merely one of covering up Fascist involvement in the atrocities of the 1940s. There was a clear attempt from within the right-wing government to *contest* Italy's historical legacy of anti-Fascism, one that defined the first Republic and provided the 'constitutional arch' that shaped the parameters and political discourse of postwar democracy. Here the battleground was not the legal terrain of the constitution itself – though many argue that Berlusconi's conflicts of interest between his media ownership and political role have even brought that into question. Rather, it was the attempt to forge a new political identity through a re-interpretation of the past. Every year on 25 April – Liberation Day, and a public holiday – Italy's piazzas are filled with people paying respects to the partisans and those who fought against Fascism. Traditionally, leading politicians and statesmen give speeches and lay wreaths. In 2002, for the first time in the postwar period, Italy's Prime Minister refused to participate in the celebrations, while others on the right looked for other historical references. President Ciampi, in his speech from Ascoli Piceno, spoke out against what he called 'improbable revisionism'. He called for 'slow and patient reconstruction' of the period. In a clear warning against the new right's agenda, he said: 'In order to avoid improbable revisionism it is important to celebrate with solemnity and a spirit of reconciliation the twenty-fifth of April'. It was crucial, he said, 'to cultivate the memory for justice not as a vendetta'.[10]

Yet Ciampi's warning went unheeded by the right. In 2003, Liberation Day was the subject of even more rancour and controversy. With Berlusconi 'resting' at his Sardinian villa, Sandro Bondi, Forza Italia's leading spokesman, set a new tone for the right's revisionist challenge. What happened in Marzabotto, according to Bondi, was the fault of the left, and the attempts by Communist partisans to 'intensify the clash' with the Nazis, who were 'in retreat' at the time of the conflict. Other right-wing politicians called for the abolition of Liberation Day, while some suggested moving it to 18 April, the date of the election of the first postwar Christian Democrat government. In Trieste, local politicians wanted to commemorate Mussolini's birthday. The left accused the government of 'not knowing' Italian history or trying to 'rewrite' it. 'Frankly, it is intolerable that the Government of Italy does not recognise the values which have inspired the democratic life of the Republic', said Piero Fassino, leader of Italy's Left Democrats, the largest opposition party.[11]

This revisionism was at the heart of the government's political outlook and began to influence policy-making. In December 2002, the Parliamentary Cultural Committee, armed with a 36-page dossier of what they saw as 'left-wing bias', gave instructions to the Ministry of Education to exercise more control over the history text books used in schools. They argued that the curriculum needed to be rewritten to eradicate the bias, following an earlier statement by Berlusconi that 'our children must no longer study history books with Marxist interpretations'.

This provoked a prompt and angry response from intellectuals, who set up a 'Hands Off Our Textbooks' campaign. Umberto Eco accused the government of jeopardising the 'health of our democratic system'. He described the government's actions as 'reminiscent of the still not distant times when the Fascist, Nazi and Stalinist regimes expressed such a right of censorship'.[12] The 'left-wing bias' that was at issue was, of course, the attention given to the Resistance and the partisans. While it does not share the historical legacy of Fascism, a defining component of Forza Italia's politics is its obsession with Communism, which it saw as a festering sore at the heart of Italy's problems. Indeed, 'Communism' and 'anti-Fascism' became synonymous for much of the revisionist new right.

The revisionist critique of the Resistance legacy finds a further expression in attempts to celebrate the lives of those who died fighting for the Italian army or were victims of Communist partisan repression. This was most apparent in the *'foibe'* tragedy near Trieste, a region with strong Fascist support, where many Italians were killed and their bodies dumped in crevasses (*foibe*), or were sent to Slovenian labour camps by Tito's partisans in the last days of the war. For a long time these deaths were hidden and subsequently often taken up by the right in the battle over the past, commemorated for example in a demonstration by Azione Giovane ('youth action'), AN's youth wing, outside Bologna train station in February 2003. There was also a poignant irony in the choice of Bologna station for this protest. Yards from where the event took place was a monument to the worst terrorist attack in postwar Italy, when 85 people were killed in 1980 as a result of a bomb planted by a Fascist terrorist group. One of the clocks remains fixed at 10.25, the hour of the explosion. There had even been an attempt by some to remove the word 'Fascist' from the plaque.

The post-Cold War era has given historians the chance to look more objectively at the *foibe* and other atrocities carried out by the Communists. The Italian government meanwhile decided that Italy would celebrate a 'Day of Memory' for the victims of the *foibe* from February 2005. However, there is a selective political memory at work in this revisionism that ignores the context of the struggle between Fascism and democracy. The attempt here is to put across the view of Fascists as 'equal' victims. The renaming of streets after MSI leaders and the creeping nostalgia for Mussolini are the most visible cases of revisionism. In Mussolini's birthplace of Predappio, not far from Bologna, you can visit his former home, now turned into a 'House of Memories'. Here you can also buy wine labelled with his vintage and baseball caps and T-shirts adorned with his images. His nearby tomb is minded regularly by a man dressed in black.

This creeping nostalgia has been given some legitimacy by recent academic work. The British historian Nicholas Farrell, who lives in Predappio, has argued that 'the resistance was a largely irrelevant factor in the liberation of Italy', that Mussolini was a 'great man' who 'remained at heart a socialist to his dying day'.[13] One of Farrell's many 'revisionist' contentions is that the 1924 murder of Giacomo Matteotti (an opposition MP whose memory has been preserved by the naming of numerous Italian streets and piazzas), an event which signalled the moment when the full brutality of Mussolini's regime first became evident, was 'probably' 'not intended'. Mussolini himself was 'far too shrewd a politician to order such a thing'. In any case, writes Farrell, Matteotti's speech had been 'provocative' and 'inflammatory'.[14]

Farrell ends his book favourably quoting the words of 'Giovinezza', the 'irresistible' Fascist song 'of hope and promise, and better times ahead...a reminder of how different Fascism once was before the fatal alliance with Hitler'.[15]

Franco Lanzarini was seven years old in the autumn of 1944 when he and his family got caught up in the German retreat on Monte Sole. They were refugees from Bologna, and his father was a partisan. Together with his mother and three younger brothers he was sent to Villa Serana, a partisan hideout where they thought they would be safe together with other women, children and the elderly. The men returned to the hills to join the battle.

At around 5.30 on the morning of 29 September they heard cannon fire, but seeing flames some way off did not think more of it. At 9.00 members of the German SS and Italian Fascists arrived at the villa and ordered everyone out. The 50 or so people were huddled together on the grass and the armed SS squadron lined up in front of them. The lieutenant waited for orders. The little boy asked two elderly men what was going to happen. 'Nothing will happen', they answered, but tears were streaming down their faces. Lanzarini turned to his mother, who was carrying his four-month-old baby brother. 'Mummy', he pleaded, 'bend down so we can die together.'

Over the next week this became a regular ritual: the SS ordering everybody out and aiming guns at them. In the event, Lanzarini's group was the one that largely escaped, though as they later made their way over the mountain in the chaos after the Germans left, Lanzarini and his family came across the decomposing bodies of the two elderly men who had tried to reassure him.

Lanzarini, now in his mid sixties, has never been sure why they were not killed along with the others, but says the strategy was 'to create a climate of fear and terror'. His father was not so lucky, killed along with other relatives in a battle on the mountain, though his body was not found until the following year. Even after they were free, the fear was not over; Lanzarini's mother had to regularly negotiate landmines and the crossfire of German and allied forces in order to get food for her children.

Francesco Pirini was 17 years old when the SS arrived on Monte Sole. As a teenage male he was thought to be a likely SS target and had escaped to the hills, missing the worst of the slaughter. Other members of his family were not so lucky. In all he lost 13 of them, including a sister and his mother, cousins and aunts. Another sister, 15-year-old Lidia, miraculously survived despite being shot in the hip and having to feign death.

Francesco tells me Lidia's story and, almost exactly 60 years after the massacre, accompanies me around the remains of the church in Casaglia where Lidia (who died a few years ago) along with around 100 others, almost all women and children, had congregated on the morning of Friday 29 September 1944, to avoid the German soldiers advancing up the mountain. They thought they would be safe in the old chapel, where Don Ubaldo Marchioni was saying the rosary.

When the SS arrived they ordered everyone to the cemetery at Casaglia, 300 yards away. Some were shot as they tried to make a run for it. When they got to the cemetery they were crammed together with a machine gun positioned in front of them at the entrance. This defenceless group were then shot to the ground with continuous machine gun fire, which was followed by hand grenades. For hours and hours Lidia lay under a dead woman's body, half-paralysed by the bullet wound in her hip. Every time the German soldiers heard moaning they would hurl in more hand grenades. After some hours a small group of wounded women who had survived managed to walk away from the cemetery, but could not take Lidia with them. Nearly everyone else had been killed. It was not until the following day that Lidia managed to move away, aided by a stick she used as a crutch. Despite a hazardous journey, in which she had to crawl most of the way and had to avoid a sniper and a marching SS squad, she made it to the shelter at Cerpiano, where she found some of her fellow survivors and after more narrow escapes made it through.[16]

We walk the same route, down into the woods along the narrow clearing and up to the brook, which opened to Cerpiano. Here we stopped at the tiny chapel in which nearly all Francesco and Lidia's relatives perished. It is hard to believe that in this tiny space 49 people, including 19 children, were crushed together, forced back by a machine gun, before being bombed by a series of hand grenades thrown through the small windows. It was here that Sister Antonietta Benni, one of the teachers at the school that was at the back of the chapel, also feigned death for hours, before leading her two surviving children to safety. All that remains now of the bombed-out chapel are some rocks and the arch, which somehow survived. Further along from the chapel, the old building used as the SS hideout is still there, with a view over the valleys. You can still pull fresh figs and other fruit from nearby trees, but there are not many signs of life. It is the silence that is now most apparent in a land previously inhabited by the oldest of communities.

For 60 years Franco Lanzarini and Francesco Pirini have carried these memories with them. Today they both stressed the need to learn from the massacre. They are both involved in educational initiatives set up by the peace school to encourage international solidarity, tolerance and understanding. Lanzarini talks passionately about the activities of the Monte Sole peace school, which has brought together Italian, German, Israeli and Palestinian teenagers in exchanges. He is proud of the Israeli girl who had recently left saying that the experience gave her the will to work more closely with Palestinians back home. A key part of the exchanges is that they visit the site of Monte Sole and talk to survivors. Lanzarini believes this is crucial in ensuring that the region's history is not rewritten by politicians. 'The truth sooner or later always comes out', he says.

As a sprightly 77-year-old, Pirini spends a lot of his time on Monte Sole, which has been preserved as an historical park and has long been cleared of the rubble, though it is still possible to find bomb fragments and remnants of carts and other machinery and utensils spread about the remains of the different peasant villages, such as Caprara. Here he welcomes visitors from all over Italy and many parts of the world and is on hand to answer questions and explain his story. For many years he could not talk about the atrocity but now feels less bitter and prefers to talk about the future. It is his quiet determination that future generations should know about what happened here that comes across most strongly. This would be an engagement with history that would serve as a vivid reminder of the horrors of Fascism, while helping Italy to renew its democratic identity. The stones on Monte Sole will need to speak up one more time.

3
Bossi's Last Shout

In the aftermath of Silvio Berlusconi's clash with Martin Schulz of the German SPD in the European Parliament, one of the few people to rush to the beleaguered Italian leader's defence was his volatile coalition ally, Umberto Bossi, leader of the Northern League. 'I am with Silvio', said Bossi, expressing 'total solidarity' in his idiosyncratic manner with Berlusconi, whom he saw as a victim of left-wing 'Jacobins' intent on building a Franco-German superstate.

Berlusconi's Nazi jibe was straight out of the repertoire of Bossi himself, whose xenophobia against immigrants and asylum seekers has brought comparisons with Jorg Haider, the notorious Austrian politician. Indeed, the xenophobia of Bossi and that of his fellow leaders of the Northern League has become the defining political characteristic of the party's politics since the election of the House of Liberties governing coalition in May 2001. The degeneration into increasing xenophobia and racism followed the growing dismay amongst Bossi and his allies that their devolution proposals were being watered down by coalition partners.

Days before Berlusconi's outburst against Schulz in late June 2003, 60 Africans died trying to enter Italy when their boat sank near the island of Lampedusa, off the west coast of Sicily. Bossi declared that, in order to stop this happening again, 'the immigrants must be hunted down, for better or worse. At the second or third warning – boom! Fire the cannons at them'. Embarrassed government allies tried to keep their distance from his remarks. 'It must be the heat', said one. 'Luckily, we are not a country of assassins', another.[1]

Bossi's outbursts on immigration, a familiar voice in the governing coalition's political discourse, came at a time when Italy was facing a severe refugee crisis, with desperate people arriving at Italian shores from as far away as Liberia, Iraq, Eritrea and Albania, while the passage from Libya has been the most common – and hazardous – journey for migrants and asylum seekers. The question of immigration moved to the top of the government's political agenda, driven to a large degree by the Northern League, whose authoritarian approach intensified as its own devolution agenda weakened. Since 2001, hundreds of African refugees have died off the coast of Sicily, Italy has seen a state of emergency, fishermen attempting to help refugees lost at sea have faced prosecution, and in 2004 the arrest and attempted prosecution of the captain of the *Cap Anamur*, the humanitarian German vessel, after rescuing a group of North Africans who had been circling the Italian seas after being prevented from landing by Italian authorities, resulted in diplomatic conflict between Italy and Germany. Despite the fact that Italy takes relatively low numbers of migrants in comparison to other EU countries, and that the majority of migrants are now from Eastern Europe rather than North Africa, the xenophobia of the Northern League and the tough populist stance taken in general by the House of Liberties coalition turned the issue into a hot topic of political controversy.

On many occasions, frustrated by the refusal of his coalition allies to pursue devolution proposals, Bossi threatened to break rank and proved a dangerous and unreliable ally of Berlusconi, while upsetting the National Alliance, which grew increasingly concerned that Italy's 'national interests' would be compromised by Bossi's regionalism. Bossi's claim that the North is a victim of 'Romecentric racism' brought persistent conflicts with the AN. They were not enamoured with his proposals for four 'vice-capitals' of Italy, as a way of taking power away from Rome; even less by his declaration that 'Milan is the real capital of Italy'.[2] His attempts to move the second state TV channel from Rome to Milan were also a matter of much contention – 'bizarre', according to Gianfranco Fini. 'The Northern League is starting to be a hassle', said Mario Landolfi, another senior National Alliance figure. His devolution proposals were subsequently submerged into a constitutional bill which sought to maintain 'national interests', with Rome keeping special powers. 'Devolution', Bossi said after the change in the proposals, 'is now devoid of any meaning.'

THE LEAGUE'S FEDERAL ROOTS

The revisions to his devolution proposals represent a major retreat from the founding ideals of Bossi's Northern League. A former guitarist, labourer and medical student, Umberto Bossi, born in 1941, came to national prominence in 1984 when he set up the 'Lombard League'. Like Berlusconi's Forza Italia, formed a decade later, the Lombard League started life as a club, which Bossi turned into a political party when he realised there was wider support for his belief that Italy's different regional cultures and traditions would be better served by a federation. At the heart of Bossi's appeal was his emphasis on territorial identity and opposition to the nation-state. Italians were becoming increasingly disillusioned with what they saw as the incompetence and inefficiency of Rome. In the North, Bossi started to appeal to those who felt their own wealth and hard-earned resources were being whittled away by Rome in the interests of 'lazy southerners'.

By the time of the 1989 European and 1990 local elections, the Lombard League's support had reached almost 20 percent of the vote in Lombardy and, following the success of other leagues in Piedmont and Veneto, it changed its name to the Northern League in 1991, with its centre in Milan and Bossi installed as its first leader. The Northern League started to campaign for three Italian republics; North, Centre and South. This proposal was not as daft as it sounded, having some links with the fractured nature of Italian historical development as well as resonating with an emerging federalism within the European Union.

The Northern League argued that the culture gap between North and South was irreconcilable. Its critique of '*Roma ladrona*' ('thieving Rome') now struck a popular chord, following the rise of Italy's *Tangentopoli* corruption scandals in the early 1990s, which brought down the ruling Christian Democrats and other leading politicians, such as the former socialist Prime Minister, Bettino Craxi. In many ways the early 1990s represented the peak of the League's influence. Its biggest strength was its status as a movement that stood against corruption and demanded reform of the Italian state. In its big electoral breakthrough of 1992, it drew support in the North from a range of disaffected voters, who wanted an alternative to the corrupt legacy of the 'Roman state', as well as attracting the more overtly 'anti-southern' vote. The argument here was that Rome, as the centre of political power, was largely responsible for corruption.

The League, at this time, benefited considerably, as Diamanti has argued, from both a renewed 'territorial identity' and a lack of trust in the Italian state, which was at its most critical moment.[3] Moreover, the populist style appealed beyond politicians. Bossi claimed to be the authentic voice of the bars, piazzas and workplaces; another outsider who brought to Italian politics a different constitutional vision. He was able to combine 'anti-government', 'anti-southern' and 'anti-immigrant' rhetoric. In contrast to Berlusconi, Bossi was a street-level populist who deliberately spurned any slick media image or sense of fashion (dressing down, using popular slang and avoiding fashionable connections). His populism inevitably resonated with a growing xenophobia over immigration into Italy from the early 1990s and did much to create and sustain a climate of fear and prejudice towards the *extra-comunitari* or *clandestini* (illegal immigrants), who were seen as the 'new southerners', taking the jobs and houses of Northern Italians. A multicultural society was not only undesirable but also unworkable according to Bossi – it would lead to the disintegration of traditional values. Territorial identity, for Bossi, was defined above all by cultural and familial continuity.

Bossi's central political objective was to replace the Catholic–Communist polarity made redundant by *Tangentopoli* and the pulling down of the Berlin Wall with a new territorial politics based on Italy's historic North–South divide. The Northern League was the party that gained most in the immediate aftermath of *Tangentopoli*, winning the mayoral election in Milan in 1993 and for a time becoming the largest single party in the North. Evidence of changes in voting behaviour shows that the League picked up significant support in some areas from former Communist voters, while in the pre-Forza Italia period, they held most of the votes of affluent shopkeepers and private sector managers. The National Alliance was yet to emerge from the remnants of the Italian Social Movement, its neo-Fascist predecessor, whose support had rarely been above 5 percent.[4]

The main obstacle to the progress of the Northern League was the arrival of Silvio Berlusconi and his Forza Italia Party in early 1994. Berlusconi appealed to much of the same constituency as the League and his own brand of populism, enhanced by massive media interests, ownership of a top Italian football club, and success as a Milanese entrepreneur, represented a threat to Bossi. Bossi feared – probably correctly – that any straight fight with Berlusconi would severely damage the League as a political force, so an electoral pact was formed with Forza Italia and the newly formed National Alliance, for the elections of 1994.

Inevitably, the Northern League lost ground in the process of reaching an electoral agreement, though it maintained a strong bargaining position within the newly elected first Berlusconi government, insisting as a condition of the League's support that federalism be prioritised. Bossi also argued that Berlusconi should resolve the conflicts of interest between his massive media ownership and his role as Prime Minister. When Berlusconi refused to concede either of these conditions, Bossi led a sustained campaign of opposition from within the coalition, eventually helping to bring down the government after seven months on a vote of no confidence. He later boasted that he 'put Berlusconi through hell' in those months.

Over the next couple of years the Northern League's political agenda shifted away from federalism towards the 'secession' of northern Italy and the foundation of the republic of Padania. From June 1995, elected members of the Northern League started to meet in Mantua, the town in Lombardy that was to be the capital of the Padanian republic, in order to produce a constitution for an autonomous northern state. Bossi was not perturbed by threats of public prosecution for 'questioning the integrity and independence of the Italian unitary state', and succeeded in generating a lot of energy for the idea of Padania, sustained by an annual 'Miss Padania' contest and other cultural initiatives.

Undoubtedly, the Padania idea was a crucial factor in the League's success in the 1996 general election, when it won up to 36 percent of the vote in some northern constituencies and was once again the largest right-wing party in the North. The projection of Padania as a 'lost nation', together with a strong feeling of Padanian identity amongst the League's own electorate, won it some crucial bedrock support. However, as Bull and Gilbert have shown, the 'invention of Padania' was the outcome of the dubious assumption that a unified ethnic identity, based on religion, language and sense of place, was waiting to be rediscovered. While such a unified identity was evident amongst the League's hardcore supporters, there was little evidence of it in the very different history and culture of parts of 'Padania', such as Bolzano, Trento, or the red regions of Emilia Romagna.[5]

By standing alone, moreover, the Northern League played a major part in ensuring the election of the centre-left and the defeat of the right-wing coalition. After the election, a future 'parliament of Padania' was proposed, and the name of the party itself was changed to 'the Northern League for the Independence of Padania'. Bossi led a ceremonial 'declaration of independence for the republic of Padania' on the banks of the River Po in 1996, in which he announced that 'Padanians no longer feel Italian'. As he started to read the declaration, 'We the People of Padania solemnly declare...', large crowds of his supporters cheered from the river banks; this was the Northern League's finest hour. Bossi's popularity was at its peak, and his party's arguments had to be taken seriously. An alternative embryonic state was envisaged, with elections to the new parliament and a mock referendum on the desirability of a Padanian state. Symbolic gestures and events proclaiming the future state of Padania took place; these included activists taking over the bell tower in St Mark's Square, Venice.[6]

The rise of Padanian nationalism was short-lived, however, and in 1998 the Northern League endured major internal divisions over what constituted the culture, symbols and character of Padania and the regional and cultural differences within and between the Padanian regions. Opinion polls showed that support for the idea was declining. In addition, the need to find an electoral strategy was pressing.

DECLINE SETS IN

By the time the current Berlusconi House of Liberties coalition was elected in May 2001, the Northern League had a much more modest set of aims. As a coalition precondition it now accepted the idea of national sovereignty – a major climbdown from its Padanian nationalist days. Its own support at the election had dwindled considerably and it only just managed to clear the 4 percent quota that guaranteed seats in Italy's semi-proportional electoral system. This vote was less than half the 10 percent it received in the 1996 election, and its number of deputies shrunk from 47 to 31. Bossi's optimism that the League would occupy a key role in the government, with himself as deputy Prime Minister, was not realised, and Berlusconi's incoming government did not have to rely on Bossi's support as it did in 1994.

In the event Bossi himself was appointed minister for devolution and institutional reforms, but with a vastly reduced remit of devolving control of schools, health and policing to the regions. The government committed itself to regional devolution, and, as the minister responsible, Bossi put forward his plans for greater powers to the regions. In the most radical aspect of his proposals, a chamber of the regions would replace the Senate. However, as this was a constitutional change, requiring separate votes in both houses to enable changes to statute, the process was a long one that tested the patience of the League. This became a long-drawn-out saga that remained a point of contention for the House of Liberties coalition. Moreover, as it no longer held the balance of power in this coalition, the relative strength of the League was much reduced.

In fact, given the suspicions of the UDC and National Alliance, who were both committed to a centralised, united Italian state and maintained strong electorates in the South, it was clear that the slow pace of reforms indicated a significant weakening of the government's commitment. Bossi's frustration on several occasions boiled over. 'Devolution or death', he announced in August 2003; if the devolution proposals were not accepted by December 2003, the League would push for 'secession'.[7] In September 2003, Bossi was still arguing that the 'Roman parties' of the coalition still continued to 'poach the money of the North'. Polls from his own supporters at this time confirmed the depth of disillusionment with the government's slow pace of reform: 50 percent of the League's supporters were disappointed with devolution reforms, while 41 percent were disillusioned with the Berlusconi government.[8]

As the Northern League's milder devolution agenda was being held up by its allies, its general political outlook careered to the far margins of the political right. Its xenophobic opposition to immigration became its defining political identity, while its catch-all populism was reduced to a rhetorical flourish. The most evident example of an authoritarian policy of the government on immigration is the Bossi-Fini legislation, widely seen as the most punitive anti-immigration legislation in Europe. It is the most significant contribution Bossi has made to the policy agenda of the Berlusconi government. This Act, approved in 2002, made it necessary for non-EU citizens to get Italian work permits before entering the country. If their jobs cease, then their work permits end. 'Immigration is not a right', Bossi has said repeatedly. 'You have to earn it by working. Those who don't have jobs should go home'.

Bossi's argument behind the legislation was the view that Italy was being taken over by foreign migrants, bringing crime, prostitution, and incompatible religious and ethical values. Much press coverage in the North, notably in the League's paper, was given over to increases in burglaries supposedly committed by immigrants, while the growth in prostitution on the outskirts of northern cities and drug trafficking were also brought into the political equation. The National Alliance, under Fini's more calculating leadership, was less outspoken than the Northern League, while the UDC was the most critical of the new legislation amongst coalition parties and managed to get the more extreme elements revised. Confindustria, the Italian business organisation (equivalent to the CBI in Britain), also condemned the legislation, fearful of the impact on business that would result from the decline in immigrant labour, while Catholic and other organisations opposed the bill on humanitarian grounds.

The law went further than any other country in attempting to 'criminalise' immigration and to police state borders. The Italian Navy, for example, was to take over powers normally given to police by being responsible for controlling the Mediterranean and Adriatic coastlines. It was given the power to intercept ships carrying immigrants looking to dock in Italy (usually along the Sicilian coast). This unprecedented power has been invoked frequently during the period of the Berlusconi government. Under this law, all non-EU immigrants are now required to have their fingerprints taken on entry, and it is an imprisonable offence to attempt to enter Italy without a job contract.

Despite the fact that Italy takes significantly fewer asylum seekers or migrants than most other EU countries, they are rigorously tested, put into detention centres and have to produce evidence of job contracts or threats of persecution from their home countries, if they wish stay for any length of time. As a result, Italy has become the hardest European country to enter as an asylum seeker, despite its location as one of the most accessible from some of the world's more repressive regimes. This law was deemed sufficiently authoritarian for the United Nations High Commissioner for Refugees to condemn the legislation.[9]

In the past, Bossi used his rhetoric to make the case for federalism against the corruption of the (Roman) state. Now he used his vision of millions of immigrants flooding to the North, terrorising and robbing honest families in Lombardy and the Veneto. *Padania*, the Northern League's paper, carries regular coverage of alleged crimes committed by immigrants and asylum seekers. 'The frontiers will open and we will have to flee to the mountains', Bossi said. Meanwhile, his rhetoric continued to turn on the South, which he saw as a drain on the prosperity of the North.

HOME DEFEAT

Relations between Bossi and his allies had always been difficult. This conflict included attitudes to Europe and the powers of the European Union, which he has compared variously to 'Stalinism', 'Fascism', or a bureaucracy run by technocrats in the interests of masons, paedophiles and homosexuals. It was this 'monstrous Europhobia' that led Renato Ruggiero, the most experienced and credible member of the Berlusconi cabinet, to resign as foreign secretary in January 2002.

From 2003, relations between Bossi and his government allies became even worse. Following the differences over the devolution proposals, the Northern League once again put up independent electoral candidates in local elections. For the crucial Friuli-Venezia Giulia election held in early June, Bossi persuaded his allies, after much wrangling, to accept a Northern League candidate at the expense of the existing incumbent, Renzo Tondo of Forza Italia. For many, this was to be a major test of the League's depth of support. For its allies it was a test of its credibility; in its own heartlands, it had to deliver.

It may not have helped the cause that the League's candidate for this election was Alessandra Guerra (with many peace banners in Italy at the time declaring opposition to the *guerra* (war) in Iraq), or that her opponent, Riccardo Illy, was an experienced politician, former mayor of Trieste and a member of one of Italy's most popular coffee-producing families. Guerra was still the clear favourite, however.

On the last official day of campaigning, predictions suggested that the race was tighter than expected. The town of Pordenone, under the control of one of the few centre-left local councils in the region, was targeted, with both Bossi and Fini speaking in adjoining piazzas. In Piazza Municipio, a tired-looking Bossi was introduced to 150 or so diehard supporters, some with the traditional green flags, neckerchiefs and ties. Another 50 or so curious onlookers sipped their *aperitivi*. Bossi's speech was a tour de force of every conceivable prejudice. As usual, he built up his rhetoric to a crescendo of shouts and gestures, even drowning out the sound of the bell-tower behind him.

The theme of his talk, such as it had any structure, was the recurrence in European history of '30-years wars', with 1968 the root cause of current discontent. This moment, he declared, was the origin of modern individualism and thereby the source of the drug addiction, hedonistic capitalism and sexual deviance that had undermined the family. It was the origin, too, of the modern left, with its class conflict and opposition to small businesses. It was the beginning of the era of globalisation and the extension of American capitalism. Therefore, Communists, bankers, hippies and immigrants were all equally culpable in moving away from the mainstream of family values and tradition.

As I waited at the end of the platform to interview Bossi in a throng of supporters and henchmen, a middle-aged Sicilian, Saverio Sinatra, pushed his way to the front and confronted him as he was climbing down. Sinatra had been looking for work for months, with two children and a wife to support. Bossi, evidently embarrassed, attempted to persuade him that it was easy to find jobs in the North. 'It is not true, I have been everywhere', Sinatra persisted. 'There is plenty of work; have you tried looking?', asked one of Bossi's aides. 'Go to Technoplast (a local employer) on Tuesday', said another league supporter, 'and you will find work. It is very easy.' When I later asked Sinatra what he thought of Bossi, he compared him to Pontius Pilate.

I asked Bossi how the local election was going. 'This is a very important election. The North is the gateway for a lot of European trade. The world is changing, and these are the years where we will need to find new solutions from strong leaders. The left and the bankers, with their big interests, have failed. Now we need ideas which are close to the people's interests.'

'What about your future relations with Berlusconi?'

'It is very simple, because whoever makes an agreement with the League will win the election. The agreement with the League allows you to win in the North. If you win in the North you win everywhere, because the South is not going anywhere. It does not have economic autonomy. The League is the determining factor which will decide who governs the country. When Berlusconi makes an agreement with us, he wins.'

Three days later, the election results in Friuli-Venezia Giulia showed a heavy defeat for Alessandra Guerra. This was marked as a turning point for the Berlusconi government. It is clear who received the blame. A 'fiasco', said one paper; 'humiliation', said another. It was a 'serious error' to go with a candidate from the Northern League, said a Forza Italia spokesman. A 'cold shower for Bossi', said the left-wing *Manifesto*.

Bossi accused his allies of not supporting Guerra. 'We always win when we go alone', he said ominously, pointing to some town councils that the League held, but with clear implications for the future of the coalition.

LEAGUE WITHOUT A LEADER

The roots of the Northern League's decline were already in place by the beginning of 2004, when another series of events that had a strong element of finality about them took place. The League received a big setback in March 2004 when Bossi suffered a heart attack. The degree to which the League had relied on Bossi became very evident in the coming months. Indeed, one feature of populist parties, whether the postmodern populism of Berlusconi or Bossi's home-grown version, is the supremacy of the leader; the charisma of the leader often serves a more effective purpose than the intricacies of policy formation. Opponents and dissidents in Bossi's party were ruthlessly dealt with, while sectarianism and opportunism had become the staple diet of its political strategy. Bossi's last major outburst before his collapse was a public rebuke of the Pope, bringing more complaint from his coalition allies. Pope John Paul had improvised a message to Roman priests and cardinals in local dialect. Bossi responded with ridicule and a promise to send the Pope three dictionaries of Northern Italian dialects, announcing that 'priests should go barefoot again' and that society was better off without 'thieving monsignors and cardinals'. 'Bossi has exceeded the limits of decency', was Fini's exasperated but now familiar response.[10]

Following Bossi's heart attack and the period he spent in a coma, the League behaved like a leaderless party. Three weeks after his collapse at the end of March, the League occupied the Chamber of Deputies after one of its members, Alessandro Cè, was expelled for 'offending the capital' by repeating the *'Roma ladrona'* claim, a familiar phrase amongst League activists and one used by Bossi himself. The ensuing rancour, in which League members accused AN colleagues of 'Fascism', carried on for hours. When Roberto Maroni, the Northern League's welfare minister, was interviewed in the following day's *Repubblica*, he put it down to 'lively DNA'. *'Roma ladrona'*, he reminded the interviewer, 'is the reason why the League exists'.[11]

It was the beginning of a serious rift. Early in April, the European Commission gave a warning to the Italian government that it needed to make cuts to its budget as it was in breach of the European Union stability and growth deficit ceiling of 3 percent of GDP. Figures showed that the Italian economy did not grow at all in the last months of 2003. As we saw in Chapter 1, the government crisis worsened in the local and European and regional elections in June 2004. These went particularly badly for the League, whose vote continued to decline; they did not even receive a sympathy vote for Bossi's incapacity. With Forza Italia in increasing difficulty, the stability of the AN and UDC strengthened the hand of the centralists, weakening the position of the League as well as Berlusconi's authority.

Following these elections, in which Forza Italia and the Northern League lost heavily, Gianfranco Fini and Marco Follini of the UDC were now able to insist on a change of political direction and new personnel in the cabinet. The League's main ally in the coalition government was a significant one: Giulio Tremonti, the economy minister, who in the past had satisfied some of the League's economic demands by bringing tax cuts to the wealthy middle classes and cutting investment in the South, and who had also been an ally in the League's campaign for devolution. Indeed, in the increasing rancour in the coalition between the AN, UDC and Northern League, the position of Tremonti was crucial in determining the future of the coalition.

Berlusconi himself, surviving at this time on populist rhetoric and the wielding of his political and media power, had became more reliant on the Bossi–Tremonti axis. The subsequent forced resignation of Tremonti was thus a major defeat for Bossi and his party as much as it was for Berlusconi. Tremonti's intended cuts in the budget for the South, backed by the League and opposed by the AN and the UDC, would not be realised. As a friend of the League and of federalism, his departure seemed to signal further decline for the League.

Bossi, having recovered consciousness, had watched the events from his Swiss clinic. On 20 July he announced that he was leaving the cabinet after being elected to the European parliament in Strasbourg, an option made possible by Italy's 'list' system, where his name had been at the top. This also meant he was giving up his seat in Italy's national parliament. This was widely viewed as a political decision based on his pessimism about the possibility of the coalition delivering the kind of devolution proposed by the League. Despite the fact that Roberto Calderoli, also from the League, was appointed as Bossi's successor, the tension between the rival parties in the coalition remained high, with the League threatening to obstruct pension reform if their devolution demands were not met.

As the government crisis unfolded, the League increased the tempo on immigration. In the middle of the government chaos following Tremonti's resignation, a ship carrying 37 African refugees attempted to land at Lampedusa, off the Sicilian coast. The German aid ship *Cap Anamur* had found their dinghy three weeks earlier and after circling the waters had helped them to the shore. However, the Italian authorities blocked them from landing, claiming that the refugees had to seek asylum in Malta, which they argued had been the first landing port. 'It would be a dangerous precedent if they were allowed to land', said a statement from the Italian ministry for the interior. This was subsequently disputed by the captain of *Cap Anamur*, who said the refugees had been picked up 100 miles from Italy and 180 miles from Malta, and that while they passed Maltese shores, at no point did they attempt to land.

The ensuing row over the *Cap Anamur*'s decision to land in Italy led to a diplomatic dispute between Germany and Italy, condemnation of the Italian government for inhumanity from international aid organisations, and the revealing of the full face of xenophobia from Northern League and other ministers. When the Italian authorities finally gave in and allowed the ship to land on 12 July at Porto Empedocle, south of Sicily, the German captain was arrested, along with another member of the crew, for 'aiding and abetting illegal entry'. Roberto Castelli, the Italian justice minister, meanwhile, was outraged at the decision to allow them to land. 'It shows Italy to be the soft underbelly of Europe. The message going out to the world is that the country has no way of controlling its own borders and anyone who wants to can enter.' According to Giuseppe Pisanu, illegal immigration was being helped by the 'cunning exploitation of laws and regulations' by aid organisations. After spending four days in jail, and with the intervention of the German government, the German aid workers were released, while the African refugees were put on a plane back to their homelands.[12]

The immigration crisis remained at the top of the Italian government's political agenda, with the Bossi-Fini law making its mark. Hundreds more refugees risking their lives set off from Libya for the 100-mile journey across dangerous seas to Sicily, only to be put on the first flight back home by Italian authorities, to the dismay of the United Nations Refugee Agency. According to them, the Italian government was in breach of human rights law by refusing the migrants the chance to provide evidence of persecution.

The Northern League had played a major part in the legislation against immigration. This would be their main legacy of the Berlusconi years. However, Bossi, from his Swiss clinic, had one last shout. The League's devolution proposals, consistently watered down, finally reached the Chamber of Deputies in Autumn 2004. It was part of a new constitutional package that would also give greater powers to the Italian Prime Minister, equivalent to that of the French President. Meanwhile, Fini and the post-Fascists were given enough sweeteners to keep them on board. The result was a bill proposing devolved power to the regions on aspects of education, health and local police administration, while reinforcing centralist powers in respect of security, immigration and defence. It appeared as a mixture of separatism and centralism. The bill was passed easily and was received rapturously by the League; they held an impromptu party with banners declaring their thanks to the sick Bossi, who remained in his Swiss clinic. Bossi returned the thanks, remembering also the contribution of Berlusconi and complimenting his successor as devolution minister, Roberto Calderoli, claiming he had 'carried forward federalism'.[13]

In reality, however, this legislation was some way from the League's original objectives. Radio Padania, the League's radio station, had been inundated in the build-up to the bill with angry calls expressing disillusionment with the proposals. Independent analysts suggested that the League might still lose up to two-thirds of its electoral support as a consequence of moving away from its original ideals. The bill, with its obvious dual intentions of consolidating the power of the Italian Prime Minister and delineating further regional inequality between North and South (removing the obligation for redistribution of assets from the North to aid development in the South), may prove to be Bossi's last major contribution to Italian politics.

Part II
Politics Again

D'Alema, react, say something, react, say something, answer, say something left-wing, say something not even left-wing, something civilised.

—Nanni Moretti, *Aprile*, 1998

4
The Failure of the
Italian Third Way

In the mid 1990s, political parties of the centre-left underwent major discussions over their policy agendas, driven by the impact of globalisation, the implications of the end of Communism, and a perceived need for a new ideological direction. Many European countries had experienced years of right-wing government. In Britain, the Thatcherite era was coming to an end, but many of its core ideas influenced Tony Blair's attempts to modernise the Labour Party on his way to power in 1997. In the view of many, his governments have marked the continuation of rather than a break from the Thatcherite era. In the eyes of some, however, his governments assumed the mantle of a new idea for the European centre-left: the 'third way'.

This new idea was given greater weight by close cooperation between Blair and Clinton advisers from the early 1990s, while the intellectual contribution of Anthony Giddens underpinned its core principles. Blair's electoral success complemented centre-left electoral victories elsewhere in Europe, notably in Germany, France and Italy; in the latter country, the Olive Tree alliance headed by the ex-Communist PDS came to power in 1996, adding to general optimism that a new opportunity for the centre-left was opening up. The Blair government was to outlast the rest of the European centre-left governments. Yet its success in winning elections in reality did not indicate an opening for the left, as it failed to break out of the Thatcherite paradigm, its questionable political priorities confirmed by its alliances with the Bush administration over the invasion of Iraq and the Berlusconi and Aznar governments over flexible labour markets.

From its evolution, the third way can be characterised by attempts to position the left within the realities of a post-Fordist globalised society. While the term has been used by many different political traditions in the past, in its most recent articulation it has come to symbolise a decisive break with the two dominant traditions that had characterised postwar societies: a 'statist social democracy' and free market neo-liberalism. More contentiously, Anthony Giddens, its leading theorist, argued that many of the old ideological divisions between left and right were no longer relevant.[1]

It is evident that a decisive historical break has been emphasised by all who have adopted the third way label. This is often achieved by the use of 'new' in the description of the party or group: New Labour, the New Democrats and the New Progressives have all assumed this purpose. In many cases there has been a significant rupture between the new idea and earlier traditions, though often this has become as much a semantic question as one based on any credible historical analysis. Thus, 'new left' in the British debate now counts as 'old left' in third way interpretations, while the modernising trajectory of the 1960s is often regarded as outdated ideological posturing and overlooked in the attempt to fashion a new politics. It is therefore a much contested term, with a lot depending upon its view of the past.

One of the defining ideas of the third way is the view that the centre-left needed to put more emphasis on individual liberty, and accept that the market has an important role to play in promoting wealth and prosperity. This meant that adherence to market principles and the pursuit of social justice were no longer to be seen as mutually exclusive but, within the context of globalisation, now depended on each other. The enterprise culture and the accumulation of personal wealth were no longer to be derided or, crucially, seen as the cause of inequality. Rather, they were now determinants of 'social justice'. According to Giddens:

> Successful entrepreneurs...are innovators, because they spot the possibilities that others miss, or take on risks that others decline, or both. A society that doesn't encourage entrepreneurial culture won't generate the economic energy that comes from the most creative ideas. Social and civic entrepreneurs are just as important as those working directly in a market context, since the same drive and creativity are needed in the public sector, and in civil society, as in the economic sphere.[2]

Certainly, Giddens felt this was an idea that had global reach, claiming countries as disparate in political cultures as Brazil,

Argentina, South Korea, New Zealand and Chile were adopting versions of the idea by the turn of the millennium.[3] Despite the universality of the third way's appeal, there were of course distinctive national characteristics and historical circumstances that shaped its development in different countries. In Italy, a country without a strong social democratic tradition but with the strongest Communist party in Western Europe in the postwar years, the crucial moment was 1989–92. The fall of the Berlin Wall, taken together with the collapse of the Christian Democrats in the early 1990s, had a profound effect in shaping the second Italian Republic, as it has been called; a new party system, with new political faultlines and polarities, began to emerge from the wreckage. The PCI, under the direction of Achille Occhetto, made its historical decision in 1991 to change its name and the identity of its party. This decision was contested by a minority of the membership, who formed Rifondazione comunista; this was to divide further in 1998 when a traditionalist grouping around Armando Cossutta formed a new Italian Communist Party, the PCd'I. The majority two-thirds of the old PCI remained in the new PDS (later DS), the Party of the Left Democrats.[4]

THE ITALIAN LEFT'S CRISIS OF IDENTITY

However, the circumstances surrounding Occhetto's historical intervention and the conflicts and upheavals that followed it testify to a crisis of identity from which the Italian left has yet to recover. The PCI, Western Europe's largest Communist party, had never been in government in Italy, except for a brief time in the immediate period of postwar reconstruction. As a party condemned to 'permanent opposition' by the continuity of DC-led coalitions, with American and Mafia support intent on keeping them out of power, they had nevertheless developed an impressive alternative political culture to political Catholicism. In the process they embraced more independent Communist solutions; from the moment postwar reconstruction began, Palmiro Togliatti, the party's legendary leader, favoured the construction of an open, democratic, mass party, as distinct from the traditional Leninist vanguard model elsewhere. He also pursued a strategy of structural reforms, whereby capitalism would be transformed by the extension of democracy to a range of social and economic institutions as a long-term strategy for socialism. This was an idea of a 'revolution as process' and much influenced by Antonio Gramsci's idea of a 'war of position', in which opposition movements seeking to take power needed to consolidate and broaden their political support through winning political consent gradually; in the process of winning consent, they would prefigure the nature of the alternative society.[5]

The PCI went a considerable distance in setting out an alternative 'Italian road to socialism'. At its height, under the innovative and charismatic leadership of Enrico Berlinguer (1972–84), the party developed an impressive mass base, including significant cultural sections, attracting in the process a range of prominent intellectuals and a reputation as the defender of Italian democracy (it helped write the postwar Italian constitution) and the initiator of broad alliances. Its 'Eurocommunist' identity was at its peak in the mid 1970s, when it received 34 percent of the vote in Italy, just behind the DC, coinciding with big turnouts for the French Communist Party (PCF) and the Spanish Communist Party (PCE). In addition, the PCI held control in a number of Italian regions and was developing a popular brand of municipal socialism. It even called its overall perspective the 'third way' to socialism, distinct from social democracy and Stalinism. Berlinguer's strategy of the 'Historic Compromise', devised from 1973 following his reflections on the fall of Allende in Chile, argued that the PCI had to make a compromise with the Christian Democrats, in order to consolidate its electoral gains. This compromise would entail withholding opposition to DC reforms in exchange for wider democratic changes. This strategy was ended abruptly and brutally by the kidnapping and assassination of Aldo Moro by the Red Brigades in 1978.

The implications of Moro's assassination for the future of his country have been discussed in this book's introduction; it also had profound implications for the future of the left. Following the death of Moro, which benefited both extreme left critics of the PCI and right-wing conservatives in the DC, Berlinguer found it very difficult to construct a new strategy. Despite his increasing disillusionment with the Soviet system, which he described in 1981 as 'exhausted', his new 'democratic alternative' strategy adopted in 1980 did not win new supporters. The rise of Bettino Craxi as leader of the Socialists (which helped it become a centre-right party that had connections to the later development of Forza Italia) brought a new electoral challenge to the PCI in the 1980s. The party's support declined gradually, suffering a major blow with the death of Berlinguer in 1984, until the events of 1989 precipitated its demise.[6]

However, the identity of the new party that would succeed it, notably its link to the past and its ideological objectives, was still a matter of contention. The conflicts and splits that persisted over the PCI's legacy and that of Togliatti and Berlinguer became open areas of debate. The PCI shared the wider crisis of the left in Europe, with particularly devastating consequences for a party of its size and mass influence. At one level of this debate was the split over whether the party should keep the word 'Communist' in its title and symbols. After all, argued Pietro Ingrao, leader of the PCI's left, the party had already moved a significant distance from the Soviet model; why did it need to renounce its past? The position of Occhetto and others, however, was that developments in Eastern Europe had hastened the end of the Communist identity and could no longer be ignored. Some, such as the *riformisti*, led by Giorgio Napolitano, went much further and argued that the new party should give up any historical opposition to capitalism and instead become a mainstream social democratic party. Others of a similar view launched an attack on Togliatti's heritage, even suggesting that his name be removed from the party's history.[7] Occhetto's response to the 'historical revisionists' was to distinguish between a *discontinuità* (decisive break) and a *demolizione* (demolition) of the past.[8] The task, he argued, was to move away from the idea that the party's subsequent strategy had to be justified in view of its historical role. In order to do this and to create a new identity after the decline of Communism, the party needed a new organisational and membership structure, one that would replace democratic centralism.

Occhetto's announcement of this need to found a new non-Communist party at a meeting with partisans in Bolognina, before he had informed his party as a whole, confirmed that old-style Communist decision-making was still in evidence. In the lead-up to the final Congress at Rimini in 1991 that would decide the name and structure of the new organisation, various attempts were made to compromise in order to preserve aspects of the party's tradition, if not the name. Such was the confusion, sensitivity and caution in the internal debates that the new organisation was referred to as 'La Cosa' ('The Thing'). Previous allies of Berlinguer such as Tortorella were also concerned that the good aspects of the party's past were in danger of being jettisoned, and formed a link with Pietro Ingrao. The old party was effectively split two to one in the final vote. A minority led by Armando Cossuta broke away to establish Rifondazione comunista ('Communist Refoundation'). Cossutta in fact was a 'traditionalist' pro-Soviet Communist who had little support. Many of those in favour of preserving the PCI's heritage decided to remain with the new party so as to avoid further damaging splits. Moreover, these were not the only points of division. Some, such as the Napolitano *riformisti*, saw the need for the new party to prioritise its governmental objectives, resisting arguments to retain strong links with social movements. The latter had remained central to Occhetto's idea and had strong support from the Berlinguerians, who saw the party as widening their support amongst the left, rather than moving more towards the centre.

In the event, the PCI became the PDS in February 1991, with a new symbol, the oak tree, replacing the hammer and sickle. One of the key reasons for the change was the view that new electoral opportunities would open up once the Communist label had been discarded and was no longer used in attacks by their opponents. Electorally, the PDS was in a very different position from the old PCI. It now had a more realistic chance of forming a government in contrast to the 'permanent opposition' the PCI had endured for virtually the whole of the last 50 years. Yet it felt it needed to dispense with much of its past, if it was to be a party of government. Ironically many of the Christian Democrats who had seen their governing party fall under *Tangentopoli* found themselves as allies in the new centre-left coalition, now termed Ulivo (Olive Tree).

The appeal of the third way for the leaders of the new Italian centre-left was clear. Viewing its Communist past as a burden, the third way offered a new direction. Speeches from party leaders in its early years were clear on the 'problematic' nature of the party's heritage. Moreover, the mistakes of the past were accompanied by the need to develop the credentials of a responsible party for government. Walter Veltroni was the most prominent 'revisionist' at this time. Another who had denounced the Togliattian tradition, he saw a major contrast between the 'oppositionism' of the old left, fixated on the past, with the innovation and modernisation of the new left, represented by parties like the DS, Clinton's Democrats and Blair's New Labour. Veltroni told the British magazine *Prospect* in 1996:

> The left has two cores, one ideological and one governmental. In Italy, the first has been dominant. The nature of this left is such that it cannot govern; it is radical for its own sake. It is necessary to break with this radical left if one is to gain credibility as a governing force. Every temptation to indulge in the past must be resisted...
>
> Either we make it to government, or, frankly, we might as well join Marxist reading clubs, sit under posters of Che Guevara and sing Chilean songs from the 1970s.[9]

In place of ideology, Veltroni proposed what he called '*La Bella Politica*', meaning 'high politics'; that is, a politics based on values, that was no longer corrupt or adversarial and that reclaimed its moral authority. Like his counterparts in Britain, he also conceived of the need for the left to claim its role as the party of the Internet and technological innovation; a need, as he saw it, to reposition the left away from its identity rooted in history. This revision for Veltroni was crucial to regaining trust amongst the electorate, while the rejection of ideology would facilitate the move towards a reconstruction of centre-left values. For Veltroni, a big admirer of John F. Kennedy, it was the American Democrats who were now to be the model party. Trust was dependent on new civic obligations, a new transparent approach to politics that would overcome political alienation between the political class and the voters.

Combined with its historical revisionism, the PDS, like its European allies, put trust and modernisation of its image at the top of its agenda. This included streamlining the internal structure of the party, the use of spin doctors and soundbites and the packaging of the party leadership, including the marketing of the private affluence of party members from Occhetto to Massimo D'Alema (who had become party leader in 1994). This reflected the personalisation of politics that was apparent in most countries. D'Alema, taking a leaf out of Berlusconi's book, was pictured holidaying on his yacht. The PDS was also marked by a significant generational shift, bringing the *'quarantenni'*, the 'fortysomethings', into the leadership for the first time – men (and like its predecessor, the PCI, its leadership remained almost completely male) like Veltroni and D'Alema.

Given the extent of upheaval in Italian politics in the years immediately following its formation, the PDS wasted no opportunity to project itself as the modernised new force in Italian politics. It helped bring in electoral reform in 1993 that was intended to end political instability and reduce the number of political parties, working to the advantage of the PDS, the largest Italian left party. Its alliance with the progressive wing of Christian democracy in the Olive Tree coalition was further evidence of the change in Italy's politics, finally bringing some of the remnants of Communism and Christian democracy together. Though this was not enough to win it victory in 1994, when Berlusconi made his triumphant and extraordinary political debut, it promised a more serious project for the election of 1996. The defining component of modernisation that drove the DS-led Olive Tree towards its electoral success of that year was its commitment to liberal market reforms. This not only moved the DS to a similar terrain to New Labour, and a decisive political break from its left-wing past, but was also part of a broader critique of the historical defects of Italian capitalism that had stunted Italy's economic development.

This included the oligarchic nature of Italian capitalism and to some degree follows a long preoccupation with the specific historical predicaments of the Italian economy originally noted by Antonio Gramsci, who wrote in the 1930s of the undeveloped nature of the Italian bourgeoisie. The emphasis on freeing up the market meant – as happened elsewhere in Europe – that the Olive Tree did not shift fundamentally from the neo-liberal hegemony prevalent in the West since the 1980s, though it helped, under the leadership of economics professor Romano Prodi, to ensure that Italy satisfied the criteria for entry into the euro at the end of the millennium.

The 1996 government was therefore elected on a platform that emphasised trust, pragmatism and financial prudence. In the aftermath of *Tangentopoli*, there was a need to modernise Italy and create new confidence in Italy's public institutions. Ulivo's modernisation package included administrative reforms, devolution proposals, and changes to business laws to free up more 'flexible labour markets'. It was these kinds of reforms that, for Massimo D'Alema, held the key to the birth of a 'normal country'.[10] The main focus for reform, though, concerned the economy, and Prodi's main achievement was guaranteeing the conditions for entry into the single European currency.

Many commentators felt that the government was a reforming one that did not get the recognition that it deserved. Yet there were significant problems that the government did not address which have a strong bearing on Ulivo's defeat by Berlusconi in 2001. It was a defeat that illustrated a crisis of identity for the Italian left. Critics like Ginsborg have suggested that the main reason for Ulivo's defeat in 2001 was the failure of the government to establish a distinctive strategy, backed by a convincing programme of social reform. 'The centre left', according to Ginsborg, 'never managed to convince the country that it knew where it wanted to go, nor to arouse enthusiasm for its policies'.[11] This view was confirmed by Giuliano Amato, the socialist third Prime Minister of the government. He stated:

> If we've suffered from a defect in these years it has been our inability to link satisfactorily the single chapters of our reform programme to a general design, capable of involving the public, and of giving the perception of leading the country towards a better society of the future.[12]

There are a variety of different possible explanations for this timidity in putting forward a concrete reformist programme. The fact that there were various changes of leadership – three premiers in five years – indicates a lack of stability and much wrangling amongst the leading members of the coalition; this was most apparent perhaps when Massimo D'Alema replaced Prodi in 1998, by a typical piece of Machiavellian gymnastics, or in the attempts – ultimately to no avail – to keep Rifondazione comunista on board. The decision of the latter to leave the government over budget cuts was used by the centre-left as the main reason for the failure of the government and led to a split between the DS and Rifondazione that was to last into the period of the Berlusconi government.

The most persuasive explanation, however, has to lie in the fact that as a country with strong ideological traditions whose movements and political parties were rooted in the historical memory of anti-Fascism, a banal and vacuous attempt to replicate the third way, constructed in very different conditions, was unlikely to succeed. Italy's postwar ideological heritage was not statist social democracy or neo-liberalism but varieties of Christian democracy and Communism. The lack of ideological principle or a clear sense of political identity seemed to be the main consequence of the third way's passage to Italy. Moreover, there was no serious commitment to long-term structural reforms. This was most graphically illustrated by the protracted and ultimately failed attempt by Massimo D'Alema to instigate long-term constitutional reform that would prevent the possibility of Silvio Berlusconi being elected as Prime Minister. During 1997–98, D'Alema spent hours with Berlusconi in the bicameral commission discussing proposals for institutional reform. Implicit in the initial negotiations was D'Alema's decision not to pursue the question of Berlusconi's ever-present conflicts of interest. D'Alema's overall objective was to further transform the party system, in the spirit of the changes to the electoral set-up in 1993 that established a 'first past the post' system with a proportional component, in order to create a majoritarian politics favouring two main parties. This would mean isolating the left around Rifondazione and helping to facilitate a mainstream 'normal' right, around Forza Italia, excluding post-Fascists and the Northern League. Establishing this political reform was as crucial to D'Alema's idea of a 'normal country' as economic modernisation.[13] Yet, as Ginsborg records, these negotiations fell apart after Berlusconi refused to cooperate in the later stages of discussions. This meant that not only did a key aspect of D'Alema's plan collapse, but Berlusconi was also allowed to continue unhindered, in fact given greater legitimation, in an unprecedented way, in his combined role as a major media baron and politician.[14]

The attempt to create a 'third way', as the Italian centre-left's route to a 'normal country', in the vision of D'Alema and Veltroni, depended to a large degree on the revision of Italy's historical memory. Yet the memory of the Resistance and the role of Communists in it had sustained the fortunes of the left in the postwar period and continued to deliver it prestige. Moreover, while the DS claimed a new modern role for itself after 1989, an assessment of its membership (a quarter of that of the PCI at the time of its dissolution) or its electoral performance (considerably lower than previous PCI performances) does not suggest a vibrant modern face of the left. Nor was the DS making inroads into the new generation. Its membership was significantly older than the PCI, and younger activists were shifting towards the more 'idealist' movements and Rifondazione comunista. In fact, from the evidence available of voting statistics, membership profiles and social composition, no convincing argument can be made to suggest that the DS is a new modernised party with a clear political identity.[15]

Indeed, when an analysis is made of the wider cultural and political legacy of the PCI, those movements and associations that imbibed left-wing culture and still exist – the CGIL and ARCI, for example, continue to prosper. Both have succeeded in sustaining a left-wing identity in non-party forms. ARCI, a cultural and political association set up in 1957 by the PCI but independent since the party's dissolution, has 1 million members in Italy and has doubled its membership since the end of Communism. It encompasses a whole range of alternative societies and recreational activities as well as political events, campaigns and legal advice for underprivileged groups. It has been instrumental in organising support for asylum seekers and migrants, while its pacifist outlook helped organise opposition to war. Its Arcigay network is the biggest gay rights movement in Italy, campaigning regularly on issues of equality and opposing discrimination, while Arciturismo has generated alternative tourism. ARCI's local presence in small towns as well as big cities has helped maintain an infrastructure and culture that has consolidated its left-wing identity.

The CGIL, Italy's largest trade union federation, also remains an important part of Italian left-wing culture. Italy's trade unions are founded on political as well as occupational status and thus historically have reflected the Catholic–Communist divide. The CISL, the Catholic union federation, and UIL, a liberal centrist federation, provided rival union bodies. The passing of the PCI had implications for the membership of the CGIL, yet it subsequently continued to occupy an important left-wing role. The extent of this role in the politics of the left, as the CGIL's involvement in the movement against labour reform and the Iraq war took shape, resulting in the rapid rise of Sergio Cofferati (its secretary) as the unofficial leader of the left, is discussed in the next chapter.

Significantly, the political identity of the CGIL has allowed it to take a broader view than is the case in other countries where trade union activities are often limited to industrial bargaining.

Rifondazione comunista, together with a range of social centres, peace groups and the emerging anti-capitalist movement, has ensured that alternative sources of left-wing identity have remained despite the modernisation of the DS. Moreover, while the DS has been shaped by the *quarentenni*, its overall ageing membership has never recruited strongly among the *ventenni* ('twentysomethings'). In this respect the late 1970s, a period in which young idealists chose to join social movements rather than political parties, has been mirrored by the contemporary left. In Italy, the movements of the 1970s were as significant in their own way as the late 1960s were in France. Links have been drawn between this movement and the anti-globalisation movement, the focus of the next chapter.

It is certainly true that the abandonment of a Communist identity was crucial to the formation of the Olive Tree. The alliance between the DS and Christian Democrats opened up a new electoral opportunity to bring the left out of opposition. Yet the political basis for an alliance with the Christian Democrats remained weak and always a matter of delicate adjustment. While some critics have seen some continuity between Berlinguer's earlier strategy and that of the DS, this argument has been unconvincing. Even attempts to revive the ideas of Carlo Rosselli, an earlier representative of a vibrant left-liberal culture in Italy, or revisionist interpretations of Antonio Gramsci, have been unable to provide a convincing argument that a new political identity was being developed.

The constant negotiations and disputes between centre-left leaders prevented any impression that a new politics was being created. D'Alema's reluctance to persevere with the reforming zeal that drove the 'Clean Hands' investigations meant that it was hard to convince the public of the validity of a new political project. The squabbling and wrangles rather confirmed that the old party politics was alive and kicking. Indeed, in this respect the Italian third way seemed to share some of the features that have evolved from the third way internationally, as it took on practical political significance. These were the new powers to party managers, a preference for pragmatic managerialism rather than ideological principle, a reduced role for intellectuals, and little time for 'movements', dissent or party activism, lest they disrupt the 'responsibilities of government'.

This timidity in regard to ideological principle was apparent during the general election of 2001. Francesco Rutelli, formerly mayor of Rome, a role for which he was much respected, was put forward as the Ulivo candidate, chosen ahead of Giuliano Amato, the outgoing Ulivo Prime Minister and a socialist. Rutelli, chosen for his good looks and Blairite image, was also promoted by Veltroni. A member of the centrist Margherita ('Daisy') party of reformist Christian Democrats, though previously a member of the Greens, he was thought to be a charismatic and telegenic figure whose personal appeal would match that of Berlusconi. Moreover, he had no Communist skeletons in his cupboard, a point noted with relief by a centre-left intent on fighting the election on small-scale policy areas. In the event, the election was won partly by the stronger of two personalities, and in reality these individuals also represented different conceptions of politics. The pragmatism of Rutelli was no match for the populism of Berlusconi.

The problem with the Italian third way lay in its project of making Italy a 'normal country'. Its way of doing this depended on searching for a political identity that was remote from its traditions and historical origins, the ideals of its membership, and the political culture – including the electoral system – it inhabited. In Britain, for example, the third way was created on the ashes of Thatcherism, the decline of the left, the absence of strong social movements, internal conflicts within the Labour Party and the vagaries of an electoral system that favoured only two main parties. In Italy, a country with strong movements, ideological politics, and respect for intellectuals, such an idea was never likely to take hold.

Events since 2001 confirmed the impression that the third way and the political trajectory of the DS remained an issue of contention. The leaders of the centre-left, increasingly concerned with constructing unity of purpose, faced new challenges. One part of this was the shifts at international level that meant fewer allies were in government. Of those that remained, the longevity of Britain's Prime Minister was achieved without any strengthening of fortunes for the European centre-left as a whole. Blair's alliance with Silvio Berlusconi and Jose Aznar of Spain on flexible labour markets, and more significantly the coalition constructed with George Bush over the invasion of Iraq, put paid to existing unity. The split between the Labour Party and centre-left European allies also marked the demise of the third way itself, an idea that was already struggling to establish any coherence.[16]

The demise of the third way, however, did not prevent the Italian centre-left seeking further attempts at 'normalisation' as it began its preparations for the next election, due in 2006. With Romano Prodi's emergence as the only credible leadership candidate to take on Berlusconi, following his release as President of the European Commission in 2004, his first declaration was to call for a united party (of ex-Communists, Catholics and the rest) on the model of the British Labour Party. Differences within the Olive Tree prevented this scenario, and the party settled on a 'Prodi list', with a view to a federation. Yet the debates about how it should position its politics – for example, closer to the 'centre' ground, or to social movements – suggested its crisis of identity was no closer to being resolved. Nor was this made any clearer by further changes of name; initially to GAD (Grande alleanza democratico), Alleanza, or L'Unione, the name it decided on in early 2005. However, by then the parties faced challenges from their own constituencies, following the rapid emergence of a range of oppositional movements and associations, less inclined to be constrained by party allegiance and growing in confidence in the aftermath of Genoa and the opposition to the Iraq war. Politics was being remade outside political parties.

'WITH THESE LEADERS WE WILL NEVER WIN'

The aftermath of the election defeat in 2001 brought much discussion within the Olive Tree, which now resembled a collection of leading individuals – Rutelli, D'Alema, Veltroni – as much as political parties. Nanni Moretti, the film director, normally loyal to the left, could not contain his dismay at the ineptitude of the leaders, in particular their inability to deal with Berlusconi's conflicts of interest. Moreover, these leaders looked haggard and divided. At a meeting in Piazza Navona in Rome in February 2002, which he attended at their invitation, Moretti told the crowd: 'We have been waiting for some self-criticism for the errors you have committed', referring to the row of leaders, including Massimo D'Alema, Francesco Rutelli and Piero Fassino, seated behind him. 'But the bureaucrats have learned nothing. I am very sorry to have to say this, but with these kind of leaders we will never win.'

Moretti's intervention proved to be highly significant. The immediate response was hostile. Massimo D'Alema walked off the platform in disgust, while Francesco Rutelli denounced the 'rantings of an artist'. Yet Moretti would be taken seriously, both in the media attention he was to get and in the future political direction of the DS, which attempted an internal debate over its political identity, future strategy and organisational structure, to which it invited intellectuals critical of its position. Moretti became the most important of these intellectuals and brought a new dimension to politics through the *girotondi* movement, at the same time opening another line of critique of the Berlusconi government. This movement started to hold regular rallies and events, focusing on Berlusconi's conflicts of interest and the dangers for Italian democracy therein.

In an extraordinarily poignant way, Moretti's arrival on the political scene saw him address the same questions of political identity, citizen participation and the crisis of the left that had occupied many of his films. These works ranged from *Palombella Rossa*, the account of a PCI leader's crisis of political identity, to *La Cosa (The Thing)*, a documentary about the dilemmas, contradictions and tribulations of the transition of the PCI into the PDS through the view of grassroots activists, to *Aprile*, which covered the election of the first Berlusconi government and the ineffectual opposition from the centre-left as well as the early stages of the uninspiring centre-left Ulivo government. In all of them Moretti used humour to depict the predicaments of the political class, while the leading characters, often played by himself, were humble, amateurish dissidents, not normally given to engaged political activity – not unlike, in fact, the *girotondini*, who from mid 2002 would fill Italian piazzas in their thousands.

The irony here, as Mazierska and Rascaroli have argued, is that Moretti in a very short space of time moved from being a despairing and helpless observer of the Berlusconi phenomenon (his real-life despair and helplessness depicted in his film characters) to being 'perhaps unintentionally, a recognised leader of the popular movement of dissent against it'.[17] Moreover, his entry into politics was a departure from the traditional role mass parties like the PCI attributed to intellectuals. In the past intellectuals were integrated into the structures of the party, often expected to defer to its cultural and organisational procedures and to offer uncompromising loyalty to its leadership. Now Moretti changed all the rules of intellectual engagement. The postmodern intellectual had more autonomy and was relatively detached from the norms of conventional politics, less constrained by ideological traditions and more free to negotiate, reflect and mediate between political movements.

Moretti, in his films, depicted the PCI and its leaders as party bureaucrats who spoke in an arcane language, were suspicious of movements, had lost touch with the popular imagination, and were therefore unable to empathise with the human condition. Their failure to construct a modern programme sufficient to inspire modern Italians was a pressing and pervasive problem. This was apparent in *La Cosa*, where the internal nature of the party's predicament predominated, and in *Palombella Rossa*, where the main character, a national PCI leader, loses his memory and in the process of reconstructing it through meetings with various members of society has to confront his political identity. In *Aprile*, Moretti, playing himself, is aghast at the inability of left-wing leaders to deal with Berlusconi's rise first time around in 1994. In a memorable scene that shows an extract from *Porta a Porta*, the news programme on RAI 1, Massimo D'Alema sits passively while Berlusconi launches into a tirade against left-wing magistrates. Moretti gets up and walks around the room holding his head, pleading with the PDS leader to respond: 'D'Alema, react, say something, react, say something, answer, say something left-wing, say something not even left-wing, something civilised.'

Aprile also covers the period of the first Olive Tree government. This first victory for the left cannot inspire the Moretti character though, as it failed to inspire many of its own supporters. In some cases, such as the sinking of a ship carrying Albanian immigrants trying to reach the coast of Brindisi, Moretti shows his despair at the indifference of the leaders of the Olive Tree to a contemporary tale of human suffering.

The crisis of left-wing identity was reflected in an inability to find a distinctive post-Communist idea. Significantly, Moretti maintained in his characters as well as in his own political actions a belief in the left, in particular a democratic, participatory left which maintained a critique of capitalism and still saw socialism as a necessary political alternative. Yet, as Mazierska and Rascaroli point out so well, this was a 'postmodern' concept of politics. This is apparent in Moretti's concern with humour in his films and in particular the use of 'liberal irony' to describe the predicaments of his characters. Mazierska and Rascaroli also note that Moretti's films emphasise the significance of language for contemporary politics (often through metaphor and autobiographical reflection), the fragmentation of a traditional community (in this case the political party and its ideology) in crisis, and how recovery depends on an engagement with social and cultural change, with a clear alternative vision to that espoused by the right. As they point out: 'Moretti's films produce new metaphors – new vocabularies to talk about our society.'[18] Moretti, they argue, provides a lesson on how to be on the left in contemporary Italy, this Italy of Berlusconi. It is

> to be indignant in the face of an anti-democratic attack on the magistrates like the one led by Berlusconi, of delirious attempts to dismember the Republic, such as the one carried out by Umberto Bossi's Northern League, but also in the face of the absence of the leaders of the left from the beach of Brindisi; it means not to be 'one of those who believes people are well, that capitalism is a society that has proved to be able to solve its own contradictions'; it means to be prepared to retell and redescribe the history of one's own community with cruel irony; it means to demystify ideology and authority in all its forms, including one's own; it means to be able to react, to say something, it does not matter if it is left wing, something civilised is enough. In short it means a great number of discourses that the left is failing to seize and organise into the new socialist project.[19]

Moretti's postmodern idea of politics is distinct from the third way in that it envisages an expanded sphere of politics, one that is a fluid and contested realm, open to reinvention and shaped by artists, intellectuals and movements, not solely professional politicians. The key failure in the battle against Berlusconi was an inability to defend liberal institutions and the democratic basis of public life. It was a failure to challenge Berlusconi on his own terms. Moretti was the first person to do this effectively. Like Berlusconi, he was an 'outsider'; a 'humble intellectual', not a professional politician but one who understood the modern world, including the media. Like Berlusconi, he stood as a critic of the bureaucracy and aloofness of traditional political parties as well as their outmoded politics and language. For Moretti, though, it had been the movements, not the leaders – the conscience of the liberal and democratic left, not the third way – ideas and visions, not pragmatism, bureaucracy and think tanks that inspired this revival. For Moretti was not a populist, but a popular intellectual who was able to stimulate a form of political association that breathed life into Italy's body politic on issues requiring urgent response, in a manner that was beyond the imagination of political parties.

5
Italy's New Opposition

DAYS OF HOPE, RAGE AND TRAGEDY: A GENOA DIARY

Thursday, 19 July 2001: A peaceful start

The ticket clerk at Camogli station, the coastal village where I am staying for the first couple of days of the Genoa G8 Summit, is determined to get me as close to the centre of Genoa as possible, the first indication of much unease amongst citizens caused by the closure of their city. On arrival at one of the suburban stations, I join up with others to board one of the free buses supplied by the city council to get us nearer to the centre.

When we arrive at the Genoa Social Forum HQ in Piazza Kennedy, the central meeting point for the activists, the place is buzzing and people are gathering around Bar Clandestino for free food and drink, provided by the 'community of San Benedetto'. Somebody is flying a kite with 'No G8' on it and the meetings that make up the 'alternative summit' are in full flow. At one of these I hear Dennis Brutus, one of Nelson Mandela's fellow Robben Island prisoners, call to bankrupt the World Bank.

As I make my way to the 'Migrants' March', the week's first demonstration, I stop at one of the entrances to the red zone, the areas forbidden to demonstrators, fenced off and guarded by *carabinieri*. I meet a group of bemused and discontented local citizens. 'I'm Genoese – why can't I walk along my own streets?', asks one. The march itself is a very joyous occasion, with music and general good humour amongst the 35,000-strong contingent. A chorus of Communist and partisan songs such as 'Bella Ciao' get the locals involved. No sign of the Tutte bianche (White Overalls), one of the leading anti-global capitalist groups, who had been prominent on previous protests and had attracted much press attention. Not a sniff of trouble on this first march. At a packed meeting that night, Fausto Bertinotti, leader of Rifondazione comunista, embraces Vittorio Agnoletto and declares the beginnings of 'an alternative left' in Italy. I share a taxi with a Dutch journalist and photographer who are following a small Trotskyist group in the 'Globalise Resistance' organisation. Outside, thunder and lightening beckon.

Friday, 20 July: Who are the black block?

I've now moved to Nervi, a posh suburb of Genoa, which becomes a key site for the protesters as it is one of the main links to the centre. Many protesters camp out amongst the palm trees. I travel on a packed bus to the outskirts of the city centre, which is as far as vehicles are allowed, and then walk the remainder of the way with a group of students from Rome. The highlight of today's demonstrations (which also include a 'Pink Silver March' promising 'tactical frivolity') is the 'Civil Disobedience' demonstration, and trouble is expected. As we approach the centre in search of this demonstration, we find the police blockades have extended well past the 'yellow zone', where access is granted but no demonstrations are permitted, and now block our street in both directions. Some locals find us a shortcut, which involves clambering down steps and through gardens. They shout words of encouragement: 'keep going, you are right'.

As we get to Piazzale Martin Luther King, we witness the aftermath of a clash with police that has left broken windows and phone boxes. A cameraman has had his equipment smashed, and is berating the line of *carabinieri* who have remained outside the Genoa Social Forum base. Where yesterday the place was a vibrant community, today there is anxiety and fear. Some of the *carabinieri* drum their shields.

Sirens sound continuously as I make my way towards the trouble spot. I bump into Claudia, a young Communist from Milan, who is very angry. 'I really hate this fucking black block', she says. 'Who are they? What are they trying to create?' The police have now blocked off the main thoroughfares and there are rumours that something major is happening near the Brignole railway station. It's impossible to get any nearer, so I walk back to Nervi and pass a trail of smashed banks and offices, including Istituto Bancario, Banco Nazionale Del Lavoro and a branch of the Italian post office. In Via Felice Cavallotti I come across the unlikely sight of a red London double-decker bus, with destination 'G8 Summit', predictably broken down. It is only when my friend Filippo rings from London that I discover that a young Italian, Carlo Giuliani, has been killed in the disturbances. Later that night, in a crowded bar, we watch Bertinotti and Gianfranco Fini, the 'post-Fascist' Deputy Prime Minister, argue over the circumstances of the killing on *Porta a Porta*, a news programme on RAI 1.

Saturday, 21 July: Middle England in protest

In possession of what seems to be the last copy of *Il Manifesto*, the left-wing daily, I am instantly popular as protesters in Nervi search for explanations of the previous evening's tragedy. Some hear the news for the first time and one girl bursts into tears. Today is the 'International Mass March', and numbers are expected to be high, despite stories that police are stopping coaches and trains.

Hundreds of protesters arrive at Nervi station and crowd on to the buses. As we head towards the meeting point of the march I notice a group of 40 or so who split and head off in another direction. Unmistakeably British by their eccentric array of headgear and other garments, I discover they are members of Jubilee 2000 and Christian Aid. My quip that they must be the hardcore anarchists goes unappreciated. 'We wanted to avoid the rabble on the corner', says Simon, who had set off from Nottingham days earlier ('rabble?'). Indeed, many have been travelling for days; some had cycled from Leeds, while others had been turfed off trains and unable to persuade coach companies to bring them. Some, including many in their 70s, have walked miles from the outskirts of Genoa. It is a heroic feat, under the circumstances.

They join a service and silent prayer session in the Boccadasse church, as part of their own campaign to cancel the debt, though this is overshadowed by the noisy procession of nearly 200,000 demonstrators, some of whom are shouting 'Berlusconi assassino! Berlusconi assassino!'. The organisers of Jubilee 2000 took the 'difficult decision' the previous evening not to join the march, so as to avoid the violence. Instead, they organise their own chain around the church: a few hundred metres further down Corso Italia, the demonstration has gone as far as it can and has been met by police lines. Outside Boccadasse church, a woman in an extraordinary straw hat is wearing a Malvern Churches T-shirt. This is middle England in protest.

The red London bus, now roadworthy again, is parked on the corner of the road. Up above, helicopters are circling. A hearty rendition of 'When the Saints Go Marching In' has to compete with the sirens of three ambulances hurtling towards Piazza Kennedy. Now they are dancing a conga, out of step with white hats flopping, as the first signs of smoke appear in the distance.

Sunday, 22 July: Carlo's shrine

The Italian press is dominated by what it sees as the destruction of Genoa. The headline in *La Stampa* is 'The Black Block Devastate Genoa'; in *La Repubblica* it is 'G8: Another Day of War'; *Il Mattino*: 'Genoa on Fire: Victory For Violence'; *24 Ore*: 'Genoa: A Devastated City'. Italian TV, meanwhile, runs continuous coverage of the trouble.

Outside the Genoa Social Forum base, where the latest battles took place, burnt-out cars and smashed-in shop fronts are the source of much interest to passers-by. The residents of the flats above the trouble spot are debating the causes of the conflict amongst themselves. TV cameras and journalists pick up the debates, which take on an operatic air as the two protagonists rise to the occasion. This is Italian 'piazza politics' being played out, where the local experiences of ordinary citizens become transformed into major worldviews.

However, the most serious story emerging is the unprovoked attack overnight by the *carabinieri* on the sleeping quarters, press and legal centres of the Genoa Social Forum. I hear horrifying accounts of demonstrators being dragged from their sleeping bags and beaten. Other journalists tell me that cameras were deliberately smashed to destroy any evidence of the attack. However, at the Genoa Social Forum press conference in the afternoon, video footage is produced which heavily implicates the *carabinieri*. Meanwhile, rumours are circulating that the 'black block' have been infiltrated by the far right as a way of undermining the anti-capitalist movement. The infiltrators include a neo-Nazi from Birmingham, who tells *Il Manifesto* that he was recruited by his 'Italian brothers'.

I am at the shrine of Carlo Giuliani, the 23-year-old demonstrator shot dead by the *carabinieri* on Friday evening. The spot where he died is marked with a range of personal donations left by fellow demonstrators: flowers, helmets, candles, a gasmask and the remnants of a petrol bomb. A young man, of similar age to Carlo, is sitting with his head in his hands and sobbing. A police car drives by and people cross themselves. Amongst the messages left, someone has written: 'J'accuse Berlusconi, Jospin, Chirac'. Another reads: 'A boy has died in the piazza where I was born'. The street sign that read 'Piazza Gaetano Alimandi' has been crossed out and amended to 'Piazza Carlo Giuliani (Ragazzo)' ('*ragazzo*' meaning 'boy'). It is a very moving scene.

Dinner with some British journalists in the evening reveals that some of the White Overalls group gave up their usual attire as a goodwill gesture in order to integrate with the other demonstrators, while more evidence suggests the far right infiltration of the 'black block'. Outside, the barriers that divided the red zone from the rest of the city have been pulled down. Traffic is busy once again and demonstrators are making their way home. In the taxi on the way back to the hotel I ask the driver what he thinks. 'The war is over', he replies. 'For now.'

A NEW LEFT?

A squatters' theatre, housed in an old warehouse in Viale Lenin, in Bologna (traditionally Italy's reddest city), provided an ideal location for a meeting to herald the rebirth of the Italian left in December 2001. It was packed with a wide spectrum of protesters, many of whom were recent Genoa 'veterans': squatters and grungies from direct action environmentalist movements, school students on strike against government proposals to introduce market reforms in Italy's schools, slick socialist veterans of 1968, and – most prominently – pacifists and other peace activists opposed to the war then in progress in Afghanistan. On one of the coldest nights of the year someone was even wearing sandals, bright red socks protruding. Italy's protests had grown sharply in the immediately preceding weeks. In addition to the big school occupations, there had been general strikes by public sector employees, a mass demonstration by metal mechanics, and Europe's biggest demonstration against the war in Afghanistan. Two of the main speakers, Fausto Bertinotti, leader of the Rifondazione comunista, and Luca Casarini of the White Overalls movement, had to pull out at the last moment because of pressing engagements elsewhere.

The keynote speaker did arrive, however, albeit over an hour late. Vittorio Agnoletto, former leader of the Genoa Social Forum, which organised the opposition to the G8 summit five months earlier, had spent the previous six hours in the company of magistrates who wanted to interview him over that summit's traumatic events. 'It's been a terrible day', he told me after the meeting as we talked en route to Bologna train station, for him a pit stop in an increasingly busy schedule. Prior to Genoa, Agnoletto had been a relatively unknown figure, working for LILA, Italy's Aids trust. His life was transformed since the summit, however, with the events having dramatic personal consequences as well as their much publicised political ramifications. As the leader of the No Global movement, he had also become a target for attack from Italy's right-wing populist government. As a result, he and members of his family received death threats, his phone calls were monitored and he had started sleeping in different houses. Unquestionably, he was the new hate figure for the Italian right. The National Alliance accused him of corrupting young people into taking drugs and, following Genoa, he was removed from government commissions on Aids prevention. Berlusconi himself blamed Agnoletto and the No Global movement for stirring up trouble in public sector strikes. However, Agnoletto found comfort from the wide support he received: 'People come up to me in the street telling me they agree with my position, and that helps me to keep going.'

On the face of it, Agnoletto makes an unlikely heir to the leaders of the Italian left. In his mid-40s, bespectacled and somewhat timid in appearance, he has been seen as a Gandhian figure, seeking peace and calm in a world of violence. His rise to prominence was rapid and reflected the new preference for movements rather than parties, the attraction of taking direct action in pursuit of big global causes rather than relying on party bureaucrats. In this respect, Agnoletto saw the experience of Genoa as crucial to the development of the anti-global capitalist movement: 'Genoa changed things because we understood immediately our importance, our power as a movement.' The death of Carlo Giuliani, the first person to be killed in an Italian piazza since 1977, had opened the eyes of a new political generation, he claimed. 'The movement grew up in Genoa. It became adult immediately. Genoa was also the first political act of the Berlusconi government and as a consequence we discovered their intolerance.'

The influence of No Global, the successor movement to the Genoa Social Forum that Agnoletto convened, had a massive impact. In the wake of Genoa, social forums sprung up in over 50 Italian cities. Berlusconi's attempt to mobilise support for the war in Afghanistan by calling a 'pro-American' demonstration was overshadowed and outnumbered four to one by No Global's own rival march. 'We are now the only opposition to the government', Agnoletto told me, dismissing the DS-led official opposition, which had been taken by surprise by the popular reaction to the Genoa events – it had adopted an ambiguous position, initially distancing itself from the protests, then declaring its sympathy for the demonstrations following the evidence of the brutality of the *carabinieri*. Agnoletto himself became a controversial figure for the DS leadership to deal with. After inviting him to speak on Aids-related issues at its congress in Pesaro the following November, the DS leadership became worried that he would venture onto the contentious terrain of anti-war protest.

In fact, Agnoletto was already convinced that the anti-global capitalist movement in Italy, having come of age in Genoa, would have no trouble being translated into an anti-war movement. Despite what he saw as a government- and media-driven attempt (in Berlusconi's Italy, these often amount to the same thing) to divide the movement by linking the protesters to terrorism, he argued that 'there was no big problem' in the ability of the movement to resituate itself as an anti-war movement. This was apparent in the opposition to the war in Afghanistan, at the time of our interview, but even more so later in the mass anti-war movement that was to grow in the wake of the US and UK-led invasion of Iraq. On the contrary, Agnoletto saw a 'dramatic opportunity for the left to rebuild itself, to think in a global way, to organise a mix between liberals committed to human rights agendas, Greens and those from the more traditional left'.

In late 2001, not everybody on the left shared Agnoletto's optimism that a new opposition was emerging. Many saw in the actions of the *carabinieri* and in the degree of public support for them, despite evidence of culpability and the beginnings of legal proceedings, confirmation of their worst fears – that the Italian government would continue to steamroll its way over the Italian constitution without effective opposition. Opposition parties still appeared divided and were trailing in the polls. Berlusconi, meanwhile, despite promises that he would resolve his conflicts of interest within a hundred days of taking office, had shown no inclination to do so; on the contrary, he was setting out to consolidate his grip on power through a series of legislative measures.

While parties struggled to deal with the impact of Berlusconi, however, the gloom for the left started to lift with the beginnings of an extraordinary set of events that not only brought a strong challenge to the government but simultaneously questioned the capacity of political parties to deliver change. These events were to confirm Agnoletto's belief that the revival of the left would come from movements rather than parties. This was a position which, until then, was viewed with a certain amount of scepticism. Moreover, the rise of the movements was to become pivotal in shifting the agenda away from what remained of the 'third way', where leaders like Fassino (the newly elected leader of the DS), Rutelli and D'Alema talked variously and vaguely about 'new beginnings', 'the end of ideology', flexible labour markets and strong united leadership, without defining what a common programme might look like. From the beginning of 2002, more traditional left values of social justice and critique of the free market began to combine with a stronger assertion of civil libertarian values in defence of an independent media, while the pursuit of peace subsequently and dramatically returned to the political agenda. These developments began to alter the face of Italian politics. Indifference to Berlusconi's excesses was being replaced by a new civic activism. The movements that started from the left became much broader in scope as very different symbols of the resistance both to Berlusconi and to global injustices manifested themselves in a range of movements and associations. Extending beyond the left, they demonstrated an idea of politics beyond populism, but also critical of conventional practice and party ideology.

The trigger for the new wave of opposition was the attempt by the Berlusconi government to suspend Article 18 of the Italian constitution, which prevented employers with more than 15 employees from dismissing workers 'without just cause'. Article 18, according to the government, was arcane and intransigent: the realities of a global economy meant that employers had to have 'flexible' labour, to adapt to fast-changing economic circumstances. The proposed reforms were in fact not unlike proposals that had been considered by the previous centre-left government, and the underlying ideas were the basis of an agreement between Berlusconi and the Blair government.

The Italian workers' movement, which is organised into different political – as distinct from merely occupational – federations, responded instantly, calling for big demonstrations. The CGIL, the former Communist and strongest union federation, organised a national demonstration for March 2002. But before the demonstration took place, tragedy struck. Marco Biagi, one of the authors of a report that made the case for the government's labour reforms (though himself connected to the centre-left), was assassinated outside his home in Bologna by a terrorist group claiming to be the new Red Brigades. In the past, this sort of event, coming as it did just four days before a large national demonstration, would have had very negative repercussions for the left. However, the organisers of the demonstration, notably Sergio Cofferati, the leader of the CGIL, managed to successfully turn the demonstration into a dual attack against terrorism and for social justice. Moreover, it produced an extraordinary display of solidarity between 'older' and 'newer' social movements, namely trade unions and anti-globalisation activists, cultural and political associations, and supporters and members of the centre-left. Many people clearly saw it as an opportunity to vent their opposition to the Berlusconi government.

The result was the largest demonstration in Italy in the modern era, with estimations of over 2 million people congregated in and around the Circo Massimo in the centre of Rome. 23 March 2002 went down as the moment when the Italian left made its comeback. 'The Sun Shines Again', was the headline of left-wing daily *Il Manifesto*, in whose offices I had spent a gloomy election night ten months earlier. It was an event that gave new life to Italy's opposition.

A month later, a follow-up general strike brought twelve million workers out, sending another message to the government. By now Cofferati was leading the main opposition movement and was emerging as a potential leader of the left. He was seen as the first leader since Enrico Berlinguer to unite the different social and political forces. Those on the left could barely conceal their delight after years of ineffective leaders; to some he was the 'Totti of the left', a rising star with seemingly universal popularity. Particularly adept at keeping the various movements on board, notably the new No Global movements and the later anti-war movement, Cofferati also appealed to the left of the DS, in particular the former supporters of Enrico Berlinguer and many of those in the broad left 'Eurocommunist' tradition, who were disgruntled over the ineffectiveness of their leadership. A forgettable party congress, an uninspiring new leader, Piero Fassino, and an ambiguous position over Genoa meant that Cofferati offered the chance of a new political direction that would reconnect to a broad left identity. His position as unofficial leader of the left took off from this point.

With renewed confidence, the left of the DS called for a change in strategy and started to hold its own meetings and rallies. At one of these held in January 2003, at the football stadium in Florence, hosted by Nanni Moretti, Cofferati called for a new political direction for the Olive Tree, with a new political identity for the DS. The Olive Tree must open itself to the movements, intellectuals and associations and no longer be the preserve of party leaders, he said. Peace and the economy should be the two main priorities. Moretti hailed Cofferati as the 'real leader of the left', a phrase that covered the next day's headlines – this drew a response from Fassino that his leadership was being undermined, while Rutelli urged the left 'not to look back at the past'.[1] The left of the DS set up its own national network, *Aprile*, named after Moretti's film, with Cofferati as its first President. The press now talked of two parties, and centre-left leaders argued.

Rifondazione comunista, on the other hand, the smaller left successor to the PCI, was busily courting the No Global movement. At their congress a month after the demonstration, they took the unprecedented step of deferring to the 'movement of movements', as No Global was also called, to reform their own practices – essentially moving away from party-led strategies – and to engage with the new developments. This even reached the symbolic level of replacing the 'Internationale' with John Lennon's 'Imagine' as the congress theme tune. Agnoletto and Cofferati, the movement's two leaders, received a rapturous ovation.

The growth of the No Global and workers' movements defied orthodox explanations about the decline of the organised working class, the erosion of left–right boundaries and the inevitability of neo-liberalism. In Italy it had several implications for the left-wing opposition to Berlusconi. Firstly, it sharpened the conflict with the government. Secondly, it challenged the authority of the centre-left parties, a development that was to intensify over the coming months with the beginnings of the anti-war movement. Thirdly, however, it confirmed major divisions in Italian society, between on the one hand an authoritarian populist right, and on the other, an idealist, egalitarian new left.

However, the new opposition was not confined to the familiar left terrain of social justice and anti-capitalism. Regular protests and demonstrations were organised by Giustizia e libertà, a civil rights group, against Berlusconi's conflicts of interest. Another key player in these protests was Antonio Di Pietro, the magistrate who had led the 'Clean Hands' investigation and who now stood on an independent electoral list. His conventional centre-right politics seemed to mean little in the era of Berlusconi, whose government was committed to blocking the earlier reforming zeal of the magistrates. A series of legislation aimed at reducing the power of the magistrates and defending immunity of prosecution for politicians confirmed the regressive nature of Berlusconi's agenda, while delineating further contours of political conflict. Many of Berlusconi's reforms seemed to come back to his personal predicament: his unresolved conflicts of interest. These became an increasing concern during 2002. The inability of parliamentarians to deal adequately with this was becoming evident, not least to Nanni Moretti, who, having made his public intervention, remained dismayed at the ineffectiveness of the opposition leaders. Following his Piazza Navona speech, he had vowed to set up a citizens' movement that would keep the pressure on Berlusconi, demanding justice and media independence and committed to the defence and renewal of democracy. To paraphrase his character in *Aprile*, it would 'say something civilised'. This movement, which became known as the *girotondi* (literally the Italian name for the game of 'ring a ring a roses'), organised circles of protests and vigils in public places to keep public attention focused on the Berlusconi predicament. When he set up the movement, Moretti did not see it as anything more than 'a group of lackadaisacal voters addressing a group of shell-shocked politicians'. But it was this third protest movement that packed another of Rome's main piazzas (Piazza San Giovanni) on 14 September 2002, seven months after the Piazza Navona speech, in opposition to the latest attempt by Berlusconi to change the laws for his own protection.

2. The Italian film director Nanni Moretti addresses demonstrators gathered in Piazza San Giovanni, 14 September 2002, in Rome, Italy. Tens of thousands of demonstrators rallied accusing conservative premier Silvio Berlusconi of using political power for his personal benefit and saying opposition parties weren't doing enough about it. (Photo: Franco Origlia/Getty Images)

This protest, made up of a million people who had, in the words of *Il Manifesto*, 'arrived from all over Italy, though no trade union or political organisation had asked them', was the expression of a spontaneous non-parliamentary movement made necessary by the failures of established parties and leaders. 'They have asked me – and I have asked myself – why in these months we have done all this', Moretti told the crowd. 'It is because the situation has been made too serious to do nothing.'

THE EUROPEAN SOCIAL FORUM

The three movements gave energy and new confidence to a lacklustre opposition. The European Social Forum (ESF), held in Florence in November 2002, brought the new movements together, as well as a range of activists from beyond Italy, to discuss opposition to neo-liberalism and war and exchange ideas on new forms of democratic participation that could be alternatives to the models of political parties. The ESF, while receiving limited coverage in Europe as a whole, carried major political ramifications in Italy both for the government, which tried to prevent it from happening, and also for the centre-left, notably the DS, which was once again caught in two minds over how to respond. Indeed, the decision to hold the ESF in Florence was hotly contested by the Italian government. Following the G8 summit in Genoa, the right argued that the event should be cancelled or that, at the very least, central Florence should be fenced off. Threats to public order, desecration to works of art, and 'occupations of piazzas by insurrectionary and foreign political groups' were all predicted, while the local newspaper kept up a climate of impending doom as the ESF got under way.

'Certainly there will be devastation', Berlusconi said. In the event, only 63 out of 15,000 shops closed (including all branches of McDonald's) for the first couple of days (though an estimated 250 million euros were said to have been lost to local traders). The right's over-reaction backfired on them; nothing more dangerous than 'gentle anarchists' entered the shops, with shopkeepers being congratulated for staying open. Dario Fo, the Nobel Prize-winning left-wing playwright, who took part in the opening event in Piazza Santa Croce, talked of his 'sense of great joy and a desire to pursue the struggle not with acts of violence, but with laughter'.[2]

The ESF took a lot of sceptical commentators by surprise in its unity and sense of purpose. The Italian input was unsurprisingly huge, and its aftermath – the event was in the national news headlines for days – had further effects on the agenda of the left. Most of the critical discussion at the ESF centred on what the relationship should be between movements and parties, notably the DS. There had been much criticism of Piero Fassino, the DS leader, who kept his distance from the event. Yet, it was the DS City Council that hosted the event. The mayor, Leonardo Domenici, kept the idea of the ESF alive and took a significant risk in standing up to its opponents and going ahead with the event. The ESF was a result of his imagination and that of the Florence City Council, which adopted the theme 'Florence: Open City' to encourage a positive welcome for the activists as well as providing open civic spaces for dialogues between different groups. For Domenici, the ESF was crucial in the airing of alternatives to what he called 'the profound crisis of democracy'. Paul Ginsborg, a leading historian of Italy and left-wing activist, talked about the 'rapid disintegration of democracy' under Berlusconi, notably in its constitutional and legal forms. This, he argued, had 'dangerous implications' for the future of representative democracy that were becoming more evident by the day. The priority for the left, said Ginsborg, should be to develop new forms of participatory democracy, help strengthen civil society, and work towards the enshrining of Europe-wide democratic and civil rights.

THE ANTI-WAR MOVEMENT

Vittorio Agnoletto's claim that the No Global movement would make a comfortable transition to an anti-war movement was borne out in the Italian example. In Italy as with other Western European countries, with the exception of Britain, the centre-left opposed the invasion of Iraq from the start, believing in the authority of the United Nations and the necessity to avoid war at all costs. Renzo Imbeni, head of the Socialist Group in the European Parliament and a member of the DS, explained to me in an interview after the invasion had started that the key factor was the association of war with Fascism: 'For countries such as Italy, France and Germany, war was a reality in order to overcome Fascism and Nazism. For us war was a consequence of Fascism. For Germany it was the consequence of Nazism. In Europe, war was the decision of the dictator. At the end of the Second World War, we said "never again". For us it is impossible to imagine that you can export democracy through war.'

He also told me that all members of the Socialist Group in the European Parliament, including Labour MEPs, voted initially against the war and agreed that they needed the support of the United Nations. Once the war started most Labour MEPs reversed their positions and claimed there was, after all, a legal basis for the war. The 'deceit' on the part of Blair was obvious, he added, and carried implications for the long-term unity of the European left.

Opposition to the war in Iraq in Italy went far beyond the left, however. The desire for peace and the feeling of a civic and citizen responsibility to bring that about was clearly central to the concerns of many ordinary Italians. With public opinion strongly opposed to the actions of the US and UK, the Italian government faced more restraints and was often ridiculed for its inflated sense of importance as one of the governments supporting the war coalition. As soon as the invasion of Iraq took place, a large, often spontaneous movement of Italian activists, across the centre and left of the political spectrum, responded. Piazzas were filled with demonstrators, train stations thought to be sending arms were occupied, and *terrazzas* were covered with the rainbow colours of the *bandiere della pace*. Artists and intellectuals, of course, made their opposition clear, but the protests were extremely broad, reflecting opinion polls suggesting that 90 percent of Italians opposed the invasion. Even Veronica Lario, the wife of Silvio Berlusconi, declared herself against the war and 'with the pacifists', favourably quoting Umberto Eco on the consequences for terrorism in an interview she gave to *Micromega* in March 2003.

The churches were a strong focus for opposition, helped by the Pope's own opposition to the war. As a result, a national day of fasting in March 2003 brought an unlikely alliance between left-wing and Catholic organisations. ACLI, Rete Liliput, and local Catholic organisations and churches responded to an appeal by the Pope for a fast in support of peace. A *pasticceria* in Bologna closed its doors for the day, informing its customers with a note pinned to the door that 'there will be no cakes or brioches today, as we have closed for peace', following the call from the Holy Father. This was a scene repeated throughout Italy, with torchlight processions to piazzas and broad displays of solidarity. The headline of the left-wing *Manifesto* was 'Resistere, Resistere, Resistere!', directly above an image of spaghetti twirled round a fork.

The war itself led to new forms of political association in Italy, common interests forged between disparate groups and the introduction to politics of new generations of Italians. There were some differences over strategy. For Cofferati, now the unofficial leader of the left, opposition to the war had always been a case of '*senza se, senza ma*' ('no ifs and no buts'), while for some centre-left leaders, it was the lack of United Nations endorsement that was the crucial issue. In Italy, as elsewhere in Western Europe, opposition to the war became the 'common sense' view of the nation, a consensus that led to some of the biggest protests and demonstrations for many years. That it went beyond the left was crucial in isolating Berlusconi. Yet the involvement of a 'radical centre' also challenged the rationale of the centre-left. This 'centre' was not an ideology-free zone, indifferent to political movements or popular protest, or an anonymous electoral constituency, moved only by pragmatism and prudence. Rather, it represented social forces and political tendencies, a pacifist centre, Catholic social conscience and what Ginsborg calls the 'reflexive middle class'.[3] What united it was civic commitment to 'do something' for peace.

This civic movement for peace continued beyond the end of the war and into the period of occupation as the war coalition attempted to build a new Iraq. The commitment to peace was also evident in the large number of Italians who were part of volunteer and aid groups operating in Iraq itself. This was vividly apparent in the case of the 'two Simonas' (Simona Pari and Simona Torretta), two aid workers employed by the organisation Bridge for Baghdad who were kidnapped and held hostage for three weeks in September 2004. During the period of their captivity, ordinary Italians kept up regular vigils and protests for their release, ensuring pressure was kept on the political leaders. The two Simonas' eventual release on 28 September, after a ransom paid by the Italian government, was to an outpouring of national joy. In their press conferences, in addition to describing fear after their capture, they discussed their work amongst the women and children of Baghdad, their opposition to the invasion and their desire to return.

According to a survey for *La Repubblica* in October 2004, the two Simonas are part of a 3000-strong group of Italians who work for non-governmental organisations in the world's most dangerous places, while another 6000–7000 are on a waiting list, urgently trying to enter this kind of work. Whether it is out of pacifist beliefs, ideology, the calling of God, or some other reason, there is a latent undercurrent of global concern within Italy which is often hidden by popular representations of Italian cultural life and the rise of populism; it seems not to be reflected either in the global worldviews of Italy's politicians. Moreover, it contrasts sharply with the underlying values of the Berlusconi era. This ethos is further evidence of a wider shift towards a new associationism, a form of civic commitment that helped make peace the 'common sense' position in Italy. It was a vision that was increasingly at odds with Berlusconi, while representing a significant challenge to the official opposition.

6
The South Strikes Back

The Italian South, the 'Mezzogiorno', is often set apart from the rest of Italy. Its economic status, cultural traditions, family structures, and in particular its lack of civic culture, which has given rise to political corruption and clientelism, often compares unfavourably with the more modern and prosperous North. Yet, many of the perceptions of the Mezzogiorno have been derived from negative stereotypes, uninformed prejudice and unsubstantiated assumptions. Indeed, the Berlusconi years saw new levels of prejudice and animosity towards the South, notably through the rhetoric and invective of Bossi's Northern League, and the dominant Milanese elites that helped to bring Berlusconi to power had little time for the traditions of the South.

The Mezzogiorno is certainly poorer than the North, more given to political corruption, including Mafia influence (which includes not only the Cosa Nostra in Sicily, but the Camorra in Naples, Sacra Corona Unita in Puglia and the 'Ndrangheta in Calabria), more deferential to religion and social hierarchy, and less efficient in its institutions and sense of public duty. Consequently, fatalism is more pervasive, the problem of the state more intense and social reform more problematic. History explains much; the process of Italian unification in the 1860s was significantly more uneven and political modernisation more difficult in the South, while very different civic and political traditions prevailed in the South prior to unification. Thereafter, the liberation of Italy after the Second World War often carried different implications for North and South; the important role of the Resistance in the North was crucial in delineating subsequent political traditions and movements, while in the South liberation came from the allies. In the South there was no strong partisan legacy, which continues to influence politics elsewhere in Italy. Instead, the long hegemony of Christian democracy was at its most powerful here, reflected in paternalism and deference. Migration to the North and abroad was a route chosen by many southerners as a way of escaping from poor job prospects and poverty.

However, as some scholars have recently pointed out, the status of the Mezzogiorno has often been derived from its identification as the 'other' in a divided Italy. Its 'backwardness' is due in part to comparisons with the North and often attributed to cultural stereotypes rather than economic inequality. Southerners have long provided a large part of the northern workforce. These views, given academic credence by many writers, continue to offer dispiriting and often inaccurate pictures of the South. The text that is cited the most for legitimising the 'backwardness' of the South, Edward Banfield's *The Moral Basis of a Backward Society*, was published in 1958.[1] Banfield's main argument, based on a year's research in Basilicata, was that the development of the South had been held back by what he called 'amoral familism'. This concept was used by Banfield to explain the lack of civic awareness and the preference at all times for family interests over the common interests. The dominance of the family in providing welfare and support for its members was at the cost of wider modernisation, according to Banfield. For him, this also explained the prevalence in the South of clientelism and political patronage, and the absence of wider social solidarity and was likely to reproduce authoritarian social relations and political systems. Many have subsequently criticised Banfield's argument, pointing out that the family structure in the South is much more complex than he suggests (traditional patriarchal families are not as common as he claimed), notably because women have a much more prominent role in the family than in other parts of Italy.[2]

More recently, Robert Putnam, a much respected American academic, has attributed differences between the North and South to the different types of democratic and civic organisational structures that have existed historically. Based on 20 years of research in different regions in Italy, Putnam concluded that the very different qualities of democratic life found, for example, in Emilia Romagna and Puglia, were derived from different traditions of civic community that could be traced back to the twelfth century, where the city states in the North contrasted with the centralised Norman rule in the South. He puts much emphasis on both history and the role of institutions in shaping the behaviour of political actors and helping generate and sustain democratic performance. Putnam's research is very comprehensive and explains much about the stark differences between the regional governments and political cultures of the North and South. Some have challenged the consistency of Putnam's argument, pointing out, for example, that Fascism originated in the North, as well as the difficulties of tracing continuity of democratic traditions over such an expansive period.[3] It is also noticeable that Putnam's research, published in 1993, could not explain the *Tangentopoli* crisis, which also originated in the North and which effectively called into question the entire institutional basis of Italy's democratic life.

Moreover, as we will see, a new associationism in the South has emerged despite the existence of many of the negative aspects, such as clientelism and weak institutional structure, that Putnam identified. It is therefore necessary to rethink the South and its traditions and underlying dynamics. This includes how we define the South. Normally, the South includes the islands of Sicily and Sardinia, as well as, for example, Calabria, Basilicata, Campania and Puglia, regions that have quite different traditions. Indeed, Sicily, the subject of the next chapter, is a place full of its own paradoxes. Moreover, we will find that there is a new South emerging, which has its roots in economic changes that have taken place over the last 30 years, but which arose from the shadow of the Berlusconi era. The passivity of the past is still current, but it is now possible to find new forms of association, between movements and networks, involving a mix of political actors. Corruption and clientelism continue to eat away at the body politic in some places, while familism remains very strong – yet generational changes and in particular the changing aspirations of young women are challenging old certainties. Religious symbols remain pervasive – with busts of Padre Pio and symbols of the Madonna watching over many towns and houses – but these coexist with new freedoms. Fatalism, one of the biggest problems of the South, has been usurped in some parts by new forms of civic resistance that have often been one step ahead of political parties. Moreover, the southern economy, which has long trailed the more prosperous North despite receiving government resources from the *Cassa del Mezzogiorno* (the scheme used to fund social and economic development in the South), has shown clear signs of change.

In his book *Christ Stopped at Eboli*,[4] Carlo Levi, sent to political exile in a remote corner of Basilicata in southern Italy by Italy's Fascist government in 1935, described his time in

> [another] world, hedged in by custom and sorrow, cut off from History and the State, eternally patient, [a] land without comfort and solace, where the peasant lives out his motionless civilisation on barren ground in remote poverty, and in the presence of death.

The 'remote and barren' landscape he describes (and, during his time there, painted), is a world cut off from civilisation. His journey from Turin, at the other end of the country, opened his eyes to this other world and made clear to him a 'confrontation between two cultures' embodied in the same nation. 'No one', he wrote, 'has come to this land except as an enemy, a conqueror, or a visitor devoid of understanding'.[5]

On arrival at Aliano (he calls it Gagliano in the book), the village that was his home from 1935 to 1936, his first impressions, in addition to the desolate landscape, were the black veils of the peasant women, the doors marked with aged black pennants denoting deceased family members, and the lack of basic amenities. But his foremost impression was the fatalism and resignation of the peasants towards their predicament, their antipathy towards the state, too alien and remote for any comprehension:

> To the peasants the state is more distant than heaven and far more of a scourge, because it is always against them. Its political tags and platforms and, indeed, the whole structure of it do not matter. The peasants do not understand them because they are couched in a different language from their own, and there is no reason why they should ever care to understand them. Their only defence against the state and the propaganda of the state is resignation, the same gloomy resignation, alleviated by no hope of paradise, that bows their shoulders under the scourges of nature.[6]

During his year in Aliano, this absence of a sense of state and isolation from social and economic civilisation, combined with conflict and suspicion between the local hierarchies, Fascist functionaries, priests and smaller gentry, became a vivid memory. Yet it was the poverty that remained with him and which, following the publication of his book, did much to bring public attention to Italy's North–South divide.

Levi's sister, Luisa, while on a journey to visit him, had to pass through Matera, the capital of the province, in order to be given her clearance papers. With time on her hands she looked for the centre of Matera and later described to her brother what she encountered in detail.

A little beyond the station I found a street with a row of houses on one side and on the other a deep gully. In the gully lay Matera. From where I was, higher up, it could hardly be seen because the drop was so sheer. All I could distinguish as I looked down were alleys and terraces, which concealed the houses from view...The gully had a strange shape: it was formed by two half-funnels, side by side, separated by a narrow spur and meeting at the bottom, where I could see a white church, Santa Maria de Idris, which looked half-sunk in the ground. The two funnels, I learned, were called Sasso Caveoso and Sasso Barisano. They were like a schoolboy's idea of Dante's Inferno. And, like Dante, I too began to go down from circle to circle, by a sort of mule path leading to the bottom. The narrow path wound its way down and around, passing over the roofs of houses, if houses they could be called. They were caves, dug into the hardened clay walls of the gully, each with its own facade, some of which were quite handsome, with eighteenth century ornamentation. These false fronts, because of the slope of the gully, were flat against its side at the bottom, but at the very top they protruded, and the alleys in the narrow space between them and the hillside did double service: they were a roadway for those who came out of their houses from above, and a roof for those who lived beneath. The houses were open on account of the heat, and as I went by I could see into the caves, whose only light came in through the front doors. Some of them had no entrance but a trapdoor and ladder. In these dark holes with walls cut out of the earth I saw a few pieces of miserable furniture, beds and some ragged clothes hanging up to dry. On the floor lay dog, sheep, goats and pigs. Most families have just one cave to live in and there they sleep all together; men, women, children and animals. This is how twenty thousand people live.

Of children I saw an infinite number. They appeared from
everywhere, in the dust and heat, amid the flies, stark naked or
clothed in rags; I have never in all my life seen such a picture
of poverty. My profession [she was a doctor] has brought me
in daily contact with dozens of poor, sick, ill-kempt children,
but I never dreamed of seeing a sight like this...They had
trachoma...Most of them had enormous, dilated stomachs,
and faces yellow and worn with malaria...The thin women,
with dirty, undernourished babies hanging at their flaccid
breasts, spoke to me mildly and with despair. I felt, under the
blinding sun, as if I were in a city stricken by the plague. I
went on down towards the church at the bottom of the gully;
a constantly swelling crowd of children followed and called
after me. I thought they must want pennies, and I stopped for
a minute. Only then did I make out the words they were all
shouting together: 'Signorina, dammi'u chini! Signorina, give
me some quinine!'[7]

As a result of the outcry that followed the publication of Levi's
book, and some research into the living conditions of the *sassi*
(the old cave-like dwellings built out of the rock in the mountain)
that found 1500 of these habitations lacking water and electricity,
the Italian Prime Minister, De Gasperi, visited Matera in 1950 and,
shocked by what he saw, initiated a process of removing the people
from the *sassi*, and directed aid for replacement communities. The
official, symbolic closure of the *sassi* took place in 1953, with
residents moving to a new housing complex outside the centre
of Matera, though many stayed until the 1960s, until further laws
ensured the removal of all *sassi* residents.

Subsequently, as a result of the archaeological originality of its
dwellings, some of which date back to the early middle ages, the
sassi were recognised by UNESCO as a world heritage centre in
1993 and preserved as part of Italy's heritage. Today, the *sassi* are a
major tourist attraction, with hotels and new residences opening
up in the refurbished dwellings. They have provided the scenic
backdrop to many films, including Pier Paolo Pasolini's *The Gospel
According to Matthew* in 1964 and Mel Gibson's blockbuster, *The
Passion of the Christ*, filmed during 2002–03.

Matera, meanwhile, started to benefit from the economic
miracle and now has the appearance of an affluent, lively town,

3. Matera. The *Sassi di Matera,* with the new town in
the background. (Photo: Antonio Foschino, Sassiweb)

in the fastest growing province of Italy, enjoying a quality of life
that ranks among the best in southern Italy, with crime being
virtually non-existent.[8] Aliano itself, while remaining remote and
with high unemployment among young people, also benefited
from developments in economic growth, agricultural production,
cooperatives and other forms of economic association.[9]

   The transformation of Matera has been swift and suggests a new
direction for the region of Lucania (to give it its Roman name),
with its rich agricultural resources bringing claims of the 'new
California'. The old image of the backward South, dependent
on state handouts from the North, does not fit with the new
aspirations of this region. Old stereotypes and images die hard,
however, and some resurfaced after the filming and release of Mel
Gibson's *The Passion*. The *Observer*'s Italy correspondent, Sophie
Arie, in a sensationalist piece of journalism more familiar to the
British tabloids, ran a story in April 2004 on the film's release,
entitled 'Italy's Cavemen Cashing in on Passion of Mel'. In this
article Arie claimed that Gibson's Hollywood epic was 'raising the
impoverished town of Matera from the dead'.

The article provoked an indignant response from people in the town. Antonio Foschino of *Sassiweb*, a local network that helps to promote the *sassi* to tourists, took issue with the view that Matera was wild or impoverished or 'being lifted out of poverty and cashing in on the film industry', while reference to 'cavemen' was extremely offensive and ignored the fact that the caves had been evacuated 50 years previously.

'Your article', he wrote to the *Observer*, 'created an image of Matera as a desolate, poor, unknown place where we live in caves and hardly managed to survive until Gibson arrived, bringing the light of civilisation to us and the hope of survival'. In the event, the *Observer* was forced to publish a full apology, admitting that the article 'was interpreted there as reinforcing tired clichés about poverty in southern Italy'.[10]

When I visited Matera in 2004, Foschino, a local amateur historian and photographer, told me about the 'Matera miracle'. The town, he said, had been transformed over the last 30 years. He used the example of La Martella, the community housing development that had been constructed to accommodate people from the *sassi*. Architecturally, the houses were designed to reflect the close sense of community that had existed in the *sassi*. Yet the project had not been popular. This was partly because of the difficulty of recreating the older community, but it also failed because of the pace of change in the local economy and quality of life, driven by the transformation of agricultural production methods and the expansion of local industries, notably sofa production. La Martella had no school, cinema, or bars or restaurants, to keep pace with social and cultural changes. The first impression now of Matera, a town of some 60,000 people, is the quality of life, with a cluster of award-winning restaurants in close vicinity and its relaxed and contented citizens.

The Camera Club, a bar built out of a cave dwelling and the centre of Matera's social scene, buzzes nightly to the optimism of youth. The nightly *passeggiata* (the regular evening stroll that is almost a ritual in Italian piazzas) in Piazza Vittorio Veneto and along Via Roma is a packed event, attracting all generations, and is a sign of a contented and aspirational population. These changes, Foschino told me, had been under way years before Mel Gibson arrived in the town. In fact, tourism in the *sassi* since the release of *The Passion* had only gone up 20 percent in the following year.

Yet, the difficulty of projecting this reality more widely persisted. Many of the visitors to *Sassiweb* are interested in the film rather than the town. Of these, many Christian evangelists flood the message board with denunciations of the blasphemous nature of *The Passion*, or long, drawn-out theological discussions. This makes for quite a contrast with the more sedate Catholicism of Matera and the surrounding area. Christian democracy was the dominant political culture in this region and, very unusually by the standards of contemporary Italy, seems to have made a relatively painless transition to the Olive Tree coalition, providing Matera with stable centre-left local government.

Michele Porcari, the mayor of Matera, told me this centre-left Catholic tradition was a 'Lucanian phenomenon'. He also puts the economic and social development of Matera down to the 'calm' and peaceful outlook of Lucanian culture. 'People can appear very closed but in reality, deep down, we have a strong sense of solidarity and welcoming outlook.'

DAYS OF REVOLT

Sixty kilometres from Matera (but still in Matera province) lies the small town of Scanzano Jonico, with a population of 6,700 people. A relatively new town (it only gained administrative autonomy in 1974), it is situated in a remote corner of Basilicata. It does have a rich archaeological heritage, however, as the site of the first Greek settlement. As such it is a land that has seen many battles led by Romans, Saracens and Barbarians, among others.

As an agricultural economy in a region of barren and marshy land that often carried malaria, the area suffered major hardships until the Agricultural Reform Acts of the early 1950s, which allowed the development of small farm businesses and latterly cooperatives to flourish. In more recent years, Metapontino, the wider area of land that includes Scanzano, has developed a prosperous agricultural sector, producing a range of quality fruit and vegetables – strawberries, kiwis, apricots, olives, peaches, grapes and plums – as well as notable dairy and cheese farms. In addition to agricultural produce, its sandy beaches are renowned for clear uncontaminated waters, while fishing brings

4. Scanzano. Demonstrators protest against the Italian government's decision
to dump nuclear waste in Scanzano Jonico. (Photo: Giorgio Braschi)

in swordfish, tuna, cuttlefish, squid and lobster. In fact, Scanzano
is situated in an area of ecological variety and quality. Its local
council has a long commitment to 'sustainable tourism', while
the agricultural development of Metapontino has attracted the
label of the 'California of the South'.

It remains a remote location, however, with a small and
declining population in an area that carries high unemployment
of almost 20 percent and that still sees much migration to the
North from people looking for better opportunities. It was these
reasons, together with a potentially less risky electoral backlash,
that suggested to the Italian government that this would be an
appropriate place to dump Italy's entire supply of nuclear waste.
The decision, made in November 2003 without any consultation
with regional representatives, had identified an underground
dump for 80,000 cubic metres of waste. This was a very sad month
for Italians, with the deaths of 19 soldiers from a suicide bombing
at Nassiyria, southern Iraq, on 12 November. The announcement
on 13 November that a decree had been approved to locate the
waste in Scanzano was subsequently regarded as a sly move on

behalf of the government to take advantage of the sobriety of the period of mourning in Italy.

The response of the town, however, was emphatic and immediate. This was a battle which, in its own way, was as significant for its people as the ones that had taken place in the same land over the preceding centuries. Carlo Levi's observation that no one 'has come to this land except as an enemy, a conqueror or a visitor devoid of understanding' seemed to be resonant once again. Mario Altieri, mayor of Scanzano, described the decision as a 'thunderbolt...taken without our involvement'. Ermete Realucci, national President of the environmentalist group Legambiente, asserted that 'the decision to be the dustbin of nuclear waste has been arrived at without the necessary meetings with local institutions'. Simona Ianuzziello, whose diary of the days of revolt was later published, told me that when the news first broke on 13 November, the local council held an emergency meeting and phones started to ring among a disorganised, informal group of friends and activists.[11]

The immediate feeling was one of fear and the need to defend the territory. 'We have had a thousand years of invasion and domination and we are absolutely clear that this time we will not passively allow this to happen', declared Altieri, as confirmation of the news broke. He demanded to meet Berlusconi. The first demonstration took place at 7.00 pm on 13 November, a spontaneous mobilisation of local citizens. Meanwhile, Altero Matteoli, the minister for the environment, declared himself 'satisfied with the choice of Scanzano, because the government has brought to an end something that has been waiting for 20 years'. On the same day, Antonio di Sanza, head of the Basilicata group of Forza Italia, resigned his membership in protest. His unlikely ally, Francesco Caruso of the *Disobbedienti* (the No Global anarchists known for initiating direct action campaigns), announced protest actions throughout the South, stating: 'We will never allow the government to make the South the rubbish tip of Italy and Europe'.

The following day, Matteoli again praised the 'courage' of the government's decision, adding that Scanzano had been 'evaluated by a committee of experts' as the chosen site. Massimo Polledri, the Northern League spokesman for energy, also called the decision 'an act of courage'. However, the campaigners were

buoyed by the intervention of Gianvittorio Gandolfi, President
of the local tourist board, who argued that the dumping of
nuclear waste would cause 'abnormal damage to the territory'.
The coordinating group for the campaign held its first meeting
and was composed of a range of unions, commercial groups,
environmental groups, cooperatives and ordinary citizens. In an
unprecedented development, all the political parties from right
to left gave their support.

The following day, 15 November, saw the first organised
march as 1000 students stormed through Policoro telling the
government: 'Don't bury our future.' Under-Secretary for the
Environment Roberto Tortoli described Scanzano as an 'ideal
place.' 'The people always protest', he went on, 'every time a
government takes decisions'. It was, he added, 'perhaps the safest
place in the world for nuclear waste'. The following day saw the
protests increase in tempo. Traffic was closed for 25 kilometres
as a 3000-strong demonstration began, headed by the mayors of
all the councils in Metapontino, who promised the 'permanent
suspension of all activity'. The parish priest of Scanzano, Don
Filippo Lombardo, who was to play a leading role in the protests,
made his first appeal: 'The Christian community invites everybody
to oppose the decision of the government'. He also called for
'dignity' in the protest.

On 17 November, Metaponto station was blocked on the
Taranto–Reggio Calabria line for two days; the protesters also
commemorated those who died at Nassiriya, on the day their
funerals took place. Schoolchildren from Enea and Rotondella,
the closest villages to Scanzano, walked out. Carlo Jean, the
President of Sogin, the company responsible for ensuring that
the safety rules for nuclear waste are met (and who was also
the commissioner nominated by Berlusconi to originally find
the site), announced that the project would go forward. The A3
autostrada was occupied by 500 people, stopping traffic in both
directions. The first meeting between a Lucanian delegation and
government ministers took place.

The first sign that the government was starting to weaken
came on 20 November. There was an announcement that the
decree would be 'modified' after a government 're-evaluation'
of whether Scanzano was the best site. The following day, the
Northern League urged the government to hold firm and held a

counter-demonstration in Piacenza, in Emilia Romagna, a region waiting to offload its nuclear waste. 'There is a need for one united site in the national interests', they declared in an unusual bout of national consciousness.

The biggest demonstration yet took place on 23 November as the whole town, together with the rest of the Matera province, went on strike. Figures suggest numbers in the region of 70,000–100,000 attended the demonstration, with supporters from Calabria, Campania and Puglia converging on Scanzano. The demonstration took the form of an eight-kilometre snake, from Policoro to Scanzano. 'The People Rebel' was the headline in *Corriere della Sera*. 'Rescind the decree' was the unanimous call. The following day the protest was taken to Rome, with the mayor of Policoro, Nicola Lopatriello, insisting he would 'block Rome'. An estimated 3000 Romans turned up in support, including students from Basilicata studying in the city who occupied Piazza Venezia, while 22 coaches arrived from as far apart as Bologna, Milan and Naples. The head of the Greens in the European Parliament circulated a petition. Pressure was mounting on the government. Carlo Jean insisted: 'No site is better than Scanzano'.

The following day, 27 November, eight more roads, including three motorways, were blocked for two hours. Then, two weeks after the announcement of the site was made, the news that the people of Scanzano had been waiting for arrived. The government's 'modification' of the decree resulted in the removal of the name 'Scanzano Jonico' as the site of the deposit. A party took place in Scanzano, at which the 'victory of the Lucanian people' was celebrated. 'The nightmare is over', announced Filippo Bubbico, President of the Basilicata Region. Antonio Di Pietro, the magistrate who led the 'Clean Hands' inquiry, attributed the victory to the 'solidarity of regions' and the 'civic participatory demonstrations'.

After the government's U-turn, ad hoc groups of activists sustained their protests and have developed a strong civic movement in defence of their territory. The movement against the nuclear waste in Scanzano was not led by political parties, though all, including the government parties, went to great lengths to be seen to support it. At the Scanzano office of Forza Italia after the decree had been rescinded, a poster thanked both the Lucanian people and the 'sensibility of Silvio Berlusconi'.

Rather, the movement was a spontaneous revolt led by a mixture of committed individuals and groups. In many ways it was testament to the new associationism in the South, involving self-organised autonomous associations, together with traditional figures of authority, including many priests, activists from social and environmental movements and many networks that had been born out of distrust of political leaders and as a response to political inertia and corruption. Pino Mele, a local environmental activist and one of the members of the organising group, drove me to the base camp of the movement, near the intended site of the dump. He pointed out the part of the *autostrada* that was blocked by demonstrators, as well as examples of the rich agricultural terrain. He told me of his surprise at the response of the movement and the strength of feelings it had aroused. As a long-serving environmentalist he had become used to fighting lonely battles; now much of his agenda had become the common sense of the whole town. Since the government announced the decision his 'life had changed'; his phone never stopped ringing, and the campaign had become a 24-hour commitment.

The power of local feelings and a new confidence among people in the South drove the movement in Scanzano. One of the leading figures in the movement was Don Filippo Lombardo. Somewhat surprised to find himself next to anti-global capitalist activists, he told me that his role was to foster unity among a community that still looked to religion for guidance. 'The church is the people in Lucania', he reminded me. He said there were two reasons why the people of the town had become so united and had taken such determined action. Firstly, there was the 'fear' factor. 'Fear was the first thing people expressed, the danger of the nuclear waste for the community.' The second factor was the 'risk' of nuclear waste for everyone. Every sector would be affected, including the land, the development of local business, local produce and agriculture.' I asked him why he thought the government had chosen Scanzano. 'The reason is very simple; few people live here. The North doesn't want our products. And they thought that Scanzano was politically insignificant.' What did he think the significance of the Scanzano revolt would be? 'The Lucanian people are normally calm and peaceful and this was a rich experience for them.' It would have the legacy, he said, of a 'mini Resistance': 'It will be a reference point for the future. It is important not to forget. Personally I think that the phenomenon of Scanzano is part of a new southern question.'

TAKING ON CRIME

If there is a new associationism in the South of Italy, then much of it grew out of the resistance to crime, clientelism and the inertia of local government. The South had to confront immense deep-rooted problems of corruption and the lack of a sense of state, often obstructed by political parties embedded and constrained by the system. One of the paradoxes of the new South – including Sicily – is that resignation, fatalism and inertia coexist with energy, commitment and innovation. Outside Sicily, nowhere is this more obvious than Naples, the anarchic, fascinating first city of the South. Its charm and conviviality, with a strong reputation for friendliness, cannot disguise the failures of local politics. Much of this is down to the Camorra, the Neapolitan Mafia, which has earlier historic roots than its Sicilian counterpart, the Cosa Nostra, and which continues to control a large part of the city, in particular its economy. As Behan has pointed out in his study of the Camorra, it has been able to control local markets, and mediate as 'power-broker' between politicians and the people.[12] The Camorra has been able to prosper through its control, in recent years, of the contraband cigarette industry, drugs, and extortion, and through protection rackets made up of groups of 50 or so people 'working' different districts of the city. Increasingly, it has been the battle over public contracts that has been the focus of Camorra activity, giving it unprecedented influence while depending on the duplicity of generations of politicians from across the political spectrum. Acting as 'brokers', as Behan puts it, 'not only increases their general social legitimacy, it also makes them more important in the eyes of corrupt politicians worried about getting elected'.[13]

The Camorra is therefore able to move across the boundaries of legality and illegality quite comfortably and often unchallenged. The main problem is that the Camorra is deeply embedded in the local power structures; in fact it operates not so much as an alternative to the state, but as a 'parallel state':

Once systematic criminal influence within the political structure, with its consequent protection from legal sanctions and harassment, becomes generally accepted, territorial control can take on a literal meaning. Camorra control becomes a widely known fact, conditioning both the local population and the political structure. When this position of power is reached, all manner of criminal activities can flourish, privately sanctioned by local political leaders.[14]

Fear and violence combine with a certain respect for the role of the Camorra in offering forms of employment via its various influences. In a city that regularly comes bottom of Italy's league tables for quality of life, including levels of employment, any reforms must also have a long-term economic strategy. All these factors make the prospect of reform complex and difficult. Many hopes were invested in the election of reforming leaders, notably Antonio Bassolino, the DS mayor, elected with massive majorities from 1993–2000. While Bassolino did succeed in cleaning up parts of the city, and indeed helped create optimism in the city in the mid 1990s that the Camorra could finally be defeated, he was unable to address the long-term structural issues and left before the end of his tenure to become leader of the province.

The problem of the political parties' assimilation into the world of the Camorra, together with the need to address the problem at a popular and grassroots level, has meant that movements and associations outside official politics have often taken the lead. A dispute in 2004 in one of the small towns just north of Naples, Acerra, symbolised the complexities and difficulties of reform in and around Naples. Acerra is a town known for its Camorra connections and, along with neighbouring towns, is part of what is locally called the 'triangle of death'. Following a long-running dispute over the failure to dispose of the town's rubbish – an issue which brought people to the streets in many other places in the South – the region, unable to find a place to dispose of the rubbish and with all local waste disposal centres saying they had reached maximum capacity, outlined its plans to set up a factory with an incinerator, with potentially grave environmental and health consequences for the town.

This decision brought major demonstrations and conflicts with the police and the local state. Its significance, however, was more far-reaching. The town, whose mayor, Esperito Marletta, was a member of Rifondazione comunista, had developed a militant tradition in recent years, despite the pervasive influence of the Camorra. The demonstrations, which reached their peak in August 2004, saw many violent clashes and arrests. Marletta himself was arrested in mid August, after police opened the gates of the factory without his permission. At the end of August, a 'human snake' of thousands, stretching a kilometre long, descended on Acerra, and many shops closed in protest. According to Marletta,

> the demonstration was a sign of the maturity of the citizens, residents and demonstrators who have chosen to come to the piazza to say no to the installation of the rubbish incinerator. There has been no dialogue with the forces of law and order and we will not remain silent and accept the solutions that have been handed down to us by others. The institutions must listen to the voices of the people.[15]

The response of the citizens of the town was massive, the indignation and resilience to an alien state very evident. The stench of uncleared rubbish was apparent in and around the streets of Acerra, while opposition to the proposals was flagged in red writing on white sheets, hanging from *terrazzas* along the rubbish-strewn streets. 'We want to live'…'No to the factory of death; protect our children!'…'Incinerator = death'. Posters in shop windows called for the immediate suspension of work and closure of the factory. Posters advertising rallies and demonstrations, under the signatures of many local organisations and networks, called on the people of Acerra 'to recover our identity and our civic sense'. Low-cost clothes shops and cafés, with the unemployed sitting around, testified to the economic plight of the town, but there was still an unmistakeable mood of resistance.

Yet the Acerra dispute reflected the bigger dilemma of clientelism and corruption of the South. In recent years the Camorra had won many public sector contracts, and there were claims that they supported the demonstrations and were stirring up trouble for this reason. The mayor of Acerra protested his surprise at this, as he had organised his election campaign against the Camorra and previous left-wing rallies (such as that of 1995) had seen activists killed by Camorra violence. What it suggested, however, was that the Camorra was so deeply embedded in the culture of Naples, its institutions and city life, that it even absorbed attempts at reform. The intensification of Camorra violence from late 2004 evoked memories of Palermo in the 1980s (described in the next chapter). The strength of local feeling here gave hope, but the future remained uncertain; the Camorra was still in control.

MODELLO EMILIANO?

The port of Bari in Puglia has shared similar problems to Naples on a smaller scale in recent years. Bari, like Naples, suffered for years from criminality, a stagnant economy and urban degeneration. The old part of Bari – the Cittavecchia – made up of narrow, maze-like streets, had suffered years of neglect, was crime-ridden (the notorious Baresi scooter thieves were only part of the problem in this violent part of the city), and had long been in control of the local Mafia, the Sacra Corona Unita. The right-wing Forza Italia administration that had run the city since the mid 1990s had made some cosmetic changes to the old part of the city. It had supported new pubs and restaurants, but it had not provided a long-term social programme, or work for the residents. Bari's social problems, notably unemployment, lack of basic socioeconomic infrastructure, children leaving school early (some as young as twelve) to work for dangerous Mafia projects, pollution of the beaches and a lack of support for immigrants, would only be resolved by a long-term programme of reform. As in other places, the role of the local Mafia was significant in resisting long-term change. In Bari, the Mafia provided an alternative welfare system, offering black market work for children and support to their families.

The prospects of change for Bari were not promising in a city that had adopted the Berlusconi ethos of quick money and turned a blind eye to illegality. In the lead-up to the election for mayor in 2004, there was much discussion over the alternative candidates to the right-wing council. The left-wing parties did not have a strong tradition in Bari. Moreover, in order to succeed, the coalition had not only to be broad, but also to have the courage to take on criminality.

The candidate who emerged from this was Michele Emiliano, an anti-Mafia magistrate and a citizen of Bari with a strong following in the city. Emiliano was an independent candidate, and not officially attached to any political party. This was to be a great asset during the election campaign. He maintained his independence in his discussions with the centre-left and indeed was openly critical of the 'snobbism' that had characterised previous attempts by the left in the city in its attitude towards the Baresi. Being a Baresi was clearly an advantage for Emiliano, while his status as a magistrate was important in emphasising his authority and commitment to change. Crucially, however, it was his ability to bring together a broad range of associations and organisations into his electoral coalition that secured an unlikely victory in the election of June 2004. This coalition included not only all of the centre-left parties, but also anti-Mafia groups, ARCI and ACLI; it was a coalition founded and sustained by the new associationism. This lasted until after the election, following Emiliano's decision to set up a forum, based on the experience in Barcelona. This forum involved the associations as well as elected councillors in developing long-term projects for the city. It was an early experience of how the new associationism in the South could impact on local politics and generate social change. The previous administration had no dialogue with the associations. It shared the populist dilemma that was Italy's problem, eschewing the need for the processes of politics in favour of short-term lucrative business interests.

According to ARCI's Livia Cantore: 'Emiliano will bring new opportunities to the town. We have great expectations of Emiliano because he has the instruments for change. He knows what Bari needs. He has made alliances with associations which never happened before'. In particular, she pointed to the need for 'cultural change' in order to address the problem of children leaving school early, the relationship between men and women, and projects for integrating migrants, for which she had special responsibility. Emiliano's victory brought hope in these directions because he was committed to changing the infrastructure, supporting long-term projects and – as he had done in his previous job as a magistrate – taking on the Mafia.

Cantore had responsibility within ARCI for immigration and spent much of her time organising legal defence and support for migrants and refugees seeking asylum. One of these was Sajjad Sardar, a Kashmiri refugee whose story reveals much about the realities of Berlusconi's Italy, as well as the nature of the new associationism. Sardar had been a member of the opposition Socialist Party in Kashmir, a state lacking any democracy. His party had been made illegal by its government, which meant that he and his colleagues had to organise in a clandestine way. In 2002, following a peaceful demonstration against the government, the Kashmiri Prime Minister ordered the police to break up the demonstration; this they did in a particularly brutal way, opening fire on the demonstrators. 'This changed my life', Sardar told me. Now a marked opponent who was unable to continue his job as a teacher, he told his family that he had to leave Kashmir. He travelled first to Iran, then on to Turkey, where he had to pay $1200 in order to take a boat towards Europe. Stopping in Libya he found the Libyan police brutal, stealing money from the many people waiting to travel. The journey across the Libyan seas towards Sicily, one made by thousands in recent years, was hazardous, with many people taken ill on board.

On arrival at Lampedusa, off the coast of Sicily, Sardar was forced to wait for four days before being moved to a detention centre at Bari. Along with 1000 other immigrants he stayed for a month, as Italian authorities attempted to interrogate those seeking asylum. Eventually he was moved to another detention centre at Lecce, where he found himself in cells with a range of criminals, including low-level *mafiosi*. The regime at Lecce, he told me, was brutal, presided over by a priest, Don Cesare. With five people to a cell, conditions were desperate, and there were many cases of people harming themselves in order to be removed from the centre. Others suffered severe psychological problems. In the early hours of the morning, police would arrive with instructions to deport people. 'Everybody would wait for this time, wondering if they will be next.' After 50 days, Sardar fell ill, suffering dizzy spells, unable to walk or use his left arm. He told the doctor that he needed to go to hospital. He was moved back to the detention centre in Bari.

It was at this point that he came into contact with ARCI, which organised regular visits to the centre and arranged for MPs to visit, as well as organising lawyers to prepare a case for refugee status. From this time on, Sardar told me, ARCI 'never let us feel alone. They told me: "we will do something".' Eventually he was moved into hospital, while Livia Cantore and her colleagues helped organise his defence. He needed to provide evidence of the threat he faced if he returned to Kashmir. He knew many people who had been tortured. With the help of friends and contacts who had access to police documents, he was able to show that threats had been made against him and that he would be in danger. On leaving hospital and returning to the austere and hard conditions of the Bari detention centre to await his outcome, he and others appealed to the Catholic church for support. Another priest, Don Angelo Cassano, was a regular visitor to the centre and would argue with the police over the conditions of the inmates. 'These are human beings', he would remind them, and demand better treatment.

Eventually Sardar's case was heard and he was granted asylum. The next problem was to find accommodation. The Italian authorities were no help. It was left to Don Angelo to put him up at the church, to provide him with a roof over his head. Many migrants and refugees in Bari, as elsewhere in Italy, were forced to sleep in train stations. Don Angelo gave them shelter at the church, which became the meeting place for broad campaigns and initiatives in defence of migrants and asylum seekers.

Sajjad Sardar was one of the lucky ones. Most of the people he travelled with were returned to their countries of origin. In the months following his arrival others were not even allowed to present their case but were forcibly returned home, an issue that brought condemnation of the Italian government from the United Nations. 'Before coming here', he said, 'I had the concept in my mind that in Europe not only the human beings are treated well, but also the animals. But this government of Berlusconi has not treated us very well.' He doesn't know what would have happened to him if ARCI and Don Angelo had not come to his aid. Since he left the detention centre, ARCI has continued to support him, providing education and language classes and making sure he has not been alone, and organising an impromptu birthday party for him. He now hopes that others will not endure the hardships he went through and that the support he received from associations in Bari can become an example elsewhere in Italy.

Michele Emiliano was in a buoyant mood, busily conducting a series of meetings on the formation of his new *giunta*, when I talked to him shortly after his election victory. He told me that there were two areas where Bari – and indeed the Italian South generally – needed to develop. Firstly, it needed an economic strategy that would release the economy of the city from stagnation, offer a 'new deal' to the unemployed and introduce long-term cooperative schemes of work. 'Our strategy must relaunch the economy of the city by developing long-term projects', he said. Secondly, he identified the need to change the area's culture, where his council would become a 'custodian of new values'. This was a battle he had first started as a magistrate when he had taken on the Mafia in the courtroom; now he had to do the same in the city itself. This cultural change would have to put forward a new welfare system to replace that provided by the Mafia, and a new civic purpose in which ethical concern for other people would be crucial. Emiliano saw this as building on the positive aspects of the Barese identity: friendliness and local pride.

In order to work, however, the centre-left under his direction would need to change the culture of local government, a process that would need the forum to be a success. Emiliano thought that the opposition to Berlusconi could learn lessons from Bari, notably the need to change its own culture of politics, revise its relationships with the people and cultivate the involvement of associations. The '*modello Emiliano*', a term traditionally applied to the progressive social programmes of Emilia Romagna, had now found itself a new meaning in the heartlands of the South.

Part III
Another Italy?

People have realised that the fairy tale Berlusconi offered that he could make them rich has not come true. There is a kind of awakening...

—Dario Fo, December 2003

7
Civic Renaissance in Sicily

Sicily, as Leonardo Sciascia, its greatest writer, once remarked, can be seen as a metaphor for the modern world. Perhaps more than ever before, Sicily reflects the paradoxes and contradictions of the contemporary world. Located on the boundary between Europe and Africa and with a long and rich history of multi-religious communities – including Muslim ones – and cultural hybridity, it has now become (literally) the gateway to the new Europe, reflecting in the process the hopes, tragedies, conflicts, risks and uncertainties of new Europeans. The series of disasters in the Sicilian channel off the island of Lampedusa, which saw the deaths of many African refugees seeking a new start, have served as poignant reminders of what are now major tensions affecting all European countries over questions of migration, asylum and xenophobia. Sicily has, once again, become a place where the dispossessed and insecure seek refuge in the face of tyranny and economic injustice.

Sicily also has metaphorical associations with the Berlusconi era. *Furbo* (cunning) and *omertà* (silence) in the face of the law – regarded by many as peculiarly Sicilian characteristics – have resonated with the shadowy undercurrents of this moment in Italy's national history, which have realised new capacities for conspiracy and indifference. Like Bari and Naples, Sicily presents the problem of the state, the political consequences of clientelism, inertia and fatalism. This problem of the state though, so central to Italy's underlying problem and key to its future, has a particular meaning in Sicily.

The absence of a 'sense of state' in Sicily has long become Italy's problem, and the renewal of democracy and the rebuilding of a civic culture and a new public ethos is not a question confined to the island but at the heart of Italy's future. Attempts to placate Bossi and the Northern League (as a way of keeping an untrustworthy ally in the coalition) meant the worsening of the social and economic conditions of the South, and have kept political tensions on the surface. Sicily and 'Sicilians' have become a problem for a particular 'northern' discourse in Italian politics. It is clear therefore that Berlusconi's future and Italy's relationship with the rest of Europe will be profoundly affected by what goes on in Sicily. Berlusconi's coalition, after all, won all 61 Sicilian seats in the general election of 2001.

Any discussion of Sicily inevitably comes round to the Sicilian Mafia, the Cosa Nostra. The pervasive power of the Mafia was crudely exposed in the crisis years of the 1980s and 1990s, when the extent of Mafia influence in Italian politics first became apparent, with leading *mafiosi* imprisoned during the maxi-trial and the intensification of Mafia wars that culminated in the murders in 1992 of the two leading anti-Mafia magistrates, Giovanni Falcone and Paolo Borsellino. Events in Sicily at this time represented a brutal and critical challenge to the Italian state, before *Tangentopoli* brought things to a head.

At the centre of what was a complex web of duplicity was Giulio Andreotti, seven times Prime Minister, whose contacts with the leaders of the Cosa Nostra were the subject of prolonged public discussion and, from 1993 to 2004, judicial scrutiny in a range of court cases. In 2002, Andreotti was found guilty of the murder of Mino Pecorelli, a Palermo journalist, and sentenced to 24 years in Prison. In 2003 he was also found guilty of Mafia conspiracy. His eventual acquittal at the Court of Appeal in autumn 2004, on the grounds of 'insufficient evidence', meant that an 84-year-old man would not spend his last years in prison, although the Court was in no doubt that Andreotti had friendly relations with the Mafia prior to 1980. However 'insufficient' the evidence, the acquittal hardly merited the exaggerated response of Italy's political leaders from across the political spectrum, who queued up to pay compliments to a failed and ultimately compromised political figure who had gone to some lengths to oppose anti-Mafia reforms. It is no wonder that the business of dealing with the Mafia in Sicily in the 1980s and 1990s was left to others – courageous magistrates, anti-Mafia resistance groups, students, schoolchildren and, in particular, women's organisations – in actions born of frustration and cynicism, but also bursts of energy and civic commitment.

This suggests that there are reasons to think more positively about Sicily. Its impact on Italy points to its supreme paradoxes. The apparent indifference to public life contrasts sharply with the generosity of the people. The series of tragedies that has included several 'natural' earthquakes and eruptions from Mount Etna as well as political and Mafia-driven events, and that has led to prolonged bouts of despair, is countered by the idealism and hope of a myriad of vibrant activist groups and a sustained period of reform. The Palermo Spring, as it was known, led by Leoluca Orlando and discussed below, offered enlightenment from years of Mafia control and a renewal of Sicilian identity, while providing a model for dealing with the Mafia that would be used in Europe.

The conservative forces of patriarchy and hard-nosed Catholicism – still evident in black shawls, deferential attitudes and some of the more recent enthusiasm for Padre Pio – has been matched by the prominent role of women in many of the movements. Where party organisation is notoriously weak and lacking popular support, oppositional voices can be found in a range of determined and spontaneous initiatives, including anti-Mafia judges, intellectuals, writers, journalists, artists and peasant movements for social and economic reform. The Mafia, for too many both the departure and arrival point in any analysis of Sicily, has inspired a range of oppositional movements and satirical plays, hundreds of commissions and enquiries – few of them solved – and Leonardo Sciascia. Sciascia has been compared to Orwell for his commitment to the pursuit of truth and justice in the face of tyrannics, espoused in clear language and with the force of engaged political argument. The Sicilian predicament that Sciascia understands and writes about in his novels so well includes also a strain of optimism, that there is a latent desire for the Enlightenment principles of reason and justice in the face of years of state repression.[1]

SICILIAN IDENTITY

The view of Sciascia goes some way to countering the pessimism of the Sicilian predicament, which in many ways is derived from the way the past continues to constrain the present. At times, this has brought periodic inferiority complexes, and deep resignation hangs over the island. Sicily's problems have been seen as a consequence of the distrust of Sicilians towards the state, the absence of large organised workers' movements, the failures of a cohesive ideology

of liberal democracy, and the lack of a civic consciousness. Yet, its
history is full of occasions when its own conflicts and dilemmas
have been core to the development of modern Italy. Crucial in
this respect was the impact of transformism on the development
of Sicily's politics following the 'failures' of the *Risorgimento* (the
movement which led to Italian unification) in providing major
political and social change. Giuseppe Tomasi di Lampedusa's book
Il Gattopardo (*The Leopard*) gives a classic description of the period
of historical change in Sicily in which the ruling class groups
were able to switch political allegiances without undergoing
major social transformation. This 'Gattopardism', whereby the
accession to power of new political and social groups promising
major change only ensures that existing power relations remain
intact, has often been applied to various attempts to reform the
Italian state itself.[2]

As Sicilian culture and identity long predated Italian national
identity, it was not surprising that the impact of modernity on
the North and South would be uneven. The main consequence
for Sicily, one that was already apparent to Lampedusa and
that subsequently became the preoccupation of many Sicilian
intellectuals, was the problematic nature of Sicilian identity in
the face of the modernising drive of the *Risorgimento*, although
this 'problem' was not as simple as many assumed. There was
no unproblematical way of assimilating Sicilian identity, as
some, notably Giovanni Gentile, the intellectual guru of Italian
Fascism, wanted to do. One of the founding beliefs of the Fascist
intellectuals was to bemoan the lack of an indigenous national
culture and, as a Sicilian himself, Gentile saw the assimilation of
Sicilian culture into Italian national cultural traditions as the only
way out of Italian fragmentation and backwardness.[3]

Yet Sicily, through its folklores, dialect and geography, had its
own cultural identities before the birth of the Italian nation, and
they remain central – indeed, many see the hybridity of Sicilian
identity reaching outside of Italy to wider European cultures and
beyond. As Farrell has argued, one of Sicily's major anomalies is
its lack of 'national aspiration', yet many have wanted to retain
its cultural particularities: 'For the majority of Sicilian writers and
thinkers Sicily became one of those small communities, some
of which were stateless nations, dotted around the periphery
of Europe, each convinced of possessing an identity which

differentiated them from other peoples'. As he points out, this meant that one of the recurring features of Sicilian writers was the attempt to come to terms with the meaning of Sicilianness, or 'Sicilianismo', which to Farrell was 'the underside of Sicilian identity...the inevitably inward reaction of small peoples to injustices they see perpetrated by large powers with whom they are constrained by geography or geo-politics to live cheek by jowl'. In this sense, Sicilianismo was 'protective' against attempts, including benevolent ones, to look for Italian national solutions.[4]

The tensions between the preservation of Sicilian identity in the face of modernity and the drive to Italian national unity were the theme of one of the first modern Italian novels, set in the fishing village of Acitrezza on Sicily's east coast. Giovanni Verga's I Malavoglia tells the story of the lives of fishermen, above all their living conditions, family circumstances, tragedies, hopes and fears in an age when the transition to modernity, in the form of transport, travel and the unification of Italy, carried with it the prospect of a better life, without the capacity to realise it. The story focuses in particular on the attempts of the head of the Malavoglia family, 'Ntoni of Padron Ntoni', to find a new way of living free from poverty and exploitation, and by the nature of a fisherman's work, in the face of the elements. It is a fight he cannot win, however, and against the conservative force of the community he brings only shame to the family with their ensuing bankruptcy. The family are reminded of the need to accept things as they are: it is futile to move out of your environment, its loyalties and traditions; those that do fall by the wayside.

Verga described the novel, in his 1881 Preface, as 'the honest and dispassionate study of the way in which the first strivings after well-being might possibly be born, and develop, among the humblest people in society'.[5] The unique aspect of the novel is the way in which Verga presents the characters in their own Sicilian dialect, with a lot of direct speech combined with an anonymous narrator's voice in the background. Verga's approach to writing became known as 'verismo' (concern with the truth), a literary realism that focused on representing regional differences in fictional contexts. There was a wider message linked to verismo that can be found in the ways in which the future prospects of a Sicilian village were becoming tied up with a wider world; these new horizons, however, were still out of reach.

I Malavoglia was the inspiration for Luchino Visconti's neo-realist classic *La Terra Trema* (*The Earth Trembles*), made in 1947. Filmed entirely in Acitrezza, and financed by the Italian Communist Party, the film features only non-professional actors, fishermen playing themselves, together with members of their families. Given a twentieth-century update, it has a Marxist message of the class conflict between the fishermen and the owners in their struggle for survival. The lead character in Visconti's version is now a class-conscious fisherman who leads a strike against the owners, risking his family's status within the community. Unlike in *I Malavoglia*, the solution – class struggle – is more readily apparent, though still beyond the grasp of the ordinary fishermen. Like many of Visconti's films, *La Terra Trema* focused on the centrality of family and the mixture of hope and despair.

Visconti goes to great lengths in producing an authentic picture of life in Acitrezza, and the actors speak in their own Sicilian dialect. The voiceover is provided by Visconti himself, not unlike the narrative Verga supplied in *I Malavoglia*. Like the book, the film has a series of tragedies: the bankruptcy of the Valastro family; the isolation of Ntoni (called 'Antonio' in the film), the leading member of the family, from the rest of the village; and the tragedy of the girl, Lucia, one of the daughters, who has no dowry for prospective husbands. It ends with a positive dilemma, seemingly at the heart of the Sicilian paradox; namely that although this particular attempt by the family to change their world failed, there is still hope for a better life.

One of the major features of both the book and the film is the centrality of familism in the lives of the characters. This has a wider significance in Sicilian life and indeed, as Ginsborg has argued, explains much about wider Italy's social, economic and cultural settlement. For Ginsborg, while familism has often been used in very negative ways, as a way of explaining the 'backward' practices of Italian life, it has a 'modern', 'urban' dimension and should be seen as

> a particular form of the *relationship* between family, society, civil society and the state; a form in which the values and interests of the family are counter-posed to the other principal moments of human associationism...In Italy's case the very strength of family units...when linked to the relative weaknesses of civil

society, especially in the South, and to a profound distrust in the state, allowed familism to persist in its modern form.[6]

Ginsborg rejects simple equations between familism and economic, social and political change, but stresses that the balance between family–civil society–state relations is the key to understanding current Italian 'discontents'. While changes in the role of women and geographical and social mobility have changed these dynamics, Ginsborg argues that many 'families in Italy have become accustomed to developing defensive, cynical and even predatory attitudes towards much of the outside world, towards the institutions of the state, towards those wider loyalties that transcend kinship or narrow local networks of friendship'.[7]

THE MAFIA

In Sicily this defensive familism has historically taken on a particularly strong character and is the key to understanding the main bulwarks against change – notably, of course, the Sicilian Mafia. There has been much misunderstanding about the meaning of the Mafia for Italy. For an organisation that has often been romanticised in film and in popular mythology, it has strong roots in the structure of Sicilian society and many have attributed its longevity to its success in convincing people that its codes of honour, family links and protection have deep roots in Sicilian culture. It is therefore misleading to see it as merely a criminal organisation in conflict with the state. Nor is it accurate to see it as an extreme form of the freemasons, a secret society that stands apart from the mainstream. Rather, the Mafia – a term variously attributed to an Arabic origin and first used in a modern sense in the seventeenth century as standing for 'boldness, ambition and arrogance' – is deeply embedded in the hierarchies of Sicily. Distinct from 'banditry', or other forms of adventurous criminality, the Mafia gained respect as well as notoriety for its ability to weave together and consolidate ruling networks of power.[8] It has been able to do this because of its ability to provide an alternative to the state or, to put it another way, a 'state within a state'. This was possible because of the broader Sicilian values of loyalty, fear of outsiders and above all the primacy of the family in social life. For Giovanni Falcone, the leading anti-Mafia judge, eventually murdered by the Mafia in 1992 in Palermo,

> it is precisely the lack of sense of state, of state as an inner value, that generates distortion in the Sicilian soul; the dualism between society and state, the falling back on the family, the group, the clan...the mafia is essentially nothing more than a need for order and therefore for state.[9]

Perhaps the key to the longevity of the Mafia is its pernicious ability to maintain respect (the term *'mafiosi'* historically was attributed to 'men of respect') while undermining the state and its laws. Its own values, above all those it attributes to family, are in a sense above the law, while legal niceties are secondary to its own codes of honour, loyalties, ways and manners. Crucially, many of its illegal dealings are rooted in reciprocality, at the heart of Mafia operations, while the significance of *omertà* and the ostracising of *pentiti* are testament to the focus on loyalty that the Mafia demands.

Whatever its roots in Sicilian culture, the Mafia has unquestionably been a conservative force, one deeply embedded within, and dependent upon, ruling political elites, notably the postwar DC. As such, it was protected by Italy's political class. This is as true for the Mafia in its modern form as in earlier years. At the end of the Second World War, Sicily as the site of the allied landing crucial to the defeat of Fascism-Nazism, had a quite different experience from northern Italy, which had seen a strong resistance movement. This has had major implications for Italy's future political geography. The absence of a strong resistance movement meant that the ideology and historical memory that has driven (and still continues to drive) the Italian left is largely absent on the island. The collusion between the allies, notably the CIA and the Mafia, now an acknowledged historical fact in the transition to an Italian Republic, was crucial in prolonging Mafia influence and hindering the process of Italian democracy. Mafia leaders out of favour with Mussolini were released from jail in the aftermath of the war and returned to former power bases, some installed as mayors of Sicilian towns. Despite funds and support from the CIA for the Christian Democrats (who offered presents in return for votes in some places), the left was still able to win in some parts of Sicily. This included the town of Portella della

Ginestra, where peasant groups had been active in pushing for land reform. At a May Day rally in the town in 1947, Salvatore Giuliano, a well-known *mafioso*, led a group of gunmen using American weapons and dressed in US army uniforms in mowing down the demonstrators. This slaughter of unarmed civilians became a symbolic moment in the reassertion of Mafia power and confirmed, in a brutal way, the political tasks that lay ahead.[10]

Following the long years of DC rule and the fact that the main opposition party was the PCI, the Mafia's foothold in Italy's ruling political elite became entrenched. Protection from Rome gave the Cosa Nostra the freedom to run the island. Much of the DC's power base in Sicily was provided by Salvo Lima and Vito Ciancimino, successive mayors of Palermo, who ran the DC on the island and had close connections with generations of Mafia leaders. The Mafia's activities in Palermo from the 1960s onwards led to what became known as the 'sack of Palermo', in which public contracts were routinely distributed from the council to Mafia companies who then proceeded to pocket the money and leave work unfinished. Schools were run down and not refurbished as promised; instead, children were offered temporary accommodation in Mafia-owned apartments. Historical buildings were allowed to fall into ruin; these included the historic Teatro Massimo, closed for refurbishment in 1974 and not opened until 1997, when Mafia control had been broken. Large parts of the centre of Palermo, including its old town and famous fish market, the Vucciria, were controlled by protection, with entire businesses having to pay an additional rent that, according to subsequent *pentiti* confessions, provided petty cash to support the families of jailed *mafiosi*.

The most significant evidence linking Andreotti to the Mafia was his links with Lima and a prominent Sicilian banker, Michele Sindona. He was also alleged to have connections to the powerful Salvo brothers, having been photographed in their company many times, and was said to have met and exchanged kisses with Totò Riina, the acknowledged head of the Cosa Nostra. According to other evidence provided by *pentiti*, Andreotti knew leaders of both the Corleone and Stefano Bontate factions of the Cosa Nostra.

Sindona, a banker and leading member of P2, had earned his money from black market investments in the 1960s and 1970s. His accumulation of wealth and power was such that by 1973 he was estimated to be making 40 percent of all the dealings on the Milan stock exchange and regarded as the 'saviour of the lira' when the market rocked that year. Sindona attempted to make vast donations to the DC but after his companies collapsed in 1974 he faced charges of 'fraudulent bankruptcy', embezzlement, bribery, perjury and corruption, and was sentenced to 25 years in jail. His ability to escape justice by alternatively residing in the US and (after faking his own abduction) Sicily, under the protection of the Cosa Nostra and their American cousins, says much about Mafia power at this time. Sindona claimed he was being persecuted by the left for his anti-Communist views, the kind of appeal to the US (which had instigated its own charges against him) that usually worked. Courts in Palermo also pursued him on charges of money-laundering, however. The perseverance of Palermo's official receiver, Giorgio Ambrosoli, was repaid by the Mafia with his murder in 1979. In 1986, a few days after being found guilty of planning the murder of Ambrosoli, Sindona was found poisoned in prison.[11]

The conclusion of the prosecuting magistrates, as Jamieson records, was significant:

> The most serious matter in our view...is the support given to the salvage plan – an outright attempt to defraud the Bank of Italy and thus the whole nation – by the most senior political figures, amongst them the then Prime Minister Giulio Andreotti. Without Andreotti and the protection given to Sindona between 1974 and 1979 the Ambrosoli murder would never have taken place.[12]

The 'protection' that Andreotti provided for the Cosa Nostra's representatives was even more apparent in his connections to Salvo Lima, often referred to as Andreotti's 'Sicilian ambassador'. Salvo Lima was the Cosa Nostra's man in Palermo, the leader of the DC, mayor of Palermo between 1958 and 1964, and increasingly influential in cementing the link between Andreotti and the Mafia from the late 1960s.

In March 1993, the prosecution office in Palermo produced the evidence that found Andreotti's 'complicity in Mafia association' between 1968 and 1982, describing his 'actions and behaviour' as making a 'positive contribution' 'to the protection of the interests and to the realization of the goals of the organisation'.[13]

There was more damning evidence to follow. During the kidnapping of Aldo Moro by the Red Brigades in 1978, the Cosa Nostra attempted to forge a deal in prison with Red Brigades prisoners in order to ascertain Moro's whereabouts. Andreotti, however, after reading Moro's letters, sent from his place of captivity to the DC hierarchy, was threatened by Moro's revelations, and contact was refused. Tommaso Buscetta, the leading *pentito*, maintained that the Cosa Nostra could have saved Moro if Andreotti and the DC hierarchy had wanted it.[14] Following Moro's murder, journalist Mino Pecorelli and General Carlo Alberto Dalla Chiesa received copies of Moro's statements made under interrogation by his captors. Pecorelli was paid 30 million lire by the Cosa Nostra not to publish Moro's revelations, but was murdered on the orders of Stefano Bontate in March 1979. Dalla Chiesa, a former head of anti-terrorism who had a strong record of defeating left-wing terrorists and who became an uncompromising prefect of Palermo, was subsequently assassinated along with his wife and escort in 1982. According to Buscetta, both Dalla Chiesa and Pecorelli were murdered because of the threat they posed to Andreotti. More *pentiti*, notably Baldassare di Maggio, whose information led to the arrest of Riina in 1993, gave evidence against Andreotti, who was now said to have flown to meetings with the Cosa Nostra in their own private jets, influenced the court trials of *mafiosi*, and refused to help free Aldo Moro. In 1995, Andreotti was sent to trial for complicity in the murder of Mino Pecorelli.[15]

THE PALERMO SPRING

The prosecution of Andreotti and the challenge to the DC's power base in Sicily was only made possible by a sustained challenge to the Mafia from the 1980s onwards. In 1985, Leoluca Orlando, a lawyer who had risen through the ranks of the DC, was elected mayor. Orlando was elected on a clear anti-Mafia agenda, with the support of a range of anti-Mafia groups. His coalition included the left, Greens and other groups historically opposed to the Mafia. Crucially, he made a deliberate attempt to break with the DC's Mafia connections. This brought many tensions with the DC hierarchy, as well as major concerns for the Cosa Nostra itself, which switched allegiance at one point in the mid 1980s to Bettino Craxi's Socialist Party, to let it be known that the DC

5. Leoluca Orlando, the former mayor of Palermo, whose 'Palermo Spring' during the 1980s undermined the power of the Mafia. (Photo: Sicilian Renaissance Institute)

could not depend on its automatic support. Orlando's first period of office from 1985 to 1989 was termed the 'Palermo Spring' because of its break with the past, its search for new beginnings, its refusal to accept Mafia instructions and its determination to face political corruption and Mafia violence head-on. It was his ability to mobilise diverse sectors of the Palermo population not traditionally involved in such public initiatives that distinguished Orlando's period of office. It became, in Ginsborg's words, 'one of the most unexpected and welcome aspects of Italy in the 1980s'.[16] The most significant example of this new approach was evident in the maxi-trial, which opened in 1986 and which became a tortuous process that, when appeals are taken into account, only ended in 1992 with the decision of the Supreme Court to hand out major life sentences to leading *mafiosi*. In all, 476 suspected *mafiosi* were put on trial. Along the way, lawyers for the Cosa Nostra made numerous attempts to hold up proceedings. Large numbers of relatives of *pentiti* were murdered, while magistrates who had refused to capitulate to Cosa Nostra demands were assassinated. Yet 1992 was regarded as a major turning point and established new legal precedents for prosecuting the Mafia. Many *mafiosi* gave themselves up, while Ignazio Salvo, Palermo's leading *mafioso*, convicted at the maxi-trial, was murdered for failing to protect Mafia interests.

Yet the tragedy of the Mafia's legacy in Palermo, which in the mid 1980s was compared to Lebanon for the daily conflict and violence it entailed (averaging five deaths a week at one point), had not ended. After a period of relative calm through the maxi-trials of the 1980s, the confirmation of life sentences for leading *mafiosi* in January 1992 signalled a resumption of hostilities. This was also a challenge to the state in Rome, in that it questioned who was in control. Giovanni Falcone and Paolo Borsellino, two senior magistrates who were leading the fight against the Mafia, were both assassinated within two months of each other in 1992. Falcone, together with his wife and bodyguards, was killed by a bomb returning from Palermo's Punta Raisi airport in May. Paolo Borsellino, assistant chief prosecutor in Palermo, was killed two months later on the doorstep of his mother's house. Both Falcone and Borsellino had been sentenced to death by Totò Riina at a meeting of leading *mafiosi* in 1987. According to the *pentito* Baldassare di Maggio, a whole range of firearms was made available for their murders, as revenge for their roles in the maxi-trials.[17] Both men had survived earlier assassination attempts; they took bodyguards wherever they went and were unable to lead normal lives. Indeed, both were certain of their eventual assassination. In 1992, in the aftermath of the maxi-trial, a new attempt on their lives was made. During their investigations they had faced numerous obstructions from Rome. Following the two murders, which sent Italy spiralling into a new wave of panic, many people were advised to leave the city, and there was great fear that the Mafia wars were about to recommence. The people of Palermo, however, had other ideas, and organised large demonstrations and other civic initiatives to try and ensure that the work carried out by Falcone and Borsellino would continue without them.

At the 1987 meeting of Mafia leaders, Leoluca Orlando's had been the third name on the death list. He was condemned for publicly denouncing the Mafia, breaking the DC's links with the Cosa Nostra and initiating the major legal attempts to bring the top *mafiosi* to justice. As mayor, Orlando had ensured that the Palermo City Council was the civil plaintiff in the maxi-trial, thereby making clear the opposition of the city's representatives.

For his trouble he had incurred the wrath of the DC leadership, including opposition and criticism from Andreotti, who refused to support his candidature for mayor in the 1990 election. After he was elected mayor by a large majority, Orlando found his efforts at reform obstructed by his own party, and he resigned in order to set up a new movement, La Rete (the Network), in 1991. La Rete was not a political party but a 'political movement with a limited lifespan', though one long enough to 'begin to change the conscience of Italy'.[18] Its founding members included experienced magistrates, progressive clergy and a former Communist mayor of Turin, and it succeeded in attracting the support of young volunteers and people not normally attracted to party politics, including some who had previously been involved in anti-Mafia movements. La Rete was not confined to Sicily, however, but became a national movement, winning twelve seats at the general election of April 1992, including that of Orlando as its national secretary. Its timing was crucial, as the 'Clean Hands' investigators were beginning to prepare cases for prosecution in the *Tangentopoli* scandal; coming on the back of the anti-Mafia initiatives, it gave them the confidence to pursue their enquiries. La Rete was the first movement of the new democratic anti-corruption politics.

On entering parliament, Orlando stood on a platform of explicit anti-Mafia reform, in a climate that was dominated by political corruption and the need for new directions. Following the murders of his close colleagues Falcone and Borsellino, Orlando, who since the mid 1980s had got used to eating at home, travelling in separate cars from his family and never travelling without bodyguards, was moved to police barracks in both Rome and Palermo. He was labelled 'the walking corpse' in the media and it was widely thought to be only a matter of time before he was the Mafia's next victim. When asked the inevitable question on one of Italy's prime TV shows, Orlando told the presenter Maurizio Costanzo (himself the subject of a failed Mafia assassination attempt the following year): 'If I am killed, the assassins will be *mafiosi*, but the orders will have come from the politicians.'

Orlando recounted the story to me twelve years later, from the Villa Virginia in the centre of Palermo, a family home that also houses the Sicilian Renaissance Institute, which he set up in 1999 to consolidate the anti-Mafia reforms. He explained that the experiences he went through at this time were formative in his understanding of the link between the Mafia and aspects of

Sicilian identity, and the development of anti-Mafia strategies that could be applied internationally.

'The Mafia in 1992 made a tremendous mistake. They killed too much, and this led to a reaction by the people', Orlando told me, adding that it was the women in particular who led the resistance. 'The headlines in the press were "Leoluca will be Next". When the women in Palermo read these articles they went to speak with the police chief and gave him a list of their children. They told him: "Our children are ready to stay inside the police barracks and protect Leoluca Orlando." They sent a clear message: I was not alone. They can kill a man, they can kill ten men, but the Mafia cannot kill thousands of women and children.'

Orlando told me he owed a debt to the 'civic courage' of these women, who started to encourage residents to hang white sheets from the windows of Palermo apartments, a movement which spiralled.

'Palermo was a city of white sheets hanging from the windows. You can imagine what it means in some parts of the city where many Mafia bosses lived. You can imagine the courage of the women. They met in the dark of the night, without protection. They were ready to meet the Mafia boss, living on the third floor, who would say to them: "Why are you protesting against my organisation, my family, my activities and my business?" This took real courage. They were able to do it because they became not three but three thousand women. This was "the committee of the white sheets".'

'I was called the mayor of the children. The old wise politicians said: "Oh, Mr Mayor, you are spending too much time with the children. The children do not vote." But they did not understand how important the children are in changing the moods of the parents. At home a dinner is more important than 100 political meetings, when the children ask: "Why...why do you not protest against the corruption...?"'

Orlando's experience made clear to him the need to understand the connection between identity and legality. The old Sicilian Mafia, he told me, used honour, family and friendship as the basis of what he called 'identity-based illegality'. In order to break this, Orlando argued, you must first respect the identity of Sicilians, their culture and the importance attached to the values of friendship and family. It was important to demonstrate that the Mafia 'are not worthy to be considered Sicilian'. Thanks to the movement of women and the growth of a range of anti-Mafia movements, the Cosa Nostra started to lose the connection between identity and illegality after 1992: 'I can say we won against the old traditional Sicilian Mafia, who used to justify their crimes through traditional Sicilian values.' Once the connection between identity and illegality was broken, the Mafia were seen as normal criminals.

These successes against the Sicilian Mafia meant that Italy became a model after 1992 for dealing with criminality and corruption further afield. After he was elected an MEP in 1994, Orlando passed three resolutions that incorporated the Italian anti-Mafia legislation into European law. These related to the exchange of knowledge on Mafia dealings between European countries, the criminalising of Mafia association and the right of the state to secure the assets of Mafia criminal activities.

Despite the violence in 1992, the Cosa Nostra was no longer inside the state as it had been for the entire postwar period. Palermo was a changed city; 158 churches, 400 palazzi, 55 monuments, two major cultural institutes and seven theatres, including the famous Teatro Massimo, had been restored. The number of deaths in Palermo by the turn of the millennium was less than many other cities, and virtually none were due to Mafia violence. The arrest of Totò Riina in 1993, the same year that Andreotti was first put on trial, symbolised the climate of hope and renaissance.

HOPES AND FEARS

According to media reports in 2005, the net was tightening around Bernardo Provenzano, Riina's successor as head of the Mafia, who had been on the run for 40 years. Provenzano's capture would mean that an entire generation of Cosa Nostra leaders had been removed from power. The defeat of the Sicilian Mafia in its old form was not the end of the Mafia problem in Sicily, however. Orlando argues that a new Mafia had been given legitimacy by Berlusconi's own promotion of a 'culture of illegality'. He told me: 'There is something new in this scenario. The new Mafia does not use the old traditional Sicilian values of honour, family and friendship. The new Mafia uses other values: "freedom without rules", "richness and wealth without development". In my view this government is promoting the opposite of Italy after Falcone and Borsellino.' There was a key difference between the Mafia links of Andreotti and Berlusconi. Orlando regarded his old foe Andreotti as 'historically, politically and culturally responsible for the Mafia'. His role as 'protector of the system' was given legitimacy by the US in the period of the Cold War when many Mafia bosses were released and installed as anti-Communist mayors in parts of Sicily. This meant that Andreotti was able to declare that many of his actions were carried out 'in the name of freedom, of democracy and in the name of God'.

Berlusconi, on the other hand, did not need to meet Mafia leaders. By sending the message, through legislation and his own personal dealings, that illegality was not going to be countered, he created the basis for a new, more global, less traditional Mafia. The new Mafia, which involved some of the older families, welcomed the election of Berlusconi. In 2001, all of Sicily's 61 parliamentary seats were won by Forza Italia and its coalition supporters. Berlusconi's old friend and colleague Marcello Dell'Utri has been charged with Mafia association, and Berlusconi himself has been named by the *pentito* Antonino Giuffrè as having 'direct contact' with the Mafia's representatives in 1993.[19] However, as Orlando points out, 'Berlusconi didn't win the election because he won the votes of the Mafia. He won because normal honest people believed as a successful businessman he could lead Italy to success.'

The fight against the Mafia continues in Sicily, and not only in Palermo. Claudio Fava, the centre-left candidate for Catania in the provincial elections in 2003, came from a family with a strong history of anti-Mafia activity. His journalist father, Giuseppe, was murdered in 1984 because of his anti-Mafia investigations. Fava was fighting the election on the slogan 'The courage to change'. He told me that the choice was between the clientelism of the right and the democratic agenda of the centre-left. 'Work is the key', he said. 'Either you accept the system of getting work by connections or you try and break it.' The practice of 'buying votes' was still prevalent in some areas.

With unemployment at 20 percent and cafés filled with men passing the time of day, socioeconomic depression is still evident in Catania and the surrounding area. In May 2003, just after I visited Catania for the first time, the mayor of Acicastello, the next village to Acitrezza, was shot dead along with four other council officials and members of the public. First thoughts of Mafia involvement were dispelled when it became apparent that Giuseppe Leotta, the man who carried out the killings, bore a grudge against the mayor for not giving him a job as a chauffeur. Leotta had previously been employed on a short-term contract, which had not been renewed. In the small piazza where he killed his first victim, an elderly pensioner sitting on a park bench, a quote from Mussolini about the centrality of work is engraved on one of the municipal buildings and is still visible in the background, a harrowing reminder of Sicily's economic and political exploitation.

Leotta had a history of mental health problems. After stealing a car and avoiding roadblocks amid general panic in the village, he shot himself in a church later that day. This incident in a Sicilian village once again reflected the Sicilian tragedy of dashed hopes of a better life. As *La Repubblica* reported, it was as if Leotta had 'settled his account with everything, with colleagues, with his obsessiveness, with his place, with above all the mayor, with the village where he wanted to be, but could not be, happy'.[20]

Visconti probably wouldn't appreciate the irony, but back in Acitrezza, the village immortalised in *I Malavoglia* and *La Terra Trema*, the fishermen support the post-Fascist National Alliance. The new Mafia still keeps its fingers in various local pies such as housing developments, fish markets and the tourist industry, while, according to local knowledge, helping to keep the crime rate down in Catania. The village itself has changed enormously, with tourism a new dominant industry, while the position of women has also changed significantly.

Despite the success of *La Terra Trema* at the Venice Film Festival in 1948 and its subsequent international acclaim, the actors involved (with the exception of one of the child actors who returned with Visconti to Rome as one his servants) remained in the village after the film came out, most returning to their former jobs. Lucia, the 'girl without the dowry', is now 73 years old (real name Agnese Giammona) and married to the owner of the Giovanni Verga restaurant, which looks out over the quay where many of the film's scenes took place.

She told me that when she and her sister were invited to play the two daughters of the main Valastro family, her father wasn't

6. Agnese Giammona as 'Lucia' in *La Terra Trema* and as she was in 2003.
(Photos: International Media Films Inc. and Natalie Guziuk)

happy, particularly when he heard of the roles they were to play. 'At first, he didn't want us to be in the film...It sounded to him like a form of prostitution.' Visconti persisted and eventually won the father round. Like the other actors, Agnese was paid for 15 days' work (the filming lasted six months) and as one of the central characters she was lucky enough to get a train ticket to the Venice Film Festival in 1948 when the movie won awards. She was wearing the gold watch she was given at the Festival for our interview. That none of the actors went on to star in other movies confirmed *La Terra Trema* as a neo-realist classic, and Agnese was intrigued, though not overly excited, when I told her that her photograph was next to Burt Lancaster's during the Visconti season that was then on at the National Film Theatre in London. She told me that the film had been a very positive experience that had given her hope for the future, and that her life had changed, though not in the way that Visconti's film implied.

Italy's erotic blockbuster of 2003, *100 colpi di spazzola prima di andare a dormire* (*100 Strokes of the Brush Before Bed*), by the 17-year-old Melissa P, was set in Catania and its environs. It sold 850,000 copies. This graphic description of a teenager's sexual awakening from the age of 14, with its details of group sex, bisexual encounters and sadomasochism, shocked as well as enthralled the nation. Perhaps what was more remarkable, in a land where 50 years before women hid in black veils and talked to their prospective partners from the safety of a window ledge, was her self-assurance. 'I have no remorse...It's not much use debating whether it's good or bad. If I had the chance, I'd do it all again', said the girl from Acicastello.[21]

At the European elections of 2004, Claudio Fava, the local centre-left candidate in Catania once again, was finally elected after having received more votes than any other candidate on the island. Along with other results, this was seen as a significant development, as a challenge to Berlusconi and the right in one of their strongest areas. It also offered the prospect of a Sicily no longer dependent on the Mafia. The same Claudio Fava had written the screenplay for *I Cento Passi*, the film that told the true story of Peppino Impastato, the young son of a *mafioso*, whose short life was dedicated to opposing the Mafia and dreaming of another Sicily.

8
Slow Food in the Fast Lane

The Berlusconi years saw the increasing globalisation of the Italian economy and cultural life. Globalisation, under neo-liberal hegemony, was transforming all aspects of Italian life, with a government keen to endorse the global marketplace; after all, its own Prime Minister was himself a global entrepreneur. As elsewhere, neo-liberal globalisation, often linked with the economic and cultural power of the US, made its mark on Italy, with whom the US had always had a complex relationship. Waves of Italian emigration from the South of Italy in particular to the US, the role of the US in helping to overcome Fascism, US intervention in Italian politics (for example, in the general election of 1948, when the Communists were seen to be a major electoral threat), and suspicion on the part of Italy's left towards US 'imperialism', made relations between the two countries an important, if contentious, issue.

In terms of its cultural life, the US appealed to many Italians for its Hollywood movies and glamorous lifestyles. Berlusconi's admiration for the American presidential system was well known, while many of the programmes on his channels had been imported from the US. Its food, however, was generally less attractive to the diet-conscious Italians, whose commitment to cuisine and good living is beyond the comprehension of many other nationalities. Tobias Jones' contention that Italians obey only two rules, namely how to dress, and how to dine, may be an exaggeration, but food remains central to the Italian way of living.

Yet by the turn of the millennium, evidence was emerging that the US 'live-to-work' culture was impinging on Italian society, and not only in hard-nosed, work-conscious Milan. According to a survey for the Italian newspaper *Il Messaggero* in the summer of 2001, 34 percent of vacation-bound Italians were suffering from 'office separation syndrome'. As they took their holidays, many became 'depressed' or 'hyperactive', even bringing along 'souvenirs' from the office, thereby sustaining a 'sense of nostalgia' for the culture of work. Eating habits too were becoming a cause for alarm, with an estimated 4 million obese Italians in October 2001, or 9 percent of the population (the figure was 23 percent in the US). As a response, a 'National Obesity Day' was established where action plans and advice would be provided for overweight individuals. 'Stress' (Italians use the English word) was also a problem, affecting 60 percent of the Italian population, according to a study by Riza Psicomatrica in September 2004.[1] Shifts in the work–life balance, in favour of the former, fuelled by the need to be efficient and to be in control, were having undesirable consequences, with family crisis, over-eating and increased loneliness the outcomes. Indeed, taken together with Italy's extremely low birth rate and ageing population, loneliness had become a social problem. Italians were made aware of this in 2004 when Giorgio Angelozzi, a 79-year-old former classics teacher, went on primetime TV advertising himself for adoption. He had taken this dramatic step after spending years on his own, following his wife's death and losing contact with other family members.

Globalisation at one level, then, meant increased uniformity in ways of living. It also meant fast living. It is one of many paradoxes of contemporary Italy that the normally relaxed and serene disposition of its citizens should change as soon as they are behind the wheel of a car, and most Italians need at least one mobile phone to keep them up to speed. The information society, according to James Gleick, has led to a

> quick-reflexed, multi-tasking, channel hopping, fast-forwarding citizenry. The modern economy lives and dies by precision in time's measurement and efficiency in its employment. If money is the visible currency of trade, time is its doppelganger, a coin over which companies and consumers battle, consciously or unconsciously, with ever-greater urgency.[2]

Eating on the move was part of this cultural standardisation, with fast food outlets steadily multiplying, if at a lower rate than in other European countries. Food, in Italy, has always been a cultural and social phenomenon and the centrepiece of family life; now it looked as if it was in danger of becoming the tasteless ritual it had become elsewhere. Yet, as many countries and cultures have found, resisting the march of neo-liberal globalisation seemed an almost impossible task. It was, after all, regarded by politicians and business leaders as an inevitable development. In order to lead the fast life, people would adapt. While there were many critics of globalisation, including those who had protested at Genoa, there were fewer indications of practical alternatives to neo-liberalism, or a vision of what an alternative society could become.

This had particular consequences for the left. With the critique of capitalism at the core of its politics it always seemed to have difficulty in demonstrating that it could offer an alternative, or forming a vision of what the good life might look like. Moreover, given the many puritanical attitudes towards good living that existed on the left, it had particular difficulties in getting across the message that a more egalitarian society would also bring a higher quality of life, as well as being more fun.

FROM ARCIGOLA TO SLOW FOOD

The founding of the Slow Food movement was an attempt to address this and other problems of the contemporary world. The idea of 'Slow Food' has its origins in the left-wing cultural movements of the 1970s and 1980s. The movement's founder and President, Carlo Petrini, was the national organiser of the cultural association ARCI, then officially attached to the Italian Communist Party. He had also made his mark by being the founder of Radio Bra, Italy's first free radio station. Arcigola ('*gola*' meaning 'gluttony') represented the gastronomic dimension of ARCI's cultural agenda and was established in 1986 out of a mixture of left-wing groups, shortly after ARCI had established its 'Lega enogastronomica' (League for Food and Wine). With a regular presence at the PCI's national festival (Festa L'Unità), where there was competition between the best restaurants, its membership grew rapidly from 500 to 8000 between 1986 and 1989. In 1987, to complement this development, the left-wing *Il Manifesto* started a column entitled '*Il Gambero Rosso*' ('The Red Prawn'), which was given over to discussion of food and wine. Petrini himself organised the first Slow Food demonstration in 1986, attended by thousands of protesters, armed with bowls of *penne*, outside an intended McDonald's site near the Spanish Steps in the centre of Rome.

Prior to the 1970s, the Italian left had given time to cultural matters, in the traditions of its major thinker, Antonio Gramsci.

Yet gastronomy had never been a concern for the left, despite occupying a big presence in the life of Italians. Slow Food's emphasis on food therefore brought into question long-standing left-wing assumptions about 'pleasure'. 'Pleasure', Petrini wrote in his account of the origins of Slow Food, 'still has a faintly dubious ring. A man devoted to work and raising a family is assumed to be an upright citizen, but a man dedicated to pleasure – you never know. Would you want your daughter to marry someone like that?' Pleasure was seen to be the 'luxury of the few, artificial, undisciplined and shameless'.[3]

The 'right to pleasure' was to become a crucial part of the philosophy of Slow Food; the organisation's founding declaration declared itself 'an international movement in defence of the right to pleasure'. The founding of the Slow Food movement officially took place in Paris in December 1989, the bicentenary of the French Revolution deemed appropriate for an organisation heralding a new dawn of 'slow living'. In its founding manifesto, Slow Food launched its attack on the 'fast life':

> We are enslaved by speed and have all succumbed to the same insidious virtues. Fast Life disrupts our habits, pervades the privacy of our homes and forces us to eat fast food...In the name of productivity, Fast Life has changed our way of being and threatens our landscapes. So Slow Food is now the only truly progressive answer...
>
> A firm defence of quiet material pleasure is the only way to oppose the universal folly of the Fast Life. Our defence should begin at the table with Slow Food.[4]

SLOW FOOD: THE LOCAL DIMENSION

Founded in Paris, the Slow Food movement made its home in Bra, a small town in Piedmont, northern Italy, in a region renowned for its Barolo and Barbera wines and the white truffles of the Langhe region. The sense of place was important and the emphasis on territory was to become crucial in the development of Slow Food. Bra had been the centre of Arcigola's work, but equally importantly was in a region with long agricultural traditions. Many of them, including wine vintages, had been lost in the race for efficiency and productivity. A major part of Slow

Food's purpose is to revisit traditional local cultures and educate local communities about the 'lost' history of food, the social context of eating and the relationship between food and ways of living. In the case of wine in Bra itself, this has meant using oral testimony from local people and researching the histories of particular cellars. In Zibello, in Emila Romagna, it meant the rediscovery of *culatello*, a lost variant of prosciutto, made from the hind leg of a pig. This discovery led to several local festivals and a reassertion of local identity in the town. Elsewhere, local events, organised to educate and publicise the role of food and wine in the community, including wine-tastings and cheese shows, have gradually extended into education programmes for schools. School garden projects, wherein children are educated about horticulture and the environment, and talks by nutritionists and other experts on the history of food are examples of Slow Food initiatives.

The expansion of the Slow Food movement since 1989 has been made possible by the growth of a unique organisational structure. Each regional group is organised into local 'convivia'. The term itself denotes a marked cultural contrast with official politics, traditionally organised around the party branch where, as a special treat, a 'social' may be put on for members. The role of the convivium leader is to organise food and wine events, to 'create moments of conviviality' amongst the group and the wider community. This might include 'taste workshops', where local delicacies can be introduced. Each convivium has the wider purpose of raising the profile of particular products, local artisans and wine cellars, and facilitating dialogue between producers and consumers. Italy has convivia in all its major towns and many villages, and in all has 35,000 members. The membership of the Slow Food movement worldwide, since its foundation in 1989, had grown to over 80,000 in over 100 countries by the end of 2004. In addition to the large Italian membership, the movement has developed an expanding presence in the poorer South, while the US, the home of fast food, has a particularly strong association.[5]

The emphasis on the 'local' has two more important dimensions for the movement. Firstly, much emphasis has been given to the rebirth of the *osteria*, the traditional eating environment in Italy renowned for hospitality and value as well as the quality of its food. The *osterie*, according to Petrini, were the 'symbolic locus of traditional cuisine, run as a family business, with simple service, a welcoming atmosphere, good quality wine and moderate prices'.[6] In this way, they helped 'foster local identity'.

Secondly, Slow Food was built on developing local produce and involving local artisans, tradespeople and small businesses. It rejected what it saw as the pervasive intrusions of global food. In particular it sought to challenge uniformity and standardisation, for the damage they caused to the diet as well as the environment. 'An economy based on massive use of transportation not only has serious environmental impacts in terms of energy consumption, pollution, surface congestion and accidents, but also has the problem of an impoverished range of goods on offer', Petrini stated.[7] Slow Food condemned 'gastronomic tourism', overpriced goods and pollution.

Slow Food's strategy of rediscovering local quality has centred on the '*salone del gusto*' – literally, 'Halls of Taste' – that it organises in many towns. These are large markets run by local artisans selling their goods with support from local councils. Here, there are 'taste laboratories' which have included local specialities such as cheese, prosciutto and wine. In fact, the educative aspect of Slow Food's work is crucial to its status as a movement that seeks an alternative way of living. Educating people in matters of taste is the 'slow way' of resisting the spread of fast food. It requires a 'change of mentality', a 'different attitude to life', a long-term political and cultural agenda. For this reason, Slow Food puts a lot of emphasis on collaborative education programmes in schools, including 'Taste Week', with taste workshops to train the senses, school gardens, where local produce is grown, and visits to local restaurants, with cut-price menus. Teachers and their pupils are encouraged to identify particular pleasures and the variety of tastes. The idea is to emphasise taste, raise food awareness and link pleasure with social and environmental responsibility, the basis for a new type of food conscious-citizen:

> It won't be easy for them to flounder in the chaos of the fast life: they will be a new type, ready to defend themselves against attacks on their senses and improve the quality of their own lives. Aware consumers will come into being.[8]

THE CRITIQUE OF NEO-LIBERAL GLOBALISATION

The founding principle of Slow Food and the one most commonly attributed to it is its critique of the domination of fast food, the challenge to 'McDonaldisation'. Yet Slow Food has a holistic critique which is intended to challenge much of the underlying philosophy of neo-liberal globalisation, its 'fast' way of living, environmental degradation, the use of genetically modified products, the rise of obesity, and increasingly, global inequality – which, according to Slow Food's argument, has allowed the impoverishment of farmers and artisans in the South for the benefits of rich multinationals. As a movement, Slow Food therefore takes an uncompromising stand against global capital, while retaining an unorthodox mix of youthful protesters, restaurateurs, foodies and environmentalists.

However, Slow Food goes some way to distinguish itself from the typical anti-global capitalist demonstrator. Petrini writes in his book that the movement rejects the guerrilla tactics of activists like Jose Bove, the French farmer jailed for trying to block the establishment of a French McDonald's, despite sympathising with his ideas. 'This is not the slow style. Our choice is to focus our energies on saving things that are headed for extinction instead of hounding the new ones we dislike'. In Italy the history of McDonald's took a different direction than other countries, with the bigger cities hosting the first outlets. This meant that the provinces were initially untouched. This helps explain Slow Food's success in restoring traditional *osterie* and local food cultures, with the help of local citizens and businesses. Petrini writes:

> Others may take to the streets...Slow Food has a different idea, to rescue eating establishments, dishes and products from the flood of standardization...eclipsed for years by sandwich shops and places selling nouvelle cuisine fast food style, [*osterie*] are returning once more to the neighbourhoods of Italy...[9]

Importantly, a distinction is drawn between 'standardisation' and 'globalisation'. Globalisation is inevitable and desirable because it creates new networks of contact and communication, which could enable poor countries in the South to develop. The 'standardisation' that it causes, however, has 'swept away all the customs and habits of eating'.

This might seem reasonable in Italy, a country renowned for its strong regional culture and attention given to the pleasures of eating, but what would this mean for countries in the poorer South? It is the priority that Slow Food gives to the South that reveals its potential as one of the most important social and cultural movements that exist on a global scale. The most visible evidence of its global reach can be found at its 'Terra Madre', the 'world meeting of food communities' held over four days that takes place every two years. The idea of the Terra Madre is to bring together food communities, including cooks, fishermen, farmers, those who gather food, and food distributors from across the world in 60 'Earth Workshops'. Here global experiences are exchanged on biodiversity, hunger, poverty, sustainability, traditional food production, aquaculture, animal husbandry, the role of women in food production, and organic agriculture. At the Terra Madre held in Turin in October 2004, workshops were held on themes ranging from 'Sustainable Tourism' and 'Changing Trade Rules to Prevent Dumping' to 'Defence and Promotion of Traditional Beer Styles', 'Non-Timber Resources of the Amazon Forest' and 'Minor Cereals: Forgotten Foods or Foods of the Future?'. In attendance were 5,000 participants from over 130 countries, involving 1,200 different food communities. These included 257 food communities from Eastern Europe, 346 from Africa, 102 from North America, 273 from South America, and 224 from Asia and Oceana, in addition to many from Italy and Western Europe.

As Petrini declared in his opening speech to the Terra Madre, a mixture of pride and emotion:

> People are here from the Amazon jungle to the Chiapas mountain, from Californian vineyards to First Nation reserves, from the shores of the Mediterranean to the seas of Northern Europe, from the Balkans to Mongolia, from Africa to Australasia, all organised into what we have decided to call 'food communities.[10]

Another keynote speaker was Frei Betto, agriculture under-secretary to President Lula of Brazil. Betto took issue with Western approaches to aid. He argued:

> Famine cannot be fought with donations. There must be effective policies of structural change, including agricultural

7. Carlo Petrini, the founder of the Slow Food
movement. (Photo: Slow Food)

and fiscal reform, capable of decentralising land rents and
financial revenues. This must be supported by bold policies of
investment and credit to families, who must also be assisted by
an intense programme of education, according to the model of
Paolo Freire, thus becoming socio-economic protagonists and
political and historical actors.

Prince Charles was another of the main speakers. Paying tribute
to the 'unceasing energy of Dr Carlo Petrini' – the ex-Communist,
left libertarian, radical – Charles called for the construction of
'places and buildings that put people before cars and enhance
a sense of community and rootedness…At the end of the day,
values such as sustainability, community, health and taste are
more important than pure convenience'.

'The Slow Food movement', he concluded, 'is about celebrating the culture of food and about sharing the extraordinary knowledge...developed over millennia of the traditions involved with quality food production'.

Slow Food's involvement with poorer countries at the mercy of multinationals illustrates their determination to have an authentic appeal beyond the West, while avoiding the label of 'anti-global' or 'anti-modern'. The critique of globalisation expressed at the Terra Madre nevertheless reflected wider concerns of the anti-capitalist protest movements, and many of the solutions proposed focused on the need to allow poorer countries to develop local produce unhindered. This required respect for local identity and the protection of local economies, customs and traditions, as well as opposition to the economic dominance of Western corporations.

THE SLOW CITY

Slow Food, since its origins in 1986, can therefore be said to have a global reach and offers ideas and visions of what an alternative concept of globalisation might entail. Its attempts to involve local businesses, school students and associations in its various events – from wine fairs to seminars on biodiversity – suggest that it has an appeal way beyond a few food aficionados.

Two further developments enhanced the scope and overall strategy of Slow Food's attempts to offer an alternative way of living. The first was the setting up of the Slow Cities (*Città Slow*) movement in 1999. This was a network started by local councils who broadly shared the ideals of the Slow Food movement. At the inaugural convention it was decided that Slow Cities would apply to those with less than 50,000 residents. In order to become a Slow City, 31 criteria had to be satisfied from 60 overall conditions which included environmental policies based on recycling and re-use; the production of food using 'eco-compatible' techniques; the safeguarding and developing of typical local products through active collaboration with local restaurants, including the Slow Food convivia and local vineyards and farms; improving and promoting hospitality as a way of strengthening local community bonds; the implementation of 'infrastructural' improvements to improve the land and quality of urban spaces, including reduction of traffic and extended pedestrian areas; and raising awareness of local citizens, producers, consumers and children about the city's identity and what it means to live in a Slow City.

Slow Cities had to sign up to particular pledges on what might be called 'preferred ways of living'. They were obliged to enter into joint initiatives with other Slow Cities, promote common ideals, hold regular meetings and generally develop a clear identity of what it means to be a Slow City. The four original Slow Cities in Italy comprised Bra, Greve-in-Chianti in Tuscany, Orvieto in Umbria, and Positano in Campania. Since 1999, the number has risen to over 35 in Italy, with several in other countries including Scandinavia and the United States. In Britain, Ludlow in Shropshire and Aylsham in Norfolk had taken the mantle of a Slow City by 2004.

The first President of the Slow Cities movement in Italy was Paolo Saturnini, the mayor of Greve-in-Chianti, a beautiful hilltop town in the heart of Tuscany which could boast an *enoteca* (wine shop) on almost every street. Deep in the Chianti hills it is accessible from Florence, where a local bus will take you to the main piazza. At the time of my visit in March 2003, the hills were covered with the *bandiere della pace*, hundreds of rainbow peace flags complementing the Tuscan landscape. Local shops testified to the identity of its Slow City status; even the local travel agency was called 'Chianti Slow Travel', while butchers' and grocers' shops cultivated the image of local produce in a town that derived much of its income from British and other tourism. There was no fast food outlet in sight. This Slow City, like many others, had also become an anti-war city; on the day of my arrival, shops had agreed to close for 15 minutes at midday in protest at the war.

From his desk in the magnificent Palazzo Comunale, overlooking a traffic-free Piazza Matteotti, Saturnini told me what it meant to be a Slow City. 'Greve became a Slow City, to conserve our culture, to preserve the soul of the city, to protect its environment and ambience', he said. He denied he was launching a war against McDonald's and other fast food outlets and pointed to the widespread support given to the initiative by local people. He saw the initiative not as a big ideological struggle against global capitalism, but as a small-scale element in a wider 'jigsaw puzzle' of trying to live in a more sustainable way. 'When you think of saving energy, traffic problems, the needs of the environment, the identity of the city, then these are very pragmatic ideas', he told me. I suggested that, taken together, they offer a vision of Italy that is some way from Berlusconi's. 'Berlusconi wants to make Italy less like Tuscany', he replied.

THE SLOW UNIVERSITY

The second development was the setting up of Italy's (and the world's) first 'slow university', the University of Gastronomic Sciences, in October 2004. The idea of the university was to give academic status to the study of food from a range of disciplines covering humanities, science, ecology, sociology, anthropology and gastronomy. According to Carlo Petrini, in his introduction to the university prospectus, it aimed to fill a vacuum in the study of gastronomy that had mainly been left to scientists who focused on narrow areas of food science and nutrition. 'It is truly incredible', he wrote, 'that such an important feature of our lives and a field so vast...has never achieved academic recognition'.[11]

The breadth of disciplines involved in the study of gastronomy can be found in the university's curriculum. These include philosophy, anthropology, botany, agriculture, biology, economics, sociology, agronomy and nutrition science. Wine journalists, food critics and leading restaurateurs are on hand to offer specialist lectures, while academics from the full range of disciplines are involved in teaching, many flown in from international universities. The 60 students entering the first year, chosen competitively from over 400 applicants from across the globe, can study a variety of interdisciplinary courses. A student might choose 'History of Cooking and Gastronomy' in the first year, followed by 'Geography of Wine' in the second year and 'Sociology of Consumption' in their final year. For the two-year 'specialisation degree' they could take 'Gastronomic Literature' and 'Consumer Psychology' in the first year, followed by 'Business Marketing' and 'Food Law and Legislation' in their final year. The university also offers thematic and regional field seminars that take students not only to Tuscany and Sicily but to Californian wine regions, Champagne vineyards in France and gastronomic centres in Japan and South Africa.

Laptops, laboratories and multimedia libraries are all provided for students, which means that studying in the slow lane does not come cheap, though scholarships are available for successful applicants who need them and the university has received generous sponsorship. The two campuses are located in regions close to the heart of the Italian food lover. The main site, which also contains a hotel and restaurant vastly superior to normal student refectories, is situated deep in the Langhe wine region at Pollenzo, close to Slow Food's headquarters in Bra, which also provides accommodation for students. The second site is at Colorno in Emilia Romagna, near Parma, in an area known for its prosciutto and Parmesan cheese.

THE FUTURE IS SLOW

It was at the Pollenzo campus of the university that I met Carlo Petrini to talk about his movement. The ex-ARCI campaigner, a product of the radical milieu of the 1970s (a movement often now regarded as utopian), seemed to be much closer to achieving many of his earlier aspirations, albeit through a more unexpected route. What was distinctive about the origins of ARCI and many of the movements of the earlier era was their emphasis on culture, on the idea that popular culture was a vital terrain of politics, not an afterthought or an appendage to the bigger economic sphere.

This view for Petrini's generation in Italy was much influenced by the political and cultural writings of Antonio Gramsci. The former Italian Communist leader, whose famous works were written from one of Mussolini's prison cells, emphasised the importance of political movements embedding themselves in popular culture. The Slow Food movement seemed to satisfy many of these criteria, and I asked Petrini for his own views about the legacy of Gramsci. 'I think that Gramsci's thought is still very relevant today; in particular the concept of popular culture and the relationship of the intellectuals to the people and their local identity', he said. He pointed to Slow Food's own work amongst peasant communities in different countries and other initiatives adopted to develop the local economy, derived from a knowledge of and identification with local identity. This, he felt, was close to Gramsci's idea of rooting a movement empirically in the cultural and economic conditions of the people and intervening in politics through culture. This was the 'Gramscian dialectic' that Petrini saw as central to Slow Food's own approach. In this way, we had to recognise that 'seeing the world through gastronomy was to address a number of political, cultural and social questions'.

Petrini was proud of the global impact Slow Food was having and stressed the importance of practical initiatives and cooperation between local producers, consumers, associations and councils. He pointed to the Ark of Taste (so called because of the 'long stormy voyage ahead of us'), an initiative set up by Slow Food in order to catalogue and publicise 'forgotten flavours', and the Presidia, which gave awards for the preservation of products threatened by industrial standardisation. A New International Ark Commission had been set up to look into deserving cases of lost foods. Examples of the work of the Ark of Taste included Italian Valchiavenna goat, American Navajo-Churro sheep, Greek Fava beans grown on the island of Santorini, and the last Irish cattle breed, the Kerry. The Presidia had obtained sponsorship from regional tourist boards, agricultural councils and cooperative producers to support its initiatives on protecting biodiversity. Petrini felt that Slow Food had made unique links with a diverse range of associations and was involved in a number of collaborative projects such as manifestos on the future of food as well as areas of policy formation. Its political influence also worked at different levels involving a diverse range of social groups in civil society, forming dialogues with political parties, local governments and even national governments. Petrini pointed out that Letizia Moratti, education minister in the Berlusconi government, had spoken at the opening of the University of Gastronomic Sciences.

Petrini saw Slow Food in part as a response to the 'crisis of the left' of the late 1980s and 1990s, notably its antipathy towards the 'right to pleasure'. He clearly still sees himself as part of the left. Indeed, as we sat down to lunch, he took a call from Fausto Bertinotti, the leader of Rifondazione comunista, who rang to welcome him back from his holidays. However, Slow Food's origins and subsequent development went much beyond the left. Slow Food was essentially an attempt to 'see the world' differently. As far as globalisation was concerned, Petrini regarded it as an 'irreversible phenomenon', but one which could have 'positive' or 'negative' dimensions. 'At the moment we have negative globalisation', he stated. On the positive side he pointed to the growing contacts beyond Europe and in third world countries and the growing influence of Slow Food initiatives in these countries. He had recently given advice to the finance minister of Lula's Brazilian government. 'Today we have developed good links in Japan, the US, Australia, Canada, Mexico and Argentina, Brazil, Peru and India. Slow Food brings three positive features to the globalisation debate. Firstly, respect for the environment. Secondly, respect for social life, and thirdly, the right to pleasure. This should be seen as a universal right', he told me, over a glass of Barbera d'Alba 2001.

9
From Postmodern Populism to Postmodern Politics?

This book opened with the argument that Silvio Berlusconi's government was characterised by postmodern populism. This became effectively a mode of governance – that is, a particular way of ruling – that was derived from Berlusconi's unique role as a major media entrepreneur and politician and constructed on the back of the failures of the *partitocrazia*, the historic problem of the Italian state and the crisis of mass representative politics. Along with his coalition allies, helped notably by the historical revisionism of the National Alliance, Berlusconi challenged the basis of Italy's postwar political settlement, which had been founded on the values of anti-Fascism. The Northern League offered a different populist vision, based on a rejection of the Italian state and the failures of representative democracy by pushing first for independence, then for a federalist solution, while its xenophobic opposition to immigration posed a challenge to European liberal values.

It has also been argued that Berlusconi's distinctive populist approach hastened the development of an 'anti-politics'. It ignored conventional political structures, collapsed the boundaries of legality and legitimacy and carried a strong authoritarian streak. Crucially, it has to be seen against the background of wider societal changes. These changes, which have their own 'Italian' expressions, nevertheless resonate with wider shifts in the nature of contemporary societies. Berlusconi was one particular response to the crisis in mass politics and representative democracy, a characteristic feature of many European countries. Berlusconi's impact followed the decline of the 'grand narratives', in this case political Catholicism and Italian Communism, which had lost ideological legitimacy and were no longer able to structure people's beliefs, mobilise their opinion at election times or sustain their allegiance through cultural festivals and rituals. Moreover, the new political parties that replaced them on the centre-left did not come to terms with the consequences of the postmodern world and have been slow to engage with those looser, spontaneous and generally more fluid forms of political association that have emerged and which had some grasp of the new social realities.

The new Italian right, represented by Berlusconi and his allies, responded first to the political vacuum that followed the crisis of 1992–94. It was helped by the fact that its new electorate was highly dissatisfied and critical of the old party system.[1] It was able to respond in this way, despite the first ill-fated Berlusconi government, because the centre-left did not modernise and did not understand or engage effectively enough with the new society. Berlusconi was particularly effective at undermining the status of professional politicians; the centre-left, for all its rhetoric about new beginnings, remained paralysed by older forms of political leadership and was too cautious to closely identify with the more radical associations. Indeed, Berlusconi's risk-taking was another mark of distinction between his government and its lack-lustre opponents, particularly in the early years. His particular interpretation of the new risk-driven world of the information society and globalisation was more convincing than the centre-left's attempt to import the third way, while the latter's prolonged ambiguity in its relationship to the new social forces in preference for seeking out the 'centre ground', something it never attributed with a set of coherent beliefs, was particularly inept.

Postmodern populism, which organised Berlusconi's agenda, was a mode of governance that appealed to Italy at a particular moment. Populism has not been confined to Italy, of course. Other populist experiments have been apparent in the West such as Ross Perot's intervention in US politics, Jorg Haider in Austria and Jean Marie Le Pen in France. Margaret Thatcher's governments in the UK in the 1980s were described by the sociologist and political thinker Stuart Hall as being driven by 'authoritarian populism'. The Blair governments have not escaped either; the term 'populist' applied frequently to his strategy of appealing to (some would say 'appeasing') 'middle England', while the managerialist focus of his governments have been described by Anthony Barnett as 'corporate populism'.[2] Yet Berlusconi's version of populism has been more threatening and far more substantive in its critique of conventional politics. This has allowed it to accommodate, however uncomfortably, different ideological constructions within the coalition parties; in the case of the Northern League and the National Alliance, even competing and contradictory ones.

Consequently, as we have seen, it has posed a significant threat to the autonomy of public life that is essential to democratic politics. The conflict between the Italian Prime Minister's private interests and the public interest, and the overrunning of normal procedures of representative government by appealing directly to the sentiments, emotions and prejudices of an 'imaginary public', have only weakened an already fragile liberal democracy. For populists, according to David Marquand:

> Legitimate power springs from the uncorrupted people, and only from the people. Constitutional checks and balances are therefore suspect. They impede the expression of the popular will and will chop up the power which emanates from the people into self-stultifying bits. The people are a homogeneous and monolithic whole...There is a paranoid streak in the populist mentality. Against the pure, virtuous people stand corrupt, privileged elites and sinister, conspiratorial subversives. The latter are forever plotting to bring down the former.

'Populists', he carries on, in a description that would be particularly apt for Berlusconi, 'offer...certainty, security and glamour in place of the drab, confusing greys of the ordinary politician'.[3]

Margaret Thatcher's governments in Britain are among the examples Marquand uses in his discussion of populism and its effects on public life. Like Berlusconi, Thatcher also filled a political vacuum, in this case the one that followed the decline of the postwar Keynesian consensus. Yet there are significant differences between Thatcherism and the Berlusconi phenomenon. Thatcherism represented a major ideological critique of the postwar consensus, and in its place proposed a more elaborate neo-liberal way of understanding the world, one that continued to shape the priorities of the Blair governments. It depended on a long-term defeat of the British left and the social forces that had driven it. Like Berlusconi, Thatcherism successfully 'appropriated' the 'new times', post-Fordist shifts in work and the new aspirations of the working class.[4] However it had a long-term strategy, took many unpopular decisions and benefited from stable electoral majorities.

Berlusconi on the other hand, while imposing a vision, a new language and style of politics, has always struggled to provide a convincing worldview beyond short-term gains and objectives. The splits in his coalition indicated the lack of ideological coherence and the fragility of his rule. He depended upon nearly 100 lawyers to keep his show on the road. Unlike Thatcher, he also reneged on many of his promises, notably in the economic sphere.

Nor has the Italian left as a whole, beyond the party leaderships, suffered the same kinds of defeats as the left in Britain. A left-wing and 'social movement' infrastructure, together with a cultural form of politics, remained from the 1970s, while the legacy of Berlinguer (particularly noticeable amongst DS members on the twentieth anniversary of his death in 2004) and the PCI more generally still informs political debate on the left. One of Berlinguer's major strengths, as the leader of a mass party, was to engage with the grain of political and cultural change and sustain broad appeal amongst different social groups. The structures of mass parties like the PCI would now be deemed too bureaucratic for many of the movements, but for a while the rise of Sergio Cofferati offered a type of political leadership that was largely in the traditions of the broad democratic left. The ideas of Antonio Gramsci continue to be discussed, if in more contested, revised and dispersed forms. The historical memory of the left remains strong, if often divided.

Parts of this left-wing legacy have influenced the new associationism, which has emerged as an alternative embodiment of a postmodern politics. Here, the more conventional, mainly left-wing trade union and social movements which resonated to some degree with the libertarian, anarchist and direct action strategies of the 1970s (symbolised by the anti-global capitalist protests in Genoa) have been joined by less conventional movements such as the spontaneous protest against nuclear waste in Scanzano Jonico. Indeed, overall, there are significant differences between the new associationism and the movements of the 1970s. The social movements of the 1970s had a much stronger ideological base, were more radical in their militancy, and more 'anti-state' in their objectives (often influenced by varieties of Marxism). Violence was more common in the conflict between the movements and the state, and sections of the extra-parliamentary left remained convinced that, given the power and conspiratorial nature of the state in the 1970s, some form of violent struggle was inevitable.

The new associationism, on the other hand, was defined by a renewed sense of civic purpose and the development of new forms of solidarity and association, and has, moreover, reflected diverse regional variations, political outlooks and social composition to a greater degree than before. A commitment to peace and non-violence, despite the clashes at Genoa, is also more evident in the new associations, perhaps partly due to the greater number of women who are involved in associations than are involved in parties (in which they remain virtually invisible) and, in the South, the role of religious leaders in many of the movements. The defining feature, though, was a commitment to strengthening civil society with the more long-term objective of recreating a sense of state.

The diversity of the social composition of the new associations was also significant. The movement in Scanzano, for example, attracted environmentalists and peace activists, while parish priests and other local community figures played an important role in a region that maintained strong Christian democratic traditions. La Rete, the network set up by Leoluca Orlando, drew on a distinctive set of activists that crossed the boundaries of right and left; deliberately short-term, it epitomised the spontaneity and transparent nature of contemporary political movements. Nanni Moretti's intervention was a further example of a different political actor. It reflected the possibilities for a more fluid relationship between intellectuals and conventional parties, amplified in Moretti's own example as a film director who had previously made interventions through this medium and who was reluctant to leave things to politicians. The *girotondi*, the protests Moretti organised, were also distinctive, bringing together committed groups and individuals in more informal and autonomous organisations. The core group of the *girotondi* was perhaps close to Ginsborg's idea of the 'reflexive middle class', often found in the public sector and the professions. It provided a contrast with Berlusconi's own core middle-class supporters, who were businessmen and private sector employees. The middle class, like other social groups in a very divided country, continued to fragment and develop looser and more fluid political identities than before.

The Slow Food movement, through its convivia, the Presidium, the Ark of Taste, the Terra Madre and Cheese Week, brought together a unique range of people – local producers, farmers, intellectuals, gourmets and wine experts, educationalists, nutritionists and social movement activists. Moving between the boundaries of culture, economics, politics and gastronomy, it provided a holistic critique of a 'way of living', namely neo-liberal American capitalism, but appealed to a diverse range of supporters. Its particular type of associationism was of a unique local and global dimension, bringing together new forms of association between producers and consumers.

In the anti-Mafia protests it was the resistance of the women that was ultimately decisive, while the election of Michele Emiliano in Bari was testament to the active role played by magistrates, whose status, having risen dramatically during the 'Clean Hands' investigation of the early 1990s, subsequently took a battering as one of Silvio Berlusconi's prime targets. As a magistrate, Emiliano was part of the professional group that had done more than any other to change Italy's political system. Many of the associations and movements were not entirely composed of new actors, of course; rather, the less structured or ideologically determined forms often allowed a 'new mix' of political actors drawn from earlier traditions; the 'No Global priest', in the case of Don Angelo in Bari, was a typically Italian postmodern construct.

In addition to this unusual social mix, there are three other distinctive dimensions to the new associations that will remain crucial for the future of Italian politics. Firstly, these associations were all committed to doing politics differently. Here, the emphasis on civil society, in a country regarded for its unaccountable state powers and weak civic sense, is significant, and suggests the basis for a new politics of the future. The peak of this influence was the moment in 2002 when a combination of the three largest movements came together, namely the CGIL-led opposition to labour market reform, the *girotondi* protests in defence of liberty and democracy, and the peace and No Global movements. With the continuing crisis on the centre-left, these movements with their regular mass demonstrations and other public initiatives appeared as the main opposition to the Berlusconi government. The demonstration in March 2002 against the suspension of Article 18 of the Italian constitution, when over 2 million people congregated in the centre of Rome, was probably the largest demonstration in the history of the Italian Republic.

Demonstrations aside, the new associations offered different ideas of politics. The historian Paul Ginsborg, who is also a prominent member of the *girotondi*, is involved locally in Florence with the Laboratorio per la democrazia ('Laboratory for Democracy'). This initiative, he told me, had two main objectives: to both defend and renovate democracy. The group organises local initiatives, for example in defence of the autonomy of the magistrates, and is also interested in developing new forms of democratic participation. This has been influenced by Ginsborg's own 'bitter experience' of attempting to work with parties. Despite the relatively strong Florentine civil society, evident when it created an 'open city' during the European Social Forum in 2002, and the extraordinary number of 47 civic committees representing a range of local concerns, the DS, the party that governs the city, is in Ginsborg's view unreceptive to new ideas and ways of working. He contrasts the five minutes allowed to each speaker in the Laboratorio with the rambling monologues of party politicians and regards the local centre-left government as a 'classic example' of the old ways of working. At the 2004 mayoral elections, the Laboratorio, allied to Rifondazione comunista, took 12 percent of the vote and forced a second ballot.

At the peak of the impact of the new oppositional movements in 2002, Ginsborg was also involved in negotiations with Nanni Moretti and Sergio Cofferati over setting up a new broad left political organisation. He laments a lost opportunity for a 'critical left' that has a potentially large constituency but no formal political home. The three reasons why this did not work out, he says, were the lack of flexibility in the older established organisations, the difficulty of keeping a disparate range of people together, and the role of Cofferati, its obvious leader, who was reluctant to break with the DS. Cofferati's loyalty to the party was a reminder that political parties retain a strong role even for the more critical sectors of Italian politics and will not disappear in the postmodern period. The point is whether they choose to develop more open and accountable structures and more flexible ways of working with associations. Though the mass party is over, many of its features remain, notably the centralisation of power and the inability to reform.

The second distinctive aspect of the new associations was the use of new forms of technology and media. The anti-global capitalist movement, to take one example, is often described as being backward and 'Luddite' in its view of global and technological change. In reality, the protest movements have been sustained by innovative use of technology. This includes the role of Indymedia, the alternative media group that covered the Genoa events and provided an alternative to mainstream 'mass' TV coverage. The various Genoa Social Forum, No Global and other websites were crucial in mobilising activities, avoiding roadblocks that prevented access to the city, and providing accommodation for demonstrators. The websites also provided a source of political identity, whereby forums and debates consolidated or challenged political beliefs and assumptions. The invisibility and spontaneity of the websites was crucial to the mobilisation of political action. Latterly, they provided a source of information on how to take action against police brutality and offered support for victims of violence. Mobile phones, digital cameras and conventional independent filming recorded the events and provided images that were often used to counter official reports.

The use of websites has become more mainstream as a tool of conventional politics, in ways ranging from early attempts at 'e-government' to the websites of political parties. Yet, for the associations, the Internet takes on a unique role, by virtue of being less controlled, more short-term and spontaneous, and essentially enabling political communication between unconventional political actors. In Scanzano Jonico, websites and email lists became one of the main forms of mobilisation of protest, often at very short notice. The ability to reach people over a vast rural area, with poor transport, was crucial, as was the pressure exerted through demonstrations.

The final defining feature of the new associationism was the more fluid ideological configurations apparent in many of the associations and movements. Although these movements were often focused on particular issues and campaigns, it is important to recognise that these were not 'post-ideological' in their aims and objectives. While often more limited than those of political parties or the bigger social movements, and often fractured or loose, they nevertheless often assumed an ideological form. If we consider ideology as a set of ideas and beliefs that have sufficient coherence to mobilise political action, offer a framework through which to understand, interpret and seek to change society, and offer a form of social identity, then it is possible to conceive of these movements as either linked to existing or older ideological traditions (as critiques or revisions) or embryonic ideologies of the future. For example, within the anti-global capitalist movement there are varieties of Marxist, anarchist and libertarian left-wing ideological positions that offer critiques of neo-liberalism, but also provide contested spaces within the movement. In many cases, such as the protest in Scanzano, different ideological traditions such as environmentalism and Christian democracy coexisted together, as they did on a larger scale in opposition to the Iraq war. Unsurprisingly, differences emerged over strategy, for example within the peace movement, and there were also ideological conflicts within many of the movements. Yet, the common goals and spirit of unity persisted in these unlikely alliances.

In many important ways, therefore, the new associations helped to renew ideology, though in very distinctive ways that were often not reducible to traditional left/right categories. Michael Freeden has described ideology as the 'vehicle of dissent', because of its role in providing contending viewpoints. These viewpoints have an indispensable role in helping to 'reinvent politics'; they provide a 'vital and energizing ingredient in the fashioning of group identities and policies.'[5] In Freeden's view, the problem with many contemporary uses of ideology is that they are seen as totalitarian and all-encompassing, or else only belonging to a world of political extremes. This view seems to have been popular among the leaders of the Italian centre-left like D'Alema and Veltroni in their search for new directions and in their determination to move away from the past. An 'end of ideology' trajectory certainly seems to inform much of the third way debates, where managerialism and pragmatism take over from ideology and dissent. During the election campaign of 2001, I saw Francesco Rutelli, the centre-left opponent of Berlusconi, arrive in Parma, one of Italy's poshest cities and a key battleground in the election. He arrived by train on the 'Rutelli Express', a trip that had taken him the length of the country. His reception party was a very provincial affair. A local band played the national anthem as he stepped off the train, looking very serene in his train guard's hat. The very best Parmesan cheese and prosciutto was available, along with local wines. It was a very civilised gathering, with polite conversation and cheery optimism about the forthcoming election. It was the epitome of that respectability the centre-left craved; as near as one could imagine to an ideology-free zone.

Yet ideology remains vital for politics. As Freeden states: 'Far from witnessing the end of ideology, a plethora of new ideologies has continued to emerge...while older ideologies have been undergoing continuous processes of breaking up and regrouping... not only are there new movements adopting ideologies but an explosion in the usages of ideology'. These range from what he calls 'grand full ideologies to thin, partial or eclectic ones'.[6] The tendency in the postmodern era, following the collapse of older traditional ideologies, he argues, is for fragmentation and differentiation. He concludes: '...if it is at the same time impossible for us to conceive of a world without political ideologies...we are now conceptually prepared for a world of ideologies in which re-combinations are normal and frequent and in which boundaries are there to be traversed'.[7]

Moreover, even in those associations that extend beyond the left and in some cases could not be defined in traditional political characterisations at all, ideology remains important. Pacifism, the production of food, participatory democracy, sustainability, anti-capitalism are all driven by wider beliefs about how society should be organised. A lot of myth is attached to the 'centre', a political space that is assumed to have no ideology, devoid of political commitment, conservative in its social attitudes and political orientations, perhaps a little authoritarian on issues to do with immigration, while sensible on the economy. Above all it is the epitome of 'normality'. This construct, similar to 'middle England' in the UK, is even more difficult to define in Italy. Yet it continues to organise much of the attention of the leaders of the centre-left. Indeed, the centre-right, under Berlusconi and his allies, has been much more adventurous in giving its political groupings some active sense of what is wrong and how society needs to change.

This concern over the vacuity of the centre has been expressed by a growing number of centre-left intellectuals. Massimo Cacciari, the left-wing philosopher and mayor of Venice, has talked of the need to recapture ideology in its 'good' meaning, in order to give direction to politics, provide political leadership and elucidate a sense of political identity amongst the electorate. The failure of the centre-left to distinguish between older ideological formations, including redundant ones, and new ideological configurations, meant that it could not mobilise opposition to the Berlusconi government effectively. Instead this was a task taken up by others.

The new associationism has demonstrated that ideology, the importance of beliefs and values, will still influence political actors even if the individuals involved are not in political parties or established social movements. The *girotondi* shared with anti-Mafia protests a commitment to rebuilding liberal democratic norms, defending the autonomy of public life, and strengthening political pluralism and liberty. The mobilisation against the Iraq war was driven by the return of pacifist beliefs in Italy, uniting different political groups under the universal symbol of the *bandiera della pace*.

Therefore, the new associationism represented the defence of liberal representative democracy in the face of the populist challenge from Berlusconi. Yet it also posed a challenge to the status, credibility and organisational strength of political parties. The new associations will not replace parties; nor will parties disappear, despite falling membership, deterioration of their public esteem and organisational shifts such as the personalisation and centralisation of power, which has been as evident in its own way amongst the centre-left as it has been on the right. Indeed, Italian political parties, including the new forms that emerged after 1992–94, remain strong and bureaucratic; it is one of the continuities of the first Republic. Yet it is equally absurd to see the future of politics as belonging exclusively to parties. Therefore, a new kind of relationship between associations and parties, made more urgent by the fragmentary nature of postmodern cultures, becomes essential. It is particularly important for the parties of the left, in their attempt not only to defeat Berlusconi electorally but also to renew politics and ultimately rebuild public life and develop a new civic culture. In the future, the associations can play an important role in facilitating public debate, as intermediate channels of participation, and in helping to define the boundaries between private and public interests. They will become important in helping to renovate the institutions of the state by providing new channels of accountability and participation. In this way the associations have already started to challenge populist assumptions by strengthening what Marquand calls the 'perimeter walls of the public domain'.[8]

One of the few thinkers to attempt to outline a role for associations in the political order was Paul Hirst, in his book *Associative Democracy*. He saw associative democracy as a solution to weak civil societies, over-powerful states, unregulated elites, privatisation and deregulation, which had become prominent in many advanced Western societies. Italy, with its inefficient state, weak civil society, increasing power of unregulated elites but emerging associations, would appear to be ripe for change. Associative democracy, whereby voluntary organisations would become self-governing as well as allowing for more decentralisation from central government, was regarded as a supplement rather than a replacement of representative democracy. In reality it was seen by Hirst as necessary to address the 'crisis' in representative democracy, and a preferable contemporary alternative to statism or neo-liberalism. According to Hirst, associationism 'attempts to construct a political framework with which individuals and the groups they create through voluntary associations, one with another, can pursue different public goods whilst remaining in the same society'.[9]

THE FIRST POSTMODERN ELECTION CAMPAIGN?

The victory of the centre-left in the mayoral election in Bologna in June 2004 provided a good example of what an alternative 'postmodern' politics, built on an associationist critique of populism, might become. The existing incumbent, Giorgio Guazzaloca, had been the first right-wing mayor of Bologna in the postwar period. He had been elected in 1999 on the 'civic list', namely an independent slate, though following his election he received the support of the main right-wing parties, notably the National Alliance and Forza Italia. Guazzaloca, a local butcher and entrepreneur, made much of the fact that he was not a member of a party. He always maintained that he had been elected as a 'Bolognese'. He knew the local culture and had direct experience of local business. He could be described as a 'provincial populist', reflecting disenchantment with party politics and allowing popular local concerns to shape his alternative. He was elected at a time when the Olive Tree was in power for the first time nationally and Bologna had seen over 50 years of uninterrupted left-wing local government, led by the PCI. Whoever was to take on Guazzaloca had to deal with his populism.

The candidate eventually chosen by the left to fight the election was Sergio Cofferati. After his rise as the unofficial head or 'real leader' of the left (in Nanni Moretti's words), Cofferati posed a threat to the leadership of the DS and subsequently the Olive Tree coalition. At the same time he gave new hope to the left, including the left wing of the DS; many in the DS in Bologna, with its left-wing traditions, were supportive of Cofferati, who was the leading figure in *Aprile*, the group on the left of the party. After much discussion, it appeared that Cofferati, as far as the DS was concerned, was the ideal candidate. A strong national figure, he appealed to traditional left-wing supporters while offering a solution to the DS leadership. If he was preoccupied with becoming mayor of Bologna, he would not be able to become a rival national leader. Polls among the left's own electorate showed him to be the most popular choice as a national leader of the left, ahead of Veltroni, D'Alema and Fassino.[10]

Cofferati needed to win the support of Bologna 2004, the assortment of 85 associations that had come together after the previous defeat to plan to win back the city for the left. This list of associations ranged from trade unions to cultural organisations. According to Roberto Grandi, vice-rector of Bologna University and a specialist on media politics, who later co-wrote a book on the Cofferati election campaign, Cofferati's early dialogue with the associations was crucial in his subsequent victory. Not all the parties were initially in favour of Cofferati's candidature; the centrist Daisy party, for example, had doubts about Cofferati's left-wing past. By attending many meetings of the associations, Cofferati was able to win them over, and this increased his overall legitimacy. Crucially, it also allowed him to address the charges made by his opponent, Guazzaloca. Guazzaloca's frequently cited argument against Cofferati was not the usual one made by the right: 'I do not say that he is a Communist, I say that he is not Bolognese' (Cofferati was from Cremona in Lombardy).

Essentially, Guazzaloca saw Cofferati's candidacy as one that was imposed by the parties. According to Grandi, this raised questions that Cofferati needed to address. He needed to redefine what it meant to be Bolognese, and he had to convince the citizens of Bologna that he had some relative autonomy from the parties.[11]

Guazzaloca's campaign, such as it was (he actually denied he was engaged in one), was shaped by his Bolognese identity. Under his leadership, as he saw it, the Bolognese ran the city while he himself was autonomous and avoided traditional political mediation or what could be seen as the conventional places of politics. Grandi points out an instance of Guazzaloca visiting an old people's home where he played cards with the residents but avoided discussion of political or social problems. He often refused to give interviews to journalists, and his definition of being Bolognese was clearly a limited one, linked to local knowledge, business experience, and enthusiasm for tortellini, mortadella and traditional Bolognese food. It was a view of political leadership that sought to bypass conventional politics.[12]

Cofferati's task, therefore, was a complex one. He had to find a strategy that was political while avoiding the pitfalls of conventional party control. In addition, he had to provide an answer to the 'Bolognese question' that seemed at the heart of the election. According to Grandi, the role of the associations was crucial in both these matters. Apart from the process of nomination, Cofferati enlisted the help of some 750 volunteers, individuals who were members of associations or parties or who had no alignment other than a wish to be involved in an important election campaign. This would not be an election campaign dominated by party militants. This helped Cofferati's autonomy in a positive way as well as extending the breadth of his campaign. It also allowed him to develop another idea of Bolognese identity, one that was rooted in the varied experiences and needs of groups of local people. Grandi told me that Guazzaloca's problem was 'that he attempted to impose his model of what it means to be Bolognese as the only model'. He argues that the long meetings Cofferati held with associations paid off and eventually removed that particular question from the campaign.

Cofferati had to overcome other problems, however. Much of the local media was under the control of the right. This included the main daily newspaper of Bologna, *Il Resto del Carlino*, which following its earlier support for Fascism had reverted to more conventional right-wing politics. Cofferati's attempt to get around this was one of the most innovative parts of his campaign, going beyond the traditional relationship between political parties and the mass media and prompting Grandi's description of the election campaign as the first of the postmodern variety. 'Cofferati', Grandi told me, 'saw that RAI didn't cover what he was doing. He wanted to give a sign that if the traditional mass communication didn't cover you, you can do something else. You have to do something else.' Bologna had been the first city to offer its citizens free Internet access, and as a university city with a transient population, it offered an alternative way of connecting with Bolognese culture to that offered by Guazzaloca. The projection of Bologna 'La Dotta' ('The Learned') recreated another image of Bologna, as the informed, innovative, enlightened city. A 'three-day marathon' of art, shows and music symbolised a different use of public space. Piazza Maggiore, Bologna's main piazza and the centre of so many demonstrations and rallies over the years, was turned into an open space for local citizens. According to Grandi, the campaign saw the creation of new structures of communication between citizens and institutions. Citizens no longer wanted to be 'bombarded by vertical communication', where they were at the mercy of the 'big communicator', but instead wanted 'horizontal communication'. This horizontal communication was more dispersed and interactive, with space for a reciprocal dialogue between citizens and political leaders.[13]

In the postmodern election campaign, the mix of different types of communication, including some from the pre-modern era such as oral communication, becomes crucial. In place of the hierarchical top-down relationship between mass party, the mass media and the elector, there is more emphasis on 'diffuse communication', with 'direct' and participative forms of democracy, often facilitated by the Internet, to make up for the limitations of representative politics.

Cofferati's ultimate victory of 56 percent to 44 percent was considered to be a significant turning point in Italian politics. Along with other results such as Emiliano's victory in Bari and gains in Milan and Sicily, it was interpreted as a significant advance for the centre-left. Whatever the significance for national elections, the Bologna events suggested the possibility of a more substantial shift in the movement against populism. Following his election victory, Cofferati's relationship with the associations remained important. During the campaign he had promised, if elected, to spend two months talking to the associations before deciding on his programme for office. This offered an unusual opportunity to influence the programme for the following five-year term. For Grandi it reflected a distinctive 'pre-figurative' strategy, whereby Cofferati 'showed during the campaign, some taste of what will happen, to give an idea for the electorate, the style of listening before deciding. It prefigured the style of the administration, the relationship between the mayor and the city'.

It would not be surprising if Bologna were to become the model of a new politics for the centre-left. After all, in the 1970s and 1980s, the 'Modello Emiliano' was much admired beyond the traditional left. Its municipal government and day centres, as well as forms of participatory democracy amongst neighbourhood committees, were some compensation for the PCI's isolation from the centre of power.[14] Bologna is in Italy's most prosperous and innovative economic region. Its standard of living ranks among the highest, it has the lowest birth rate in the country and its overall quality of life is generally regarded to be the finest. It is Italy's largest gay capital and has the reputation of being one of the most tolerant and free-thinking cities in Europe. As a city of culture and a university city, it boasts Umberto Eco – professor of semiotics, one of the world's most well-known intellectuals, and a key ally of Cofferati in the latter stages of his election campaign – and a vibrant independent film, bar and music culture.

During the 1970s Bologna was at the cutting edge of municipal reforms. The preservation of its architectural heritage was accomplished by keeping property speculators out of the medieval part of the old city. Yet it was also a city where the dominant party sub-cultures, Catholic and Communist persisted.[15] Indeed, the PCI in Bologna was not only the largest party of the left, it was also, as ex-mayor Renato Zangheri would often point out, the biggest Catholic party. Parties remained strong; indeed, in the election of Cofferati, the DS, as the largest party, remained decisive in securing his candidature, despite the involvement of the associations.

DECLINE OR RENEWAL?

Bologna represents one part of the hopes of the new associationism, namely the reinvention of politics as the only way of challenging populism in the long term. If there is a postmodern context for this reinvention of politics then it is not one that warns of the 'end of ideology', but one that recognises ideology in its more fluid forms; it does not, as some 'postmodernist' accounts imply, simply veer towards relativist or overly revisionist accounts of history. On the contrary, following the dissolution of mass politics and the erosion of the grand narratives of political Catholicism and Communism, the postmodern era in Italy offers the chance to reconnect with earlier political traditions drawing, for example, on the legacies of democratic anti-Fascism, older forms of participatory democracy, and looser organisational structures. The new associationism reflects much of this emerging trajectory.

The clash between populism and associationism, a conflict between two contending doctrines, is likely to continue. The general election scheduled for 2006 is likely to be another decisive moment in the turbulent history of Italian politics and could signal the process of rebuilding the public culture. However, its outcome is uncertain, and there are more pessimistic scenarios. Italy under Berlusconi has been a country entering rapid and serious decline. As Paul Ginsborg has argued, while 'crises' are a familiar part of the landscape of Italian politics, decline is something relatively new.[16] Economic decline over the decade since 1994 has been evident in low rates of GDP, a significant decrease in exports, high inflation linked to the euro and sharp falls in competitiveness.[17] Italy's public debt after four years of Berlusconi's government remains huge. Despite the idealism of its people on global issues, the Italian government provides the second lowest percentage of GDP (0.17) among advanced nations in aid to developing countries (the US providing the lowest).[18]

Italy's overall international standing, assessed by the quality of its institutions, efficiency of its public services, and competitiveness of its businesses, has dropped 20 places from 26 to 46 between 2001 and 2004.[19] To long-term structural economic decline can be added increasing regional divisions between North and South, despite persistent rhetoric of national reconciliation, falling social mobility, a significant decline in public spending on the arts, and a major population imbalance of smaller numbers of young people in comparison to older people. Michele Porcari, the mayor of Matera, told me that despite many promises, the only significant commitment to the South had been the agreement to construct the Messina bridge to link Sicily directly to the Italian mainland, and even this has been thwarted by claims of Mafia involvement in the project. Indeed, the impetus gained from earlier anti-Mafia reforms has fizzled out in recent years; the centre-left government of 1996–2001 was very cautious not to endorse the more radical magistrates, while Berlusconi's attempts to free up business have arguably given legitimacy to the activities of a new Mafia. Naples remains a city crippled by the actions of the Camorra.

Italy's international status among its European allies was in freefall by the end of 2004. The rejection of Rocco Buttiglione as the European Commission's justice commissioner by the European Parliament in October, after he was nominated by the Italian government, was further indication that Italy was out of kilter with the European consensus on justice. Buttiglione, a close friend of Pope John Paul, had spoken of his personal opposition to homosexuality and been openly critical of single mothers. Buttiglione claimed he was discriminated against for his personal (Catholic) opinions. In fact, his record as an Italian government minister and the widening disdain for Berlusconi seemed the most likely explanation, while one of the prime opponents of Buttiglione was Martin Schulz, the recipient of the earlier 'Nazi Kapo' jibe.

There was renewed hope for those seeking another Italy beyond Berlusconi, following the regional elections of 2005. The rout of the House of Liberties coalition in these elections, where they lost seats in some of their strongest areas, precipitated Berlusconi's biggest political crisis. Having forced him to resign and form a new government, the UDC and National Alliance called for more resources for the South, criticised the devolution policies put forward by the Northern League and hinted at a future realignment of the Italian right after Berlusconi's demise. Gianfranco Fini, Italy's foreign minister since November 2004, maintained his leadership ambitions, prompting the possibility of an ex-Fascist becoming Italy's new leader. Forza Italia, rocked after another dismal election performance, gave the impression of a party in freefall and likely to collapse further in the event of its leader's removal from power in 2006. It now depended on the Northern League for support, with Umberto Bossi, in the twilight of his career, proving a more resilient ally of Berlusconi than many predicted; this suggested, however, that both populist forces would increasingly depend on each other in the near future.

The biggest challenge to Berlusconi came from the South. Driven by new forms of political association and increased optimism over the prospect of social change, the voters of the

Mezzogiorno delivered a damning verdict on the Berlusconi government in the regional elections. Calabria and Puglia joined Campania and Basilicata as centres of the new opposition. This was confirmed by the election of Nichi Vendola, a gay communist, as president of the normally catholic and conservative Puglia region. Meanwhile, Romano Prodi, the leader of L'Unione and the only credible centre-left candidate for prime minister, raised the stakes by accusing the right of being against 'anti-fascism', following the latter's absence from the sixtieth anniversary celebrations of Italian liberation in April 2005.

Fear and uncertainty over Italy's future formed the starting point of this book. The bomb at the offices of *Il Manifesto* in 2000 was an event that seemed to precipitate a new moment of division and polarisation in Italy, at the time Berlusconi began his ascent to power. In February 2005, a *Manifesto* journalist, Giuliana Sgrena, was kidnapped in Baghdad as she was on her way to Fallujah to talk to survivors of the earlier attack by coalition forces on that town. She was eventually released a month later on 4 March, but the celebrations were halted by tragedy. The car in which she was travelling was shot at repeatedly by a US army patrol, one kilometre from the airport, killing Nicola Calipari of the Italian Secret Service, who had negotiated Sgrena's release and who had earlier secured the release of the two Simonas. A selfless and experienced negotiator, he had been talking to Sgrena at the time of the shooting; he died after throwing himself over her body in order to protect her. In the aftermath of this tragedy there were increased calls for the withdrawal of Italian troops from Iraq, bringing more pressure on Berlusconi as his support for George Bush came under renewed criticism. The incident was made to look more questionable in light of the unconvincing explanations offered by the US army, whose claim that the car was speeding past a checkpoint was rejected by Sgrena. The scale of national mourning following Calipari's death, with the *bandiere tricolori*, Italy's national flag, fluttering in the wind alongside the *bandiere della pace*, again raised the prospect of new civic unity and cooperation, as well as confirming the strong desire among Italians for peace. It was also a message of hope and defiance. It is these values that can help reinvent politics and prevent populism degenerating further into authoritarianism. As this book has argued, this is an alternative that has already assumed very Italian – and therefore not very normal – characteristics.

Notes

INTROUCTION

1. Many of these changes are reported in a Demos-Eurisko Survey, November 2004. For the paradoxes of the contemporary Italian family, see Chiara Saraceno, 'The Italian Family from the 1960s to the Present', *Modern Italy* Vol. 9 No. 1, May 2004, pp. 47–57.
2. P. Anderson, 'Land Without Prejudice', *London Review of Books*, 21/3/02.
3. For an interesting discussion of Italy's foreign policy under Berlusconi, see James Walston, 'The Shift in Italy's Euro-Atlantic Policy. Partisan or Bipartisan?', *The International Spectator* Vol. 4, 2004.
4. L. Sciascia, *The Moro Affair*, Granta, 2002, p. 78.
5. Ibid., p. 29.
6. This was a letter signed by 50 of the DC's hierarchy, quoted in L. Sciascia, op. cit., p. 73.
7. L. Sciascia, op. cit., p. 78.
8. *I Cento Passi* (*The Hundred Steps*), directed by Marco Giordana, 2000.
9. His membership number was 1816. D. Lane, *Berlusconi's Shadow: Crime, Justice and the Pursuit of Power*, Allen Lane, 2004, p. 88; P. Ginsborg, *Silvio Berlusconi: Television, Power and Patrimony*, Verso, 2004, pp. 30–32.
10. T. Jones, *The Dark Heart of Italy*, Faber, 2002.

CHAPTER 1

1. *The Economist*, 26/4/01 and 1/8/03.
2. J. Klein, 'Ciao Silvio', *Guardian*, 6/6/02.
3. See, for example, M. Tarchi, *L'Italia populista*, Il Mulino, 2003; H. G. Betz, *Radical Right Wing Populism in Western Europe*, St Martin's Press, 1994.
4. P. Taggart, *Populism*, Open University Press, 2000, pp. 2, 4, 5.
5. P. Ginsborg, *Silvio Berlusconi: Television, Power and Patrimony*, Verso, 2004, p. 5.
6. P. Ginsborg, *Italy and its Discontents 1980–2001*, Allen Lane/Penguin Press, 2001.
7. *Il capitalismo molecolare*, Einaudi, 1997.
8. For changing political allegiances and identities, see Anna Bull, *Social Identities and Political Cultures in Italy*, Berghahn Books, 2000.
9. P. Ginsborg, *Italy and its Discontents 1980–2001*, op. cit., p. 48.
10. Both Ginsborg (*Silvio Berlusconi: Television, Power and Patrimony*, op. cit.) and G. Fiori (*Il venditore*, Garzanti, 1995) provide comprehensive explanations of Berlusconi's rise as an entrepreneur.
11. See John Foot, *Milan Since the Miracle: City, Culture and Identity*, Berg, 2001, p. 165.

12. P. Schlesinger, 'The Berlusconi Phenomenon', in Z. Baranski and R. Lumley (eds), *Culture and Conflict in Post War Italy*, Macmillan, 1990, p. 273.
13. U. Eco, 'A Guide to Neo-Television', in Z. Baranski and R. Lumley, op. cit., p. 246. The original article appeared in *L'Espresso*, 30/1/83.
14. P. Ginsborg, *Silvio Berlusconi: Television, Power and Patrimony*, op. cit., p. 63.
15. I. Pezzini, 'Advertising Politics on Television: the Party Election Broadcast', in L. Cheles and L. Sponza (eds), *The Art of Persuasion*, Manchester University Press, 2001, p. 191.
16. J. Foot, *Modern Italy*, Palgrave Macmillan, 2004.
17. For details of Italy's changing political and electoral geography, see J. Agnew, *Place and Politics in Modern Italy*, University of Chicago Press, 2002; I. Diamanti, *Bianco, rosso, verde...e azzurro: mappe e colori dell'Italia politica*, Il Mulino, 2003.
18. P. Ginsborg, *Silvio Berlusconi: Television, Power and Patrimony*, op. cit.
19. D. Lane, *Berlusconi's Shadow; Crime, Justice and the Pursuit of Power*, Allen Lane, 2004.
20. Reported in the *Guardian*, 16/12/03.
21. *The Spectator*, 5/9/03. He was interviewed by Boris Johnson and Nicholas Farrell.
22. T. Jones, *The Dark of Heart of Italy*, op. cit., pp. 17–18.
23. G. Frankel, 'Italy's Anti-Politician Steps onto World Stage', *Washington Post*, 19/10/03.
24. Will Hutton argued this in 'The New Sick Man of Europe', *Observer*, 28/12/03. See also Marco Niada, 'Italian Capitalism Goes Sour', *Open Democracy*, 29/12/03.

CHAPTER 2

1. J. Olsen, *Silence on Monte Sole*, ibooks, 2002 (1968). For other evidence of the atrocity, see Comitato regionale per la onaranze ai caduti di Marzabotto, *Marzabotto. Quanti, chi e dove*. Ponte Nuovo Editrice, Bologna; and Renato Giorgi, *Marzabotto parla*, Marsilio, 1985.
2. This statement is republished in Jack Olsen's *Silence on Monte Sole*, op. cit., p. 372–3.
3. 'Il discorso del Presidente Rau a Marzabotto', *Associazione Nazionale Partigiani d'Italia*, www.anpi.it/marzabotto.
4. *Fondazione scuola di pace Monte Sole statuto*.
5. In an interview with Boris Johnson and Nicholas Farrell for *The Spectator*, 12/9/03.
6. Details of the change from MSI to AN and the composition of the party's membership can be found in J. Newell, 'Italy: The Extreme Right Comes in from the Cold', *Parliamentary Affairs* Vol. 53 No. 3, July 2000, pp. 469–85.
7. I am grateful to Andrea Chiarini of *La Repubblica* in Bologna for letting me see this correspondence.
8. *L'Unità*, 6/3/03.
9. *L'Unità*, 11/2/03.
10. *La Repubblica*, 26/4/02.

11. *L'Unità*, 24/4/03; *La Repubblica*, 24/4/03.
12. *Guardian*, 18/12/02.
13. N. Farrell, *Mussolini: A New Life*, Phoenix, 2004, xviii, xix.
14. Ibid., pp. 145–7.
15. Ibid., p. 477.
16. Olsen also gives details of Lidia's escape in *Silence on Monte Sole*, op. cit., pp. 238–9.

CHAPTER 3

1. For a good account of the Northern League's reaction to migrants arriving at Italian ports, see Peter Popham, 'Odyssey of Despair and not a Twitch of Conscience by Europe's Leaders', *Independent*, 19/6/03.
2. *La Repubblica*, 7/4/03.
3. See I. Diamanti, 'The Northern League: From Regional Party to Party of Government', in S. Gundle and S. Parker, *The New Italian Republic*, Routledge, 1996.
4. For details of the Northern League's social composition and political identity, see A. Bull, *Social Identities and Political Cultures in Italy*, Berghahn Books, 2000; M. Gilbert and A. Bull (eds), *The Lega Nord and the Northern Question in Italian Politics*, Palgrave Macmillan, 2001, pp. 67–104.
5. A. Bull and M. Gilbert (eds), op. cit., pp. 106–121.
6. Ibid., p. 12.
7. *La Repubblica*, 13/8/03.
8. Poll conducted for *L'Unità*, August 2003.
9. Jonathan Fowler, Associated Press, *Guardian*, 10/7/04.
10. *Guardian*, 1/3/04.
11. *La Repubblica*, 1/4/04.
12. Various reports in *La Repubblica*, 13/7/04; *Corriere della Sera*, 13/7/04; *Guardian*, 13/07/04.
13. *La Repubblica*, 16/10/04.

CHAPTER 4

1. He first argued this in *Beyond Left and Right*, Polity Press, 1994.
2. A. Giddens, *The Third Way and its Critics*, Polity Press, 2000, p. 75.
3. A. Giddens (ed.), *The Global Third Way Debate*, Polity Press, 2001.
4. See, for a comparative analysis of the third way, I. Favretto, *The Long Search for a Third Way; the British Labour Party and the Italian Left Since 1945*, Palgrave, 2003.
5. P. Togliatti, *On Gramsci and Other Writings*, Lawrence and Wishart, 1979; A. Gramsci, *Selections From Prison Notebooks*, Lawrence and Wishart, 1971.
6. See C. Valentini, *Berlinguer: l'eridita difficile*, Editori Riuniti, 2004.
7. Biagio De Giovanni, 'C'erano una volta Togliatti e il comunismo reale', *L'Unità*, 6/8/89.
8. P. Daniels and Martin J. Bull, 'Voluntary Euthanasia; from the Italian Communist Party to the Democratic Party of the Left', in Martin J. Bull and Paul Heywood, *West European Communist Parties After the Revolutions of 1989*, Macmillan, 1994, p. 10.

9. 'Italy's Baby Blair', W. Veltroni, interview with Beppe Severgnini, *Prospect*, April 1996, pp. 64–7.
10. See M. D'Alema, *Un paese normale: la sinistra e il futoro dell'Italia*, Mondadori, 1995.
11. P. Ginsborg, *Italy and its Discontents*, Allen Lane/Penguin Press, p. 303.
12. G. Amato, interview in *La Repubblica*, 2/3/01; quoted in Ginsborg, op. cit., pp. 302–3.
13. Massimo D'Alema, *Un paese normale*.
14. P. Ginsborg, op. cit., pp. 314–15.
15. Evidence for membership and voting figures for the DS in the immediate transitional period is provided in P. Daniels and Martin J. Bull, op. cit., pp. 1–30.
16. See, for example, Timothy Garton-Ash, 'Il blairismo è morto viva il blairismo', *La Repubblica*, 18/9/04.
17. E. Mazierska and L. Rascaroli, *The Cinema of Nanni Moretti*, Wallflower Press, 2004, p. 115.
18. Ibid., p. 135.
19. Ibid., p. 145.

CHAPTER 5

1. See *La Repubblica*, 10/1/04.
2. *Il Manifesto*, November 2002.
3. P. Ginsborg, *Italy and its Discontents 1980–2001*, Allen Lane/Penguin Press, 2001, pp. 43–4.

CHAPTER 6

1. E. Banfield, *The Moral Basis of a Backward Society*, Glencoe, 1958.
2. See G. Gribaudi, 'Images of the South', in R. Lumley and J. Morris (eds), *The New History of the Italian South*, University of Exeter Press, 1997, pp. 106–9.
3. For example, J. Morris, 'Challenging Meridionalismo', in R. Lumley and J. Morris (eds), op. cit., pp. 9–10.
4. C. Levi, *Christ Stopped at Eboli*, Penguin Books, 1945, p. 11.
5. Ibid., p. 12.
6. Ibid., p. 78.
7. Ibid., pp. 86–8.
8. These statistics come from a survey in *Italia Oggi* and *Il Sole 24 Ore* published in 2004 and discussed by G. Lanzillota in 'Matera e la qualità della vita', in the Matera cultural magazine *Liberalia*, March 2004.
9. Ginsborg has a short discussion of this in *Italy and its Discontents 1980–2001*, Allen Lane/Penguin Press, 2001, pp. 125–6. Detailed research on the development of Aliano can be found in R. King and J. Killingbeck, 'Carlo Levi, the Mezzogiorno and Emigration: Fifty Years of Demographic Change in Aliano', *Geography* Vol. LxxIV No. 2, 1989, pp. 18–43.
10. S. Arie, 'Italy's Cavemen Cashing in on Passion of Mel', *Observer*, 4/4/04. This was followed by the response of the paper's readers' editor,

S. Pritchard, in 'When Local Feelings Must Be Respected', *Observer*, 9/5/04.
11. The details of the 'days of revolt' can be found in English in 'An Italian Story with Few Explanations' at www.nonnulceare.com/noalnucleare.php; see also S. Ianuzziello, *Scanzano Jonico: i giorni della rivolta*, Mongolfiera and R. Montemurro, *I giorni di Scanzano*, CGIL Matera.
12. T. Behan, *See Naples and Die*, I.B. Tauris, 2002.
13. Ibid., p. 156.
14. Ibid., pp. 157–8.
15. *La Gazetta del Mezzogiorno*, 27/8/04.

CHAPTER 7

1. See, for example, *Candido* (Carcanet, 1985) and *The Day of the Owl* (Granta, 1988).
2. Lampedusa's *Il Gattopardo* was posthumously published in 1958 by Feltrinelli. It was beautifully captured in Luchino Visconti's 1963 film version.
3. Gentile's idea of Sicilian identity is discussed by Joseph Farrell in 'Considerations on Sicilian Identity', in G. Bedani and B. Haddock, *The Politics of Italian National Identity*, University of Wales Press, 2000.
4. Ibid., pp. 84–5.
5. G. Verga, Preface to *I Malavoglia*, Dedalus, 1998.
6. P. Ginsborg, *Italy and its Discontents 1980–2001*, Allen Lane/Penguin Press, 2001, pp. 97–8.
7. Ibid., p. 99.
8. For good discussions in English of the history of the role of the Mafia in Sicily, see J. Dickie, *Cosa Nostra*, Hodder and Stoughton, 2004; H. Hess, *Mafia and Mafiosi*, Hurst and Co., 1998; F. Sabetti, *Village Politics and the Mafia in Sicily*, McGill-Queen's University Press, 2002; P. Robb, *Midnight in Sicily*, The Harvill Press, 1999; N. Lewis, *In Sicily*, Jonathan Cape, 2000.
9. G. Falcone, *Cose di Cosa Nostra*, Rizzoli, 1991, quoted in A. Jamieson, *The Antimafia*, Macmillan, 2000.
10. See J. Dickie, op. cit., pp. 260–6 for discussion of Salvatore Giuliano and the Portella della Ginestra massacre.
11. A. Jamieson, op. cit., p. 218–20.
12. Ibid., p. 220.
13. Ibid., p. 220–1.
14. P. Robb, op. cit., p. 121, 131.
15. Ibid., pp. 134–5
16. P. Ginsborg, op. cit., p. 209.
17. Recounted in P. Robb, op. cit., p. 25.
18. The origins of La Rete are discussed in L. Orlando, *Fighting the Mafia and Renewing Sicilian Culture*, Encounter Books, 2001, pp. 146–8.
19. J. Dickie, op. cit., p. 434.
20. *La Repubblica*, 3/5/03.
21. Melissa P, *100 colpi di spazzola prima di andare a dormire*, Fazi editore, 2003; published in English as *100 Strokes of the Brush Before Bed*, Black Cat, 2004. The quote from Melissa P comes from the Black Cat edition.

CHAPTER 8

1. Quoted in *La Repubblica*, 4/9/04.
2. J. Gleick, 'How the World Got Faster', *Guardian*, 9/9/2000.
3. C. Petrini, *Slow Food: The Case For Taste*, Columbia University Press, 2003, p. 20.
4. *The Slow Food Manifesto*, www.slowfood.com.
5. Details of the group's activities can be found at www.slowfood.com.
6. C. Petrini, op. cit., p. 10.
7. Ibid., p. 55.
8. *The Slow Food Manifesto*, op. cit.
9. C. Petrini, op. cit., p. 28.
10. All the speeches and reports of the Terra Madre can be found at www.slowfood.com.
11. C. Petrini, *University of Gastronomic Science Prospectus*, 2004.

CHAPTER 9

1. R. Biorcio, 'Antipolitics, Political Apathy and Media in Italy', paper presented at ECPR conference, Turin, 22–7 March 2002.
2. A. Barnett, 'Corporate Control', *Prospect*, February 1999.
3. D. Marquand, *Decline of the Public*, Polity Press, 2004, pp. 101–2.
4. S. Hall and M. Jacques, 'Introduction', in S. Hall and M. Jacques (eds), *New Times*, Lawrence and Wishart, 1989, p. 15.
5. Michael Freeden (ed.), *Reassessing Political Ideologies: The Durability of Dissent*, Routledge, 2001, p. 1.
6. Ibid., p. 5.
7. Ibid., p. 10.
8. D. Marquand, *Decline of the Public*, op. cit., p. 103.
9. P. Hirst, *Associative Democracy*, Polity Press, 1994, p. 20. Hirst did some work for ACLI shortly before his death in 2003.
10. For example, the Demos-Eurisko survey of centre-left voters, 17/7/04.
11. R. Grandi and C. Vaccari, *Cofferati anch'io*, Baldini Castoldi Dalai, 2004, pp. 14–15.
12. Ibid.
13. Ibid., p. 30.
14. See M. Jaggi et al., *Red Bologna*, Writers and Readers, 1977.
15. David Kertzer's study of the two subcultures was researched in *Comrades and Christians*, Cambridge University Press, 1980.
16. P. Ginsborg, 'Hopes Unmet: Society and Politics in the Decade of Decline', paper presented to ASMI Conference on 'The Second Italian Republic Ten Years On: Prospect and Retrospect', Italian Cultural Institute, London, 26–7 November 2004.
17. Figures produced for World Economic Forum, October 2004.
18. P. Ginsborg, op. cit.
19. World Economic Forum League Tables, 2004.

Notes on Sources
and Further Reading

Writing a book about very contemporary events inevitably demands a mixture
of sources in order to capture the immediacy of the key moments. Therefore,
in addition to the books cited in the text and referred to in the Further Reading
below, I also consulted websites, now indispensable to researchers, kept diaries
and carried out interviews (in either Italian or English) with the following:
Vittorio Agnoletto, Sergio Bolzonello, Umberto Bossi, Anna Bucca, Livia
Cantore, Alessandro Cobianchi, Andrea De Maria, Ida Dominjianni, Michele
Emiliano, Claudio Fava, Agnese Giammona ('Lucia' in *La Terra Trema*), Roberto
Grandi, Simona Ianuzziello, Renzo Imbeni, Franco Lanzarini, Simona Lembi,
Don Filippo Lombardo, Pino Mele, Laura Nicolosi, Leoluca Orlando, Carlo
Petrini, Francesco Pirini, Michele Porcari, Vittorio Prodi, Enzo Raisi, Sajjad
Sardar and Paolo Saturnini. Further informal interviews and discussions were
held with members of ARCI in Bari and Sicily, Emergency in Bologna, the
Rimini Social Forum, local DS federations in Bologna, Florence and Bari, and
staff of the Slow Food office in Bra.

Italian newspapers, unlike Italian TV, provide broad coverage of Italian
political life, and the country's strong regional press (most nationals like
La Repubblica have good regional pages) helped me more than once with
important local dimensions or finding contacts. If my first source was the
Italian newspapers, the foreign press in Italy was also helpful in offering new
leads or providing useful comparisons with my own translations. Italy's rich
cultural, literary and cinematic traditions also helped to provide backdrop,
historical context, or local feeling at particular moments, and some examples
of these are listed below. My priority in this book has been to discuss cultural
questions in light of current politics; I leave deeper discussion of Italy's cultural
paradoxes to writers like Tobias Jones and Tim Parks.

The following is a very brief selection of some of the key works I would
recommend as helpful for an understanding of contemporary Italy. Where
possible I have cited the English version. The best short introduction to
Italian politics and society is John Foot's *Modern Italy* (Palgrave Macmillan,
2004). On the historical background to the Berlusconi era, a good starting
point is Paul Ginsborg's *Italy and its Discontents* (Allen Lane/Penguin Press,
2001), the seminal book on contemporary Italian history. His earlier *A
History of Contemporary Italy* (Penguin, 1990) includes the period of postwar
reconstruction and the tumultuous years of the 1960s and 1970s.

On the crisis facing the state in those years, Pier Paolo Pasolini's polemical
warnings in the Italian press about the corruptions of the Italian political class
can be found in *Lutheran Letters* (Carcanet Press, 1987). Leonardo Sciascia's *The
Moro Affair* (Granta, 2002) also probes deeply into the inertia and complicity
of the Christian Democrats. Notable films that depict the events of that era
include *I Cento Passi* (*The Hundred Steps*, Marco Giordana, 2000) and *Buongiorno,
Notte* (*Good Morning, Night*, Marco Bellochio, 2003). Another Giordana film of

2003, *La Meglio Gioventù* (*The Best of Youth*), is a six-hour epic which explores Italy since the 1960s through the perspective of a middle-class family, but omits Berlusconi's second accession to power. Joseph Farrell's biography of Dario Fo and Franca Rame, *Harlequins of the Revolution* (Methuen, 2001), and Carlo Feltrinelli's biography of his father Giangiacomo Feltrinelli, *Senior Service* (Granta, 2001), both tell us much about the wider politics of the left, while Robert Lumley's *States of Emergency: Cultures of Revolt in Italy 1968-1978* (Verso, 1990) is good on the idealism of the new social movements and the challenge to the state in that decade.

The best work in English on Berlusconi is Paul Ginsborg's excellent *Silvio Berlusconi: Television, Power and Patrimony* (Verso, 2004). This puts the story of Berlusconi's personal accession to power within the context of Italy's changing political and economic system. Ginsborg's *Il tempo di cambiare* (Einaudi, 2004) is an argument for new forms of democracy and the strengthening of civil society in the era of globalisation. It makes reference to the Italian situation in a wider context of debates about the future of politics. David Lane's *Berlusconi's Shadow: Crime, Justice and the Pursuit of Power* (Allen Lane, 2004) also looks at Berlusconi's origins and deals in particular with the darker undercurrents at the root of his rise to power. Tobias Jones' *The Dark Heart of Italy* (Faber, 2002) is a humorous, well-written and insightful analysis of Italian culture in the Berlusconi era. Following the translation of this book into Italian, Jones found himself the subject of critical attention from Berlusconi's own media. He subsequently presented programmes on RAI 3, arguably the one remaining critical TV channel.

The only major work in English on the history of Monte Sole is Jack Olsen's *Silence on Monte Sole* (iBooks, 2002) (1968), which movingly recreates the tragic events that took place in that mountain community in autumn 1944. For a major oral history study of the Fascist period, see Luisa Passerini's *Fascism in Popular Memory* (Cambridge University Press, 1987). On the history of the partisans, interesting personal stories of British partisan involvement see Stuart Hood's *Carlino* (Carcanet, 1985) and Howard Newby's *Love and War in the Apennines* (Penguin, 1990).

For more on the Northern League's arrival on the political scene and Umberto Bossi's impact on Italian politics, see Anna Bull and Mark Gilbert, *The Lega Nord and the Northern Question in Italian Politics* (Palgrave Macmillan, 2001); and Ilvo Diamanti, 'The Northern League: From Regional Party to Party of Government', in S. Gundle and S. Parker (eds), *The New Italian Republic* (Routledge, 1996). The Lega's newspaper, *La Padania* (www.lapadania.com), and its party website (www.leganord.org) give a flavour of the ideas of this movement.

While there is now extensive literature on the third way in English, including texts by Anthony Giddens, little has been written in English about the reception of the idea in Italy. Ilaria Favretto's *The Long Search for a Third Way* (Palgrave Macmillan, 2003) offers a comparative account of the Italian left and the British Labour Party. Norberto Bobbio's short book *Left and Right* (Polity Press, 1996) makes a careful statement of the durability and relevance of ideology in the context of such debates. Bobbio, one of Italy's leading political philosophers, whose major works include *The Ideological Profile of Twentieth Century Italy* (Princeton University Press, 1995), died in 2004.

There has also been very little work published in English on the contemporary Italian left and the new movements, though Ginsborg's *Silvio Berlusconi* includes a short discussion (pp. 168–74) of the interventions made by Sergio Cofferati and Nanni Moretti. Ewa Mazierska and Laura Rascaroli, *The Cinema of Nanni Moretti* (Wallflower Press, 2004), includes a section on Moretti's political intervention and makes insightful connections between his cinema and his political commitment, notably his films including *Palombella Rossa* (1989), *La Cosa* (1990), *Caro Diario* (1993) and *Aprile* (1998).

The G8 summit at Genoa in 2001 has often been seen as a time of lost innocence and has been captured as such in films like Lucio Pellegrini's *Ora o Mai Piu* (*Now or Never*, 2003). Italian texts here on the movements which emerged in 2002 include 'La primavera dei movimenti' in an edition of the periodical *MicroMega* (No. 2, 2002). On the impact of Cofferati as the unofficial leader of the Italian left, see Luca Telese's *La lunga marcia di Sergio Cofferati* (Sperling & Kupfer, 2003); on Cofferati's election campaign in Bologna, see Roberto Grandi and Cristian Vaccari, in *Cofferati anch'io* (Baldini Castoldi Dalai, 2004). The Social Forum movement in Italy generated a stream of local groups and 'social forum websites'; the World Social Forum website (www.worldsocialforum.org) is a good starting point. www.italy.indymedia.org is the Italian website of the alternative media group Indymedia, which provided alternative coverage of Genoa and other anti-global capitalist events.

The Scanzano Jonico dispute has been described in two insider accounts: Simona Ianuzziello, *Scanzano Jonico: I giorni della rivolta* (Mongolfiera, 2004); and Rita Montemurro, *I giorni di Scanzano* (CGIL, Matera, 2004). Websites provided an important source of mobilisation and information for campaigners as well as journalists. For details of the events and the breadth of the organisation, see in particular www.nonucleare.com/noalnucleare.php.; www.zonanucleare.com; and www.ilbrigantelucano.com.

There is a limited amount of literature in English on the South of Italy. Carlo Levi's classic *Christ Stopped at Eboli* (Penguin Books, 2000; the book was written in 1943–4) put southern poverty in the public domain and influenced later generations on the North–South divide in Italy. Visconti's 1960 neo-realist film *Rocco e i Suoi Fratelli* (*Rocco and his Brothers*) was partly filmed in Pisticci, Basilicata, and tells the story of a family who emigrated from the South. More recently, Gabriele Salvatores' *Io Non Ho Paura* (*I'm Not Scared*), based on Niccolò Ammaniti's novel of the same name, was made in 2003 near Melfi in Basilicata and is a gripping account of deception and violence in the Italian South in the 1970s.

Robert Lumley and Jonathan Morris (eds), *The New History of the Italian South* (University of Exeter Press, 1997) takes issue with negative stereotypical images of the South and offers new perspectives on the 'southern question' in Italian history and politics.

There have been more works published in English on Sicily, mainly because of interest in the Mafia. The best of these is John Dickie's *Cosa Nostra* (Hodder and Stoughton, 2004), which is a very comprehensive account of the history of the Mafia and its political impact. Peter Robb's *Midnight in Sicily* (The Harvill Press, 1999) mixes insightful investigative journalism on the links between the Mafia and the Italian state with the author's expert knowledge of Sicilian food. Leonardo Sciascia's fiction, notably *The Day of the Owl* (Granta, 2001), *Candido or a Dream Dreamed in Sicily* (Carcanet, 1985) and *Equal Danger* (Carcanet,

2001), addresses the Sicilian predicament with great insight and originality. Classic works of Sicilian literature, notably Giovanni Verga's *I Malavoglia* (Dedalus 1998, first published in 1881) and Giuseppe Tomasi di Lampedusa's *The Leopard* (recent edition Harvill Press, 2004, originally published in 1958), deal with the challenges of modernity in different ways, offering profound reflections on periods of social and political change in Sicily. Both these have been captured on film by Visconti: his 1963 film version of *The Leopard* was re-issued in its original uncut version in 2003, while *La Terra Trema* (1948), based on a twentieth-century Marxist interpretation of *I Malavoglia*, remains a neo-realist classic.

On the rapidly expanding Slow Food movement, the best place to start would be Carlo Petrini's *Slow Food: the Case for Taste* (Columbia University Press, 2003; original Italian version published as *Slow Food: Le ragioni del gusto*, Laterza, 2001). Slow Food's website, at www.slowfood.com, gives details of its groups and events, including those around the world. Details of the University of Gastronomic Science can be found at www.unisg.it. Carl Honore's *In Praise of Slow* (Orion Books, 2004) is good on the breadth of the Slow movement and 'Slowness' as an idea.

Debates on postmodernism and politics have been broad, interdisciplinary and not always coherent. On reflexivity, see Ulrich Beck, Anthony Giddens, and Scott Lash (eds), *Reflexive Modernization* (Polity Press, 1994) (see in particular the first chapter, Ulrich Beck's 'The Reinvention of Politics'), and Ulrich Beck's *Risk Society* (Sage, 1996). For associative democracy, see Paul Hirst, *Associative Democracy* (Polity Press, 1994) and Joshua Cohen and Joel Rogers (eds), *Associations and Democracy* (Verso, 1998).

Acronyms and Glossary

ACLI (Associazioni cristiane lavoratori italiani): Catholic workers' organisation set up in 1945 which campaigns on peace, democracy and social justice.

Alleanza Nazionale (AN): the National Alliance. The 'post-Fascist' party led by Gianfranco Fini, set up in 1994 following the dissolution of the neo-Fascist MSI (Movimento Sociale Italiano).

Anni di piombo: the 'years of lead'. The term used to describe Italy's period of terrorism in the 1970s.

ARCI (Associazione ricreativa e culturale italiana): the political, recreational and cultural association of the left, founded in 1957.

Camorra: the Neapolitan Mafia.

Casa delle libertà: House of Liberties. The name of the right-wing governing coalition, made up of Forza Italia, the National Alliance, the Northern League and the UDC.

CGIL (Confederazione generale italiana del lavoro): Italy's largest and most left-wing trade union federation.

CISL (Confederazione italiana sindacati lavoratori): the second largest and Catholic trade union federation.

Città Slow: the Slow City network.

Cosa Nostra: the Sicilian Mafia.

Democratici di sinistra (DS, formerly PDS): the Left Democrats, formed after the PCI dissolved in 1991.

Democrazia cristiana (DC): the Christian Democrats, who ruled Italy between 1946 and 1992.

European Social Forum (ESF): the annual gathering of civil society movements and networks opposed to neo-liberalism.

Fininvest: Berlusconi's holding company.

Forza Italia: Silvio Berlusconi's party, set up in 1994.

girotondi: the citizens' movement set up by Nanni Moretti in 2002 to campaign against Berlusconi's conflicts of interest and curtailments of free speech.

Lega Nord: the Northern League, Umberto Bossi's regionalist party, set up in 1991.

Mani pulite ('Clean Hands'): the investigation into political corruption led by Antonio Di Pietro.

La Margherita: the 'Daisy' network of Catholic centrist parties represented by Romano Prodi and Francesco Rutelli.

Mediaset: the name of Berlusconi's media group.

Partito Comunista Italiano (PCI): the Italian Communist Party, Italy's main postwar opposition, which dissolved in 1991.

Partitocrazia: term used to describe postwar Italy as a state run by political parties in their own interests.

Propaganda 2 (P2): the secret group of politicians, military officials and businessmen set up to infiltrate Italy's public institutions and save the country from Communism.

La Rete: 'The Network', a broad 'anti-corruption' political network set up by Leoluca Orlando in 1991.

Rifondazione comunista: the 'Refounded Communists', originally set up in 1991 and now led by Fausto Bertinotti.

Slow Food: the organisation set up by Carlo Petrini in 1986, aimed at promoting aesthetic and cultural values in politics.

Tangentopoli: literally 'Bribesville', used to describe the system of 'kickbacks' and clientelism that was found to be at the heart of the Italian political system and that led to the dissolution of the Christian Democrats.

Unione dei democratici cristiani (UDC): a right-of-centre Christian Democrat group in the House of Liberties coalition.

Index

Web benny colesanzio/ Sonia Alfano
legge di riforma web